Negotiating cultures

MANCHESTER
UNIVERSITY PRESS

theatre
theory·practice
·performance·

series editors
MARIA M. DELGADO
PETER LICHTENFELS

advisory board
MICHAEL BILLINGTON
SANDRA HEBRON
MARK RAVENHILL
JANELLE REINELT
PETER SELLARS

The series will offer a space for those people who practise theatre to have a dialogue with those who think and write about it.

The series has a flexible format that refocuses the analysis and documentation of performance. It provides, presents and represents material which is written by those who make or create performance history, and offers access to theatre documents, different methodologies and approaches to the art of making theatre.

The books in the series are aimed at students, scholars, practitioners, and theatre-visiting readers. They encourage reassessments of periods, companies, and figures in twentieth-century and twenty-first-century theatre history, and provoke and take up discussions of cultural strategies and legacies that recognise the heterogeneity of performance studies.

The series editors, with the advisory board, aim to publish innovative challenging and exploratory texts from practitioners, theorists and critics.

also available

The Paris jigsaw: internationalism and the city's stages
DAVID BRADBY and MARIA M. DELGADO (eds)

'Love me or kill me': Sarah Kane and the theatre of extremes
GRAHAM SAUNDERS

Negotiating cultures

Eugenio Barba
and the intercultural debate

IAN WATSON and colleagues

Manchester University Press
Manchester and New York

distributed exclusively in the USA by Palgrave

Published by Manchester University Press
Oxford Road, Manchester M13 9NR, UK
and Room 400, 175 Fifth Avenue, New York, NY 10010, USA
www.manchesteruniversitypress.co.uk

Distributed exclusively in the USA by
Palgrave, 175 Fifth Avenue, New York, NY 10010, USA

Distributed exclusively in Canada by
UBC Press, University of British Columbia, 2029 West Mall, Vancouver, BC, Canada V6T 1Z2

British Library Cataloguing-in-Publication Data
A catalogue record for this book is available from the British Library

Library of Congress Cataloging-in-Publication Data applied for

ISBN 0 7190 6169 5 *hardback*
     0 7190 6170 9 *paperback*

First published in 2002——

10 09 08 07 06 05 04 03 02   10 9 8 7 6 5 4 3 2 1

Typeset by Northern Phototypesetting Co. Ltd, Bolton
Printed in Great Britain
by Bell & Bain Ltd, Glasgow

To Susana, David, Carmen, Gaspar and Violeta
without whom these pages would be empty

CONTENTS

List of plates   *page* ix

Foreword: a handful of snow
FRANC CHAMBERLAIN   xi

Introduction: contexting Barba
IAN WATSON   1

I ISTA and Theatre Anthropology

1 Staging Theatre Anthropology   IAN WATSON   20

2 Transcultural dialogue: lecture/demonstrations at ISTA
   NICOLA SAVARESE   36

3 Actor as *refusenik*: Theatre Anthropology, semiotics and the
   paradoxical work of the body   NIGEL STEWART   46

4 Finding equilibrium in disequilibrium: the impact of ISTA on its
   Balinese participants   I NYOMAN CATRA AND RON JENKINS   59

5 Odissi and the ISTA dance: an interview with Sanjukta Panigrahi
   RON JENKINS AND IAN WATSON   67

  6 Interculturalism and the individual performer: an interview with
     the Odin actress Roberta Carreri   IAN WATSON   76

II Barter: performance as cultural exchange

  7 The dynamics of barter   IAN WATSON   94

  8 Border, barters and beads: in search of intercultural Arcadia
     MARIA SHEVTSOVA   112

  9 Theatre presence: sea lanes, Sardinia, 1975
     EUGENIO BARBA, IBEN NAGEL RASMUSSEN, TONY D'URSO
     AND FERDINANDO TAVIANI   128

 10 Provocation anthropology: bartering performance in Africa
     METTE BOVIN   142

 11 Invisible cities: an interview with Pino di Buduo   IAN WATSON 159

III Latin America and the Third Theatre

 12 Barba's other culture   IAN WATSON   170

 13 The house with two doors   EUGENIO BARBA   183

 14 The Third Theatre: a legacy of independence   IAN WATSON   197

 15 About islands and woods: notes on a journey to the Odin Teatret
     MIGUEL RUBIO   221

IV A dialogue with Eugenio Barba

 16 The conquest of difference: an electronic dialogue
     EUGENIO BARBA AND IAN WATSON   234

     Contributors   263

     Index   267

LIST OF PLATES

Eugenio Barba at the ISTA workshop, Brazil (1994).
Photograph: Emidio Luisi   *title page*

1 The Odissi dancer, Sanjukta Panigrahi (standing) and
  Katsuko Azuma, a Nihon Buyo performer, rehearsing a version
  of Goethe's *Faust* at the 5th ISTA, Salento, Italy (1987).
  Photograph: Tony D'Urso   *page* 88

2 Eugenio Barba rehearsing with *Teatrum Mundi* ensemble at
  the 11th ISTA, Portugal (1998). Photograph: Fiora Bemporad   89

3 A barter in a parking lot in a suburb of Bahía Blanca, Argentina,
  between local people and groups attending the Third Theatre
  gathering (1987). Photograph: Ian Watson   89

4 The Odin Teatret performing during a barter in a prison in
  Milan, Italy (1996). Photograph: Tony D'Urso   90

5 Eugenio Barba conducting a workshop at *Reencuentro Ayachuco '88*,
  the Third Theatre gathering in Huampaní, Peru (1988).
  Photograph: Ian Watson   90

6 The Odin Teatret in Ayacucho, Peru during the Third Theatre
  gathering, *Reencuentro Ayacucho '88*. Photograph: Tony D'Urso   91

7 The barter outside a Peruvian village near Ayacucho in 1978
(see Chapter 16). Photograph: Peter Bysted   91

FOREWORD
A handful of snow
Franc Chamberlain

Ian Watson has already produced an excellent introduction to the theory and practice of Eugenio Barba and the Odin Teatret in his book *Towards a Third Theatre* (Routledge, 1993). This companion volume builds on some of the insights of the earlier manuscript by developing a more specific focus on the issues of cultural exchange and interchange in Barba's work through new material by Watson himself and by the inclusion of key essays from, and interviews with, a range of practitioners and academics. The network of voices drawn from a period of twenty-five years creates a fascinating score of harmonies and dissonances which raise challenges to Barba's practice whilst at the same time affirming the practical usefulness of the work. Each of the three sections of this book are introduced by contextualizing essays and it is unnecessary for this foreword to repeat that task, or to paraphrase the earlier book. In what follows I allow my thoughts to dance around some bones of contention in order to add further provocations and challenges. I write as someone who has been alternately stimulated and frustrated by Barba's work over the past fifteen years and who, as well as making aggressive public challenges to the work, has also been a recipient of his generosity.

Eugenio Barba, despite, or perhaps because of, his distrust of language, talks and writes about his work perhaps more than any other key practitioner of the last hundred years. In the English-speaking world, he is on the editorial boards of at least three major academic journals: *New*

Theatre Quarterly, Performance Research and *The Drama Review*, and is a regular contributor to two of these. This, together with the publication of books such as *The Paper Canoe* (Routledge, 1995) and *A Dictionary of Theatre Anthropology* (Routledge, 1991), which most people refer to by its subtitle *The Secret Art of the Performer*, has ensured that his thoughts on the theory and practice of performance have been kept on the academic agenda for over thirty years. Yet Barba's impact on the practice of theatre in Britain, for example, is far less evident than that of the Ecole Jacques Lecoq in Paris and his influence on those companies and artists exploring cultural identity through form and content such as Tara Arts, Black Theatre Co-operative, Tamasha, Shobana Jeyasingh and Pan Intercultural Arts (formerly Pan Project) has been insignificant. There are British companies who acknowledge the influence of Barba, most notably Triangle in Coventry, who have also facilitated the only public perform- ances by the Odin in England as part of the Coventry Arts Alive Festival, but in general there is silence. At the European Mime and Physical Theatre Workshop Symposium held in Manchester in 1994, Enrique Pardo of Panthéâtre questioned the absence of reference to Barba and the Odin's work during the discussions which attempted to define the parameters of physical theatre. There has been little change in this situa- tion since then, although Odin's appearance at the Salisbury Festival in 2001 (30 May–3 June) introduced a new audience to their productions and working methods.

A strong link with the Centre for Performance Research at Aberyst- wyth, however, has meant that there have been Odin residencies and performances in Wales and the 1992 ISTA was hosted in Brecon. This ensured that there were more British participants in the 'internal' session than at any other ISTA before or since, yet at the same time, there was less linguistic and cultural diversity than is usual for an ISTA meeting. Per- haps this is one of the reasons why Barba was to say to me when we met again in 1995 that the meeting in Wales wasn't a 'real ISTA'. Another oddity was that the participants at the Brecon ISTA did not get to partic- ipate in a workshop with the teachers and this resulted in some frustra- tion. Whatever the reasons, the Brecon ISTA did not lead to an increased British presence in subsequent ISTAs and it is perhaps significant that the first ISTA to be held after Brecon was also the first to take place outside of Europe. It was mounted in Latin America, where Barba and the Odin have arguably had their strongest impact. The three meetings that have taken place since Londrina, Brazil in 1994 have, however, all returned to Europe. This is despite some requests by participants from Asia, whose creative work provides much of the material for ISTA, that a session be held in their part of the globe.

There may be important reasons why ISTA has not been convened in Asia, but one of the consequences is that ISTA can appear to be a kind of travelling show, similar to those parodied in 'Two Undiscovered Amerindians Visit' by Guillermo Gómez-Peña and Coco Fusco (1992), where 'indigenous' peoples are exhibited for 'education' and 'entertainment'. For those who have never attended an ISTA, this appearance might be seductive, but for those who have, there is an awareness that the exhibition of otherness is not Barba's goal. Barba's aim has always been to try to understand the principles by which a performer constructs scenic presence, not in order to produce a homogenized theatrical form, but in order to find analogies that enable communication between people from different cultures. Barba has said that the Odin, and by extension ISTA, is 'a meeting through difference' (at the Copenhagen ISTA in 1996). There appear to be two objections to this: firstly, there are those who feel that Barba is trying to reduce cultural difference in order to uncover a 'universal theatre' (see Shevtsova's essay) and second, there is an objection to Barba's method of analysis as demonstrated within the sessions themselves. The first is a theoretical objection whilst the second is based on an observation of the practice.

The claim that Barba is attempting to construct a 'universal theatre' because he is aiming to determine whether or not there are principles of scenic presence which are universal is mistaken. A study of the anatomy of the human voice and the principles which govern the production of sound, for example, does not reduce the multiplicity of languages to a universal tongue, even if there are some expressive sounds which might be considered universal. It is possible to imagine that from a set of universal principles a universal language could be constructed, but it is not clear how this would ever work in practice, even if it were desirable. No, Barba's claim is unambiguous: he respects difference because he is referring to 'analogous principles [which] are born of similar physical conditions in different contexts' and he acknowledges that these principles 'are not ... homologous, since they do not have a common history' (1995: 117). History and cultural difference are not erased and there is no intention that they should be. Some might point out that Barba has been known to say that when he was talking with Sanjukta Panigrahi he was talking with his friend 'Sanjukta' not with an 'Asian' as evidence of his desire to erase difference. By contrast, it could be taken to signify, not that Panigrahi's cultural background was irrelevant, but that it would be a mistake to reduce an individual to their cultural background because this could lead to the reinforcement of cultural stereotypes. Indeed, to reduce my friends to their cultural backgrounds could be to make them representatives of those cultures in my internal circus and to keep them in their place (and, if they followed my example, they would presumably keep me in mine). It seems to me that to reduce an individual to his or her cultural background is to simultaneously reduce the culture, which, like the individual, is always more than anyone can say it is.

The second objection is based on an observation of one of Barba's methods of working within the ISTA sessions. It is usual for Barba to invite a performer to demonstrate something of their form before an audience and then to dissect the performance by suggesting the reduction or removal of gestures, as well as to offer tasks which obstruct the usual flow of the movement. Savarese argues in his essay in this volume, that the 'dissection of the actor' has given the scholars at ISTA 'access to the smallest details of the theatre world'. This image of a dissection, however, conjures up images of Italian Renaissance Anatomy Theatres, which brought together audience, corpse and anatomist in order that the anatomist could demonstrate his expertise and knowledge through the dissection of the corpse. Unfortunately, dissection requires a corpse and the performer stands in for the corpse in Dr Barba's anatomy lesson and, if we extend the metaphor, Barba becomes a re-animator, like Galvani attempting to restore life to that which is dead. Yet the performer is not dead but very much alive and a more painful metaphor than dissection is that of vivisection. It is this vivisection of the performer which has caused some discomfort amongst those who have watched Barba at work. For some it is the cruel curiosity of a child who pulls the legs off a spider to see when it can no longer walk.

There is another confusion here, however, for it is obviously not the performer who is being cut up for the purpose of analysis but the performer's score. The performer is a conscious agent who makes editions in response to Barba's suggestions, not a corpse or someone hypnotized. I Nyoman Catra and Sanjukta Panigrahi, in this collection, both comment on how the analytical work with Barba has helped them preserve and develop their performance techniques. Another frequent collaborator with Barba, Kanichi Hanayagi has told a similar story at several ISTAs, explaining how his participation has enabled him to create new works, something which he considers vital to a dancer's development, while at the same time assisting him in the preservation of the 'old' dances. Helpful as the work may be, there is still something in the anatomy lesson which disturbs and the collaborations have sometimes been difficult, as Panigrahi indicates in her interviews with Watson and Jenkins.

Another way of getting at the discomfort is perhaps via Marco De Marinis' observation that Barba utilizes the methods of empirical science. De Marinis considers it odd that critics should require Barba to 'linger on a subject that in other scientific areas would be considered a foregone

conclusion' (1995: 121), that is, that he should have to justify the decon-
textualization of the performer for his experiments. De Marinis takes this
as evidence of the 'backwardness of theatrical studies'. However, empirical science as defined by Galileo, banned quality from the field of science,
and only those aspects of a phenomenon which were quantifiable were
the focus of empirical science. This, as has been pointed out many times,
excludes ethics and aesthetics, which are vital to theatre, and indeed are
central to Barba's work. The methodology of empirical science does not
allow us to make crucial ethical distinctions between the metaphorical
dismemberment of a performance score and the literal dismemberment
of a live human being. A number of objections to Barba's method are
ethical ones, or at least matters of sensibility, and they need to be taken
seriously. I am not suggesting that Barba should necessarily change his
approach in response to these challenges, but it is a mistake to brand
ethical objections as 'political correctness' (as De Marinis does) and to
hide behind a mask of science. Again, the threads become tangled as readers of Barba become aware of how important the ethical dimension is to
his work. No one has ever accused him of literally dismembering a performer – that would be absurd. The ethical difference between Barba's
approach and that of a criminal scientist is immense. The point is that the
methodology of empirical science would not allow us to make such a
qualitative judgement, it is a question of ethics. I remember Richard
Schechner jokingly referring to the Italian scholars accompanying Barba
as 'Barba's Mafia' and the strength of Barba's response which included a
passionate 'the Mafia kill people, we do not kill people!'.[1]

Barba's relationship with companies in Latin America has led to
significant ethical and political debates as well as actions. One of the
many things that makes Ian Watson's collection of essays distinctive is the
space and attention he devotes to this Latin American dimension of
Barba's work, and the poetics as well as politics of performance in that
region. The image of Pinochet's soldiers attacking Mr. Peanut because
that 'great friend' to Britain found it 'distasteful to host death' and of
Barba instigating an impromptu barter with Peruvian troops at Ayacucho

---

1   The exchange between Barba and Schechner occurred at a symposium entitled
    'Points of Contact: Theatre, Anthropology and Theatre Anthropology' organized by
    the Centre for Performance Research (it was the first of their ongoing Points of
    Contact series) and hosted by Leicester Polytechnic (now de Montfort University),
    Leicester, England, 30 September–2 October 1988. This was the first and only time
    that Barba and Schechner appeared on the same platform in the United Kingdom.
    Barba was accompanied by his longtime academic colleagues Ferdinando Taviani,
    Nicola Savarese and Franco Ruffini. Mette Bovin was also at the symposium and
    presented her paper on provocation anthropology (a version is included in this
    volume) together with a film of her collaboration with Roberta Carreri in Burkina
    Faso, *Dances in the Sand* (1984).

in 1988 (both described in Rubio's essay) are not ones which suggest a use of theatre as a political instrument comparable to that of Augusto Boal. Nevertheless, they are actions which focus reflection on the relationship between art and politics. Watson also considers the impact that Latin America has had on Barba and the Odin, something which is not always apparent. The participation of the Brazilian Candomblé performer Augusto Omolú with three musicians, Ory Sacramento, Jorge Paim and Bira Monteiro, in the 1994 and 1995 ISTAs, was the first time that representatives from a performance tradition that was neither Asian nor European had taken part as members of the artistic staff. That these performers were also of African descent endowed their participation with another significance.

One of the criticisms of Barba in the past was his focus on Eurasian Theatre which, it was felt, unjustifiably excluded African performance and its contribution to Western theatre. This decision not to include any of the many forms of performance from Africa at ISTA, except the Afro-Brazilian work of Omolú is a curious one. Like any researcher, Barba may restrict his area of investigation for any number of practical, theoretical and personal reasons, but as he is searching for principles of scenic presence which are universal, it makes little sense to exclude a whole continent from his research. It is doubly strange when we reflect that none of the key members of Barba's scientific staff has tested the 'findings' of ISTA against any African performance form. Mette Bovin's development and use of a provocation anthropology in collaboration with Roberta Carreri, discussed in Bovin's essay, is not an examination of the findings of ISTA. It is an adaptation of the practice of barter as an aid to conventional anthropological fieldwork. By contrast, it is Theatre Anthropology's relation to other modes of anthropology that has provided critics with further ammunition to challenge Barba's project. I have discussed the relationship of Theatre Anthropology to other anthropological approaches elsewhere (Chamberlain, 2000), but I think it worth reiterating that, contrary to most critics, I see the problem with the term theatre rather than with anthropology. Barba has stated that Theatre Anthropology should not be confused with the anthropology of performance (1995: 10), but this still leaves us with the question: of what is Theatre Anthropology an anthropology? Jean-Marie Pradier has suggested that we avoid the problem by placing a TM afterwards (1995) and Kirsten Hastrup answered the question 'is Theatre Anthropology an anthropology' with 'it's Theatre Anthropology' (1995). In the end, there is perhaps little point in arguing whether what Barba does is or is not anthropology. The more meaningful question is, how far does he achieve what he sets out to achieve, not forgetting the relevance of considering the ethics of his methodology.

Barba distinguished his use of the term anthropology from Richard Schechner's in a review of Schechner's *Between Theatre and Anthropology* (University of Pennsylvania Press, 1985), claiming that his own approach was that of 'the archaic way of physical, anatomical study' (1987: 191). In the same essay, he considered the different ways in which he and Schechner viewed the ethos of a working group. Barba characterized Schechner's view of the group as being a 'family ... without parents' while he preferred to regard Odin as a 'polis in miniature'. ISTA is the miniature polis at festival time, with the gates opened and the transmission of culture to those who have made the journey. There are lectures as well as demonstrations and, occasionally, some monastic rules such as 'no talking at breakfast'. Kirsten Hastrup has made an ethnographic study of what she calls the performers' village and identified the social structures as well as key roles which develop this image (1996).

Hastrup's notion of the performers' village owes a little to the picturesque church village of Lövånger in northern Sweden where part of the ninth meeting of ISTA took place during May, 1995. Snow fell on Lövånger and my photographs catch a few moments of laughter as staff and participants from twenty-two countries took a mid-morning break outside. For some, this was their first experience of snow, while for others, such a light dusting was barely significant. Each face carries its marks of laughter differently in the images, and exactly what each person is laughing at or about is now impossible to determine. My memory is of a group of people enjoying themselves in the snow; there is an atmosphere of fun. Of course, this overall atmosphere which I claim to remember covers over the differences in each person's experience and marginalizes the experience of those who weren't having fun at all. Not everyone is laughing in these photographs, but the appearance of these faces doesn't lead me to question my memory of the mood at that moment. Memory, like experience at the time, is not purely visual. It includes sounds and feelings, smells, tastes and touch. The memory of laughter and pleasure is not a visual image of people's faces. It is a sense of atmosphere and mood that's felt in the body. The consideration of atmosphere 'thickens' the description of the expressions in the photographs, but not enough to get at the different individual and cultural responses to the moment.

I have no idea how many languages were being spoken as we laughed in the snow, I have made no study of the various cultural codes for the expression of laughter carried by this group of people. In this action of shared laughter the emphasis is on what links us, not on what separates us. It would be easy to suggest that what linked us was our professional identity, that we were performers and performance scholars related by our engagement with performance. But at that moment we were just a group of people who had been working hard together and who were now laughing in the snow. A moment of what Victor Turner (the renowned anthropologist most often associated with theatre and performance studies) called communitas, where social roles are temporarily suspended; a moment that contradicts the hierarchical structure of ISTA. This moment of sharing is also there when we are part of an audience laughing at a performance, or listening silently, or singing together. It doesn't mean that our individual differences suddenly disappear. Our values as well as personal and cultural codes are no more erased than our perception of snow as a blanket of white erases the fact that no two snowflakes are identical or that snow is never uniform in its density or texture. Nor does it mean that we ignore the fact that snow has different values and associations for different cultures and individuals. We may forget these things temporarily, but they will inevitably return. What is important is that we make explicit in our analyses that we are consciously excluding aspects of what we are studying. For the most part, Barba has been at pains to do this.

As I remember it, the moment I have described in the snow happened spontaneously rather than being an organized action. On the last evening at Lövånger, however, we were gathered together indoors and Barba gave his instructions. He had entered the cosily warm room carrying a bowl covered with a cloth. In it, he said, was the distillation of all of his theatre knowledge. We were to sing collectively a Spanish translation of a poem by Walt Whitman, set to music by Frans Winther, and when the moment was 'right' (we had to feel it), each individual was to walk up to Barba. He would then guide that person's hand under the cloth to the piece of his theatrical wisdom that was appropriate to him or her. Within this staged event there was a powerful chorus that repeated the song over and over again, building in strength and fluidity as well as providing a backdrop for the individual journeys to Barba's theatrical wisdom. Every person's journey was their own, and different facial expressions indicated the disappointment, frustration, pleasure, anger, amusement or other emotion that each person felt as her or his hand was guided under the cloth to the cold snow that was in the bowl. What did Barba mean by such trickery? Was he cruelly ridiculing those of us who believed that there was a serious gift in the bowl? Was he playing the 'impossible' teacher trying to shake us out of our illusions? Or then again was he playing to those of us who had a philosophical bent and would reflect on snow as a metaphor for the transmission of theatre knowledge? Perhaps all of these at once. The handful of snow was a provocation, we could make of it what we would.

References

Barba, Eugenio (1995), *The Paper Canoe: A Guide to Theatre Anthropology*. London and New York: Routledge.

Barba, Eugenio (1987), 'The etymological intellectual', *New Theatre Quarterly*, Vol. III, Issue 10, pp. 188–91.

Chamberlain, Franc (2000), 'Theatre Anthropology: definitions and doubts', in Frost, Anthony (ed.) *Theatre Theories from Plato to Virtual Reality*, UEA, pp. 171–94.

De Marinis, Marco (1995), 'From pre-expressivity to the dramaturgy of the performer: an essay on *The Paper Canoe*', *Mime Journal*: Incorporated Knowledge: 114–56.

Hastrup, Kirsten (ed.) (1996), *The Performers' Village: Times, Techniques and Theories at ISTA*. Graasten, Denmark: Drama.

Hastrup, Kirsten (1995), Personal comment to the author during the ninth ISTA held in Lövånger and Umeå, Sweden (May).

Pradier, Jean-Marie (1995), Personal comment to the author during the ninth ISTA held in Lövånger and Umeå, Sweden (May).

Watson, Ian (1995), *Towards a Third Theatre: Eugenio Barba and the Odin Teatret*. London and New York: Routledge (2nd edn).

INTRODUCTION
Contexting Barba
Ian Watson

Eugenio Barba is often thought of as synonymous with interculturalism because of his cross-cultural research into performance at the International School of Theatre Anthropology (ISTA) and because of his notion of Theatre Anthropology which is predicated upon comparative studies of theatre forms from Asia and the Euro-American tradition. For anyone who knows Barba, this global fascination with performance is understandable given his professional and personal history.

Barba is a product of the 1960s avant-garde. During this explosive period of innovation and revolt, many leading theatre artists turned to cultures other than their own in order to break with the hegemony of 1950s' post-war nationalism, as a means of expanding their knowledge of theatre beyond the borders of a common language or shared history, and as a source of inspiration in their own creative work. Peter Brook, Ariane Mnouchkine, Tadashi Suzuki, Richard Schechner, and Barbas' mentor, Jerzy Grotowski, to name but a few, were fellow travellers with Barba on his journeys to performance forms far removed from his own Italian heritage or adopted Nordic homeland. Artaud and Brecht may have been beacons lighting the way for Barba's nascent interculturalism, but his apprenticeship proved to be much broader in scope. In addition to Stanislavsky, Meyerhold, Eisenstein, Grotowski and Decroux, Barba cites Asian performers and theoretical treatises, such as Kathakali, Noh, the onnogata, Barong, Rukmini Devi, Mei Lanfang, Zeami and the

Natyashastra, as central to his theatrical formation (1988: 126; 1995: 42).

Barba's personal history in many ways mirrors the cultural pluralism of his professional development. He is an Italian who emigrated to Norway and a former member of the Norwegian Merchant Marine whose assignments took him to various parts of Asia. He studied theatre for the first time in Poland, following which he founded his theatre company, Odin Teatret, in Oslo, only to move with it to Holstebro, Denmark within two years. One of the original models for his company and its work methods was the Kathakali school in Cheruthuruthy, India that he had visited and written about while still working with Grotowski. The Odin has consisted of actors from many different countries since it was formed in 1964, most of whom do not share a common native language leading to a creole of sorts both in the rehearsal room and in its productions; while the company is rarely at home since it and Barba tour extensively, especially in Europe and Latin America. Barba also spends an appreciable amount of time in Bali, Japan, India and Brazil working with the artists who attend the various ISTA gatherings. It is hardly surprising that more than a decade ago he characterized his sense of place as corporeal rather than geographic when, in examining his nationality, Barba was drawn to the conclusion that 'my body is my country' (1988a: 293).

Despite the many personal and professional influences from different cultures on Barba during his formative years and the impact these have had on his subsequent career as a director, researcher, theorist and teacher, one has to be careful in characterizing him as an interculturalist. Barba's creative pursuits and his research, like that of many others working across and between cultures, encompass a range of cultural relations. Interculturalism is but one of Barba's strategies. Rather than interculturalist, his methodologies might best be described as those of a cultural pluralist, which, regardless of its noncommittal tone and ring of political correctness, is a collective term that includes the possibility of various cultural transactions.

Cultural pluralism

Culture is a holistic complex, with an interrelated palimpsest of determinants which comprehends, among other things, socio-historical identity, mytho-religious belief systems, rituals, kinship, ethnicity, national heritage, value systems, various modes of creative expression, as well as social behaviour. A thorough study of culture is beyond the scope of this book; however, several aspects of it are pertinent to an understanding of the relations between cultures.

Contemporary cultures are, for example, living organisms which are forever on the move. They are, as James Clifford describes, a negotiated, present process (1988: 273). Culture is not a fixed, localized entity that is easily, if at all, transportable intact. Culture, like behaviour, is a discursive space that is permanently 'in action' rather than a completed product or object frozen in space and time. Thus relations between cultures are a complex interaction of entities which are in a permanent process of negotiating their own identity.

Further, as Clifford Geertz points out, culture is a human creation. It is 'a system of symbols by which man confers significance upon his own experience' (1973: 250). Whatever the nature of this 'system of symbols', it provides a basis for one's identity and reading of the world. Hence, cultures other than one's own are generally perceived as expressions of difference. Most of us see other cultures through the frame of our own and view what we see as expressive of the 'foreign' other. Culture is read etically as expression, thus it has a strong connection to performance and display, while it is lived emically as instrumental behaviour.

Culture engenders a sense of belonging, of identity and inclusion. It therefore implies exclusion, denial of membership, and borders. Borders, the lines that demarcate one culture from another, may not be as clear-cut as national borders but they are at the centre of cultural relations. It is the meetings at these borders, the 'in between' spaces as Homi Bhabha refers to them (1994: 1), that define the relationships between cultures.[1] These liminal spaces are discursive; they are sites of discussion, conflict, eruption, compromise, debate, and above all, negotiation (Bhabha, 1994: 22). But not all negotiations are the same. There are at least four major different types of negotiation: transcultural, cross-cultural, multicultural and intercultural; and most, if not all, meetings between cultures involve a combination of two or more of these. Putting aside questions of cultural hegemony and the politics of cultural relations, which I take up later in

---

1 The in-between spaces that Bhabha refers to can be both physical and conceptual. The no man's land between warring rival street gangs is a physical space that is at least potentially a site of neutral contact and negotiation. However, the conceptual dimension of the borderland is far more encompassing than its physical counterpart. This is where the symbols, myths, beliefs, and enculturation of the various socio-national/ethnic realities interact.

The relationship between the physical and conceptual has a historical dimension. In colonial times, physical distance played a major role in the relationship between cultures. Colonies such as India and those in Africa, were 'out there' in relation to the cultural 'centres' of Europe. The impact of these colonies on their European counterparts was limited by distance and technology. In today's high-tech, postcolonial world, the situation is very different. Immigration, the mass media, computers and relatively cheap air travel have all led to the space between cultures shrinking both physically and conceptually.

'Staging Theatre Anthropology', a knowledge of these different processes is important in order to understand Barba's cultural pluralism.

The transcultural refers to a relationship in which culture plays no significant part. As the name implies, it involves an all-inclusive dimension of human expression that eclipses or subtends culture. It is, as Patrice Pavis puts it, a transcending of particular cultures in search of the universal human condition (1992: 20); a pre-cultural dimension, if you will, that is the cultural equivalent of Carl Jung's notion of psychological archetypes. Peter Brook's early work with his Paris-based theatre company, Le Centre International de Recherche Théatrale (CIRT) was, for example, an attempt to discover the transcultural nature of the theatre event. His experiments with a fabricated language in *Orghast* and the journey with his actors through sub-Saharan Africa were predicated upon the understanding that theatrical reception has a universal dimension that is independent of culturally specific factors such as language and/or familiarity with particular, culturally based, theatrical styles.

Unlike the denial of culture in the transcultural, the cross-cultural refers to a situation in which many cultural influences or fragments coexist explicitly in one cohesive object, space, event or ritual. These cultural traces, which retain their individual integrity rather than becoming diluted creolizing factors, are appropriated as a means of explicating the cultural discourse at the centre of the transaction. Mnouchkine's early 1980s Shakespeare cycle (*Richard II, Henry IV, Twelfth Night*), for instance, was framed by what Andrzej Wirth describes as 'the occidental cultural matrix of Shakespeare's chronicles' while 'using stereotypes of commedia dell'arte, Noh and Kabuki as a kind of overpainting, ornamentation and stylisation' (1991: 290). Various cultural influences were clearly evident in the cycle. But, Mnouchkine's creations were rooted in a Eurocentric framework and sensibility overlaid with appropriated cultural stereotypes that brought a new understanding of each play's relevance to its equally Eurocentric audiences.

The multicultural, like the intercultural, has become somewhat of a hackneyed phrase in contemporary society because it is used to describe almost every situation in which different cultures are in any kind of sustained contact. This intemperate application aside, the multicultural is most frequently used to describe the racial and/or ethnic make-up of major cities like New York or Los Angeles in the United States. In these and similar cities there are many ethnic groups, each with its own socio-national culture, living in the same and/or adjacent neighbourhoods. The fact that these groups remain in contact over extended periods of time has led to multiculturalism being associated with harmony, equality, a 'celebration of difference', and peaceful co-existence. One hardly needs to be an urban scholar to know that the reality is somewhat more complex. Nevertheless, the multiculturalism that is at the root of the term is evident in books like *By Means of Performance* (1990) edited by Richard Schechner and Willa Appel. Schechner's and Appel's book is a collection of essays by different authors which examine various aspects of performance including theatre, rituals, sports and display behaviour from different cultures without privileging Western theatre over the Yaqui Indian Easter Pageant or how character is portrayed in Kathakali. This multiculturalism is mirrored in events such as the 1990 Los Angeles Festival that featured artists from twenty-two different countries around the Pacific Rim, without favouring Korean shamans over Maori dancers, Japanese Taiko drummers over Inupiat Eskimo performers, or Australian Aborigines over Angelenos.[2]

Interculturalism describes a merging, mixing or creolization. It is a transitive, dialectical process in which at least two cultures fuse and/or suffer partial disculturisation to create what the Cuban anthropologist Fernando Ortiz termed a 'neoculture' (in Taylor, 1991: 61–2).[3] As the creole metaphor that describes interculturalism confirms, the most obvious examples of the intercultural are linguistic. The Puerto Rican community in New York, for instance, has developed a form of Spanish which is deeply rooted in the language of Castille but has absorbed and/or adapted enough English words so as to be difficult at times for a person whose native language is European Spanish to understand. Interculturalism is hardly limited to language. Anne Bogart's production of *The Medium* at the New York Theatre Workshop (spring of 1994), for example, drew heavily on intercultural elements. The production, which was Bogart's take on the life and ideas of the Canadian media critic and guru Marshall McLuhan, combined the conventional Stanislavsky-based American acting tradition, her own Viewpoints technique, and the Suzuki Method to develop a performance style that blended movement, voice and a fragmented dramaturgy typical of the postmodern. This production may have owed much to its historical antecedents, but these antecedents were interwoven, adapted and used as points of departure during the collective creation phase of rehearsals to develop material far

---

2 For a description of the Los Angeles Festival see: Burnham, 1991; and Phelan, 1991.
3 Ortiz developed the notion of neoculture in reaction to the attempts by his North American colleagues in the 1930s to describe cultural acquisition in terms of acculturation, that is, the absorption of a minority culture by its dominant counterpart. Ortiz maintained that rather than one culture being absorbed by the other, the process is one in which both cultures suffer a deculturisation and combine to create an entirely new, neoculture (Taylor, 1991: 61–2). Ortiz, incorrectly in my opinion, described this process as transculturisation. What he in fact was describing is what I prefer to term interculturalism.

removed from any of the techniques that were the genesis of the piece. In short, they were fused into a neoculture.

Regardless of the differences between the transcultural, cross-cultural, multicultural and intercultural, rarely are any of them mutually exclusive. Most negotiations between cultures involve two or more of these processes since contacts between cultures are multifarious. Such interactions can encompass confrontations, conflict, collisions, appropriation, overlapping, withdrawal, separation, harmony, inclusion, unity, adaptation and change. Equally, the transactions they represent are not static. They are in a constant state of flux.

Barba and cultural pluralism

Cultural pluralism, rather than the intercultural alone, is at the heart of Theatre Anthropology and especially its research arm ISTA which incorporates the multicultural, transcultural and intercultural in its methodology.

Most of the research done at ISTA is multicultural. During ISTA sessions, Barba and his colleagues investigate the acting process primarily by comparing and contrasting performance forms from different cultures. Excluding occasional lecture/demonstrations of improvisation techniques in which performers from various traditions work together, these investigations are done with each of the cultural forms intact and separate from the others.

The major findings of this research are the principles that underlie what Barba terms the pre-expressive. This pre-expressive level of performance is concerned with presence, with how, in Barba's words, a performer can engender and project 'a presence which immediately attracts the spectator's attention' (Barba and Savarese, 1991: 188).[4] The pre-expressive is transcultural since it has its roots in the physiology that all performers share. It is unconcerned with the expressive performance codes of Noh theatre, Odissi dance, or psychological realism because they are culturally specific ways of shaping an actor's energy. The pre-expressive is predicated upon the fact that the human body functions in particular ways, no matter if that body is engaged in a theatre form from Japan, China, North America, Brazil or Bali.

The application of these findings – which Barba intends for the benefit of the Western performers who attend ISTA because, he argues, the traditional Asian genres already have the pre-expressive principles

---

4 For a detailed explanation of the pre-expressive see: Barba and Savarese, 1991: 8–22, 186–204; and Watson, 1995: 32–7.

imbedded in their performance codes – is intercultural. Euro-American performers are expected to combine their particular cultural form of expression with the principles of pre-expressivity. The expressive mode has its roots in the cultural performance tradition of the particular form, be it conventional realism, absurd theatre or street performance. The pre-expressive, on the other hand, is transcultural since it is engaged prior to expression. There is a dialectic relationship between the expressive techniques of the genre and the transcultural/pre-expressive, which results in a neoculture of sorts: a vital stage presence within the particular form. A brief example may clarify Barba's intended application of performance principles across cultures. One of his basic pre-expressive principles lies in the manipulation of balance and one's centre of gravity. In forms such as the classical Indian Odissi dance and Noh theatre (both of which he has researched extensively at ISTA), performers are required to alter their normal centre of gravity and distribution of body weight by the way in which they manipulate their spine, place their feet, and bend their legs. These alterations, which are far removed from the daily use of the body, call for greater amounts of energy merely to stand or move than do similar tasks in everyday life. This additional energy infuses presence into the actions on stage. A Western actor playing the role of Hamlet can, without attempting to copy the Odissi or Noh forms, apply these same principles of altering his centre of gravity and distribution of body weight into his portrayal in order to inject his performance of Hamlet with presence.[5]

Cultural pluralism is not limited to ISTA and Theatre Anthropology in Barba's work. It underlies virtually all of his professional activities. His performer training system, if one might call it that, for instance, is predicated upon the pre-expressive. His training at the Odin is essentially geared to exploring the transcultural performance principles that engender presence and underlie expression rather than focusing on mastering a collection of vocal, physical or technical skills that mark the virtuoso performer.

---

5   The notion of infusing a performance with presence through a physical adjustment of the body is not all that far removed from some Western acting techniques that owe little, if anything, to comparative cultural research. The manipulation of body centres and the use of animal-based models to alter one's physical base in the Adler approach to character work, for example, has at least part of its origins in the notion that each character has a unique rhythm, centre of gravity, and movement pattern that is related to that of the actor portraying the role. One of the performer's major tasks during rehearsals using this technique is to discover the ideal relationship between his/her physicality and that of the character in order to inject the portrayal with a believable vitality.

Many of Barba's productions are equally rooted in cultural pluralism. Several of them, for example, have their thematic origins in more
than one culture. Even his first Odin production, *Ornitofilene* (The Bird
Lovers – premiered in October, 1965), was decidedly multicultural in its
concern with a 'meeting' between cultures. It dealt with a group of
wealthy foreign investors who decided to build a tourist hotel in a small
Norwegian village. The poverty-stricken village needed the investment
and the jobs it would generate. But, the ecology-conscious foreigners
insisted that local people give up their only pastime, hunting birds, or
they would withdraw their offer. The villagers were outraged, an outrage
which was compounded by the fact that the 'wealthy foreigners' were
former Nazi soldiers who, twenty years before, tortured and killed many
of their neighbours when they occupied the village.

Ferai (premiered in June, 1969), the production which established
Barba's international reputation as a director, on the other hand, leant
more toward the intercultural through its interweaving of two myths of
very different cultural origins. These myths, one Greek (the legend of
Alcestis, the princess who sacrificed herself for the sake of her husband)
and the other Nordic (the saga of the Danish king, Frode Fredegod, who
was so revered by his people that, in order to retain the political and social
harmony of his reign after he died, his soldiers removed his intestines,
salted his body, and carried his cadaver around the kingdom in a chariot
as a symbol of national unity), were fused with the newly emerging Odin
theatrical style. The final *mise-en-scène*, which included characters from
both tales, had a myth-like religious quality born of its ritualized action,
expressionistic images, and archetypal conflict between what Christopher
Innes characterizes as male and female principles (1981: 179).

This preoccupation with thematics drawn from different cultures has
continued throughout Barba's career. Two of his productions from the
1980s, *Oxyrhincus Evangeliet* (premiered in March, 1985) and *Talabot*
(premiered in August, 1988), for instance, had their origins in a variety of
cultural elements blended in a mixture of the intercultural, multicultural,
and cross-cultural. *Oxyrhincus*, which combined the intercultural and
multicultural, had its roots in a mixture of Hassidism, a Coptic city where
some of the oldest known Christian manuscripts were found in the early
part of the twentieth century, the popular literary and filmic tradition of
South American cowboy-like outlaws, as well as the Vargas Llosa novel *The
War of the End of the World*; while *Talabot* whose origins lay in the writings
of a contemporary Danish anthropologist, Kirsten Hastrup, as well as the
'Huldrefolk' (hidden people) of Nordic legend, shamanism, and historical
figures such as the Danish explorer Knud Rasmussen, Antonin Artaud and
Che Guevara, placed a greater emphasis on the cross-cultural.

A number of Barba's productions have also incorporated cultural pluralism in their *mise-en-scènes*. *The Million*, for example, grew out of a sabbatical taken by the actors in the late 1970s during which they travelled to various parts of the world to study different performance forms. The ensuing production was an episodic piece with no clear story-line. It consisted of a series of vignettes in which a variety of exotic characters – such as Balinese dancers, a lion from the Japanese Kabuki, the Hindu Monkey King, a clichéd version of a Mexican in a huge sombrero, stilt figures in elaborate costumes and masks inspired by Haitian models, as well as a samba-dancing bear sang, danced, and/or played out simple, wordless scenes to the accompaniment of Asian, Latin and popular Western music. This *mélange*, though intercultural in many ways, included a strong cross-cultural component, especially in the costuming (much of which was culturally authentic), and a multicultural musical score.

Other productions Barba has created outside of the Odin have also combined various cultural elements in different ways. His *Teatrum Mundi* that are mounted at ISTAs, for instance, involve all of the artists attending the particular gathering in a single cohesive production while each performer retains his or her own particular cultural form; and his version of *Shakuntala*, presented at the 1993 *Festuge* (Festival Week) in Holstebro, combined a score written by a Western trained composer (Frans Winther) and one of India's leading musicians (Raghunath Panigrahi), a libretto by Winther, and a cast consisting of professional opera singers, a European chorus, Indian musicians and singers, a group of classical Western musicians, and the Odin actors accompanied by the Odissi dancer Sanjukta Panigrahi.

Barter is another example of cultural pluralism in Barba's work. These barters, in which performance replaces money as the currency of exchange, are a subversion of the traditional economic art model. The conventional transaction of my creativity for your gold becomes one of your culture's heritage and preoccupations for my theatre. Barters are a point of contact between cultures, a meeting that is realized through the trading of cultural products. But, as is taken up in greater detail later in 'The dynamics of barter', there is no question of unequal reciprocity in barter since there is no pre-established value for the performances that are their currency. All items are performatively and culturally equal in a barter, implying that they are a multicultural phenomena in which difference, equality, and exchange are all important.

This is not the entire story, however, because, even though most barters involve a simple form of reciprocity in which both groups of participants remain culturally separated, intact, and alternate their performances, cross-cultural factors are also involved. These cross-cultural factors are most obvious in barters such as the one the Odin mounted with the Candombe singers and drummers of Montevideo (Uruguay, April 1987). Instead of following the traditional format of having one group's performance precede the other, it was decided that the Odin actors and the Candombe artists would perform together. This called for a brief rehearsal where the Odin actors and their Candombe colleagues devised the rough outline of a scenario in which each group retained their fixed fragments of performance, as they might in a more conventional barter, except that they were now integrated loosely into a single, cohesive performance. Each of the Odin and Candombe performers retained his role, costume and score, as he would in a traditional barter, but the individually identifiable cultural fragments were subsumed into a single unit. The episodic, vaudeville-like dramatic structure of individual unconnected acts, which characterize most barters, was discarded for the sake of a single, unified, cross-cultural performance text.

All this is not to say that the Montevideo event negated the multicultural because, excluding the finale, in which both groups of performers danced together to the beat of the Candombe drums, the Odin actors and Candombe dancers took turns performing their individual, culturally inscribed fragments, much as they would have in most barters. Just as the conventional barter incorporates the cross-cultural, if one considers it in its entirety rather than merely as an accumulation of unrelated scenes, the Montevideo event consisted of both cross-cultural and multicultural elements.

In reality, every barter falls along a continuum between the cross-cultural at one end and the multicultural at the other; some barters are closer to the multicultural while others are nearer the cross-cultural. Whatever their cultural valence, all barters are a combination of the cross-cultural and the multicultural.

Even though Latin America is a continent made up of many countries, it is collectively Barba's 'other' culture. He and his Odin colleagues have, since their first appearance in Latin America at the Caracas Festival in Venezuela in the mid-1970s, often returned to tour, teach, and to help organize international gatherings of group theatre in various parts of the continent.

Barba's relationship with Latin America is dealt with in greater detail in the last section of this volume but, suffice to say, it has always been a significant relationship marked by reciprocity. He has had a major impact on group theatre throughout the continent. As well as providing a theoretical framework for these independent groups, Barba and the members of his company have shared their strategies for economic subsistence and models for artistic survival with their Latin American colleagues, and passed on their training and dramaturgical methods.

Latin America, in turn, has influenced Barba. It has been an important factor in several of his productions, ranging from the thematics that have generated them (as in *Oxyrhincus* discussed earlier) to providing geo-cultural influences to help shape them (the initial work on *Talabot* was done in Mexico with this intention); and from suggesting historical characters (Che Guevara in *Talabot*) to playing a role in a production's design choices (the costuming in *Oxyrhincus* included authentic gaucho clothing).

Barba's contact with Latin America is marked by a combination of the multicultural and intercultural. Latin American theatre artists are, understandably, primarily concerned with their own culture, which is separate and independent from Barba's Eurocentric preoccupations and Odin practice. But, the meeting and extended interaction between these fellow theatre workers from different continents has frequently resulted in a syncretism of sorts, a creolization of expressive forms that tends towards the neocultural. In Peru, for example, Barba first taught his training and dramaturgical methods at the International Group Theatre Gathering in Ayacucho in 1978. The organizers of the gathering, Mario Delgado and his group Cuatrotablas, as well as others who are now leading figures of the independent group theatre movement in Peru, such as Miguel Rubrio and the members of his company, Yuyachkani, have adapted and passed on what they learned over the succeeding years. So much so, that in the late 1980s group theatre in Peru was dominated by young groups combining their Peruvian social and political concerns with forms bearing the clear hallmarks of the Odin's theatrical style as taught to them by their older colleagues. Coincidentally, Barba's work, as described above, bears the hallmarks of his contact with Latin America.

The relations between Barba and Latin America could be represented, as in earlier examples of similar contacts, by a continuum with multiculturalism at one end and interculturalism at the other. Most of the cultural transactions between Barba and his Latin American counterparts fall somewhere along this continuum.

The continuum highlights a major difference between barter and Barba's contact with Latin America. Barter is essentially static. The relations it generates between cultures are limited to a single event with a relatively clear beginning, middle and end. It is predicated upon a celebration of difference, a cultural plurality that implies contact, give and take, but no change in the cultures involved. In Latin America, on the other hand, the cultural transactions are dynamic, they are part of an ongoing process continually moving from the multicultural to the intercultural. These transactions imply an interactive process, a penetration and reciprocity that takes place 'inside' the cultures rather than at their outer edges or borders.

Whether dynamic or essentially static in nature, cultural relations for Barba are concerned with engagement. His focus is on contact, meeting and interaction. He is less concerned with what delineates, marks or defines a particular culture than with exchange. The nature of Barba's various exchanges in Theatre Anthropology, barter, and Latin America are the focus of this collection of essays.

Fusion versus reductivism

During his opening address at the 1996 ISTA symposium on 'Theatre in Multicultural Society' in Denmark, Barba characterized the theatre as a site in which there is a 'meeting through difference'. Theatre is the common ground in which difference is displayed and, most importantly negotiated. As Robert Livingstone puts it, theatre is 'a site for the active transformation of culture' (1995: 196). But this active transformation is hardly the same in every instance. It is a process which can take one or other of several forms.

It is at least theoretically possible that two or more theatre cultures could occupy the same site simultaneously with few or no repercussions for either of them. Some barters, for instance, at least appear to have little more than negligible consequences for both of the cultures involved beyond the presentation of self-contained, cultural products. These barters may be a site of difference and meeting, but the meetings have little more import than polite strangers exchanging social niceties as they pass each other in a corridor.

Metaphorical strangers aside, the theatre is generally speaking an active site of consequence with regard to cultural relations. These relations are most often one of two types: fused or reductivist. Cross-culturalism, multiculturalism and interculturalism are all forms of fused transactions in the theatre because fusion is the product of cultural integration. This integration can have its genesis in an amicable exchange between cultures or in a more abrasive, disruptive clash. The defining characteristic of fusion is not how a product is arrived at, but rather whether the various cultural components which generate it are imbedded in a single, cohesive aesthetic frame. Fusion encompasses the apparently seamless interweaving of various performance traditions from Indonesia, India, experimental theatre, and Latin as well as North America that mark Julie Taymor's creative work, as well as the postmodern eruptions born of the collisions between the Chicano world, the reality of contemporary

America and the culture of Mexico that one finds in Guillermo Gómez-Peña's pieces.[6]

Not to overdo the continuum paradigm, fusion involves varying degrees of interaction that can best be understood as fitting somewhere along a vector at one end of which is total integration and the other separate incorporation.

Works like Peter Brook's *Mahabharata*, which interwove Indian mythology, training in classical Indian performance forms such as Kathakali, a cast drawn from a variety of acting traditions, and a *mise-en-scène* that drew heavily on Brook's background in the English classics, belong more closely to the total integration end of the continuum than Barba's *Teatrum Mundi*. The latter, with each of the artists remaining faithful to their particular cultural tradition within the context of a single performance text, is an example of separate incorporation. Most fusion productions, like those of Mnouchkine's Shakespeare cycle, mentioned earlier, or her *Les Atrides* series in which she drew heavily upon Kathakali aesthetics in her vision of the classical Greek chorus, fall somewhere along the continuum.[7]

Aside from the *Teatrum Mundi*, most of Barba's productions are closer to the integration end of the continuum than its separate incorporation counterpart. Since a barter, on the other hand, is a single event made up of separate performance pieces with little, if any, causal or narrative connection between them, it falls closer to the separate incorporation end of the continuum than his productions; while the interculturalism that is at the root of Barba's relations with Latin America implies a greater degree of integration than separate incorporation. By far the most interesting and unique elements in Barba's work are the

---

6   Richard Schechner has a much more benign view of fusion. He regards fusion, along with multiculturalism, as a 'utopian scheme' that 'cloak[s] power arrangements and struggles' (1991: 30). His somewhat Pollyanna-like view of fusion stands in stark contrast to his view of interculturalism which is championed by those who 'probe the confrontations, ambivalences, disruptions, fears, disturbances and difficulties when and where cultures collide, overlap or pull away from each other' (1991: 30). In making a distinction between fusion and the intercultural, Schechner is confusing process with product. Fusion is arrived at in different ways, the intercultural being one of them. But, excluding Barba, whose work is reductivist rather than fused in nature, the artists he cites as interculturalists, Gómez-Peña, Salman Rushdie, Peter Brook and Tadashi Suzuki, all create material in different ways that fuses various cultural elements into a single, cohesive aesthetic frame.

7   Marvin Carlson provides a related topography of cultural pluralism. But, in using the spectator's relationship to the performance material as his point of reference, his elaboration is more extensive than the continuum I suggest. His topography begins with conventional performance in its home culture and ends with an imported cultural product that disregards local traditions (1990: 50).

reductivist notions that underlie Theatre Anthropology, his ISTA research and, in turn, most of his training practice.

Theatre Anthropology is concerned with universals. Most of Barba's early definitions of Theatre Anthropology, of which there are several, are best summed up in the definition he provides in the *Dictionary of Theatre Anthropology*, 'the study of human beings' socio-cultural and physiological behavior in a performance situation' (Barba and Savarese, 1991: 8). But, the truth is that Theatre Anthropology, as his more recent definition in *The Paper Canoe* reveals, does not have such a broad agenda: 'Theatre Anthropology is the study of the pre-expressive scenic behavior upon which different genres, styles, roles and personal or collective traditions are based' (Barba, 1995: 9). As Marco De Marinis points out, Theatre Anthropology is a partial rather than a global theory (1995: 129), its province is 'pre-expressive scenic behavior' not 'socio-cultural and physiological behavior in a performance situation'. Yet, despite the fact that the pre-expressive is synonymous with stage presence, Barba maintains that it has nothing to do with cultural expression. It is a universal that underlies all performance.

Unlike other theatrical 'universalists' of the second half of the twentieth century, such as Brook or Grotowski, who have pursued universality either as a mode of dramaturgical expression (Brook) or as a process in which one generates and projects a personal epiphany that in turn induces a similar experience in the spectator (Grotowski), Barba's universality is concerned with technique: a technique which, as De Marinis notes, privileges the physical over the mental, verbal or dramaturgical (1995: 128). As touched on earlier, the pre-expressive consists of what Barba describes as 'shared common principles' (Barba and Savarese, 1991: 8), these principles are physical rules of scenic practice that explain the nature of presence and how a performer can generate it, whether he be a Kathakali dancer, a Stanislavsky trained actor, a Kabuki *onnogata*, or a member of the avant-garde.

Barba has been severely criticized, especially by Rustom Bharucha, for his focus on techniques that ignore cultural expression (Bharucha, 1993: 57–60, 244). Most of this criticism questions the very nature of the pre-expressive by maintaining that it is impossible to separate cultural expression from a mode of engagement that supposedly underlies it. Unfortunately, the arguments that support this assertion tend more to hearsay than to empirical evidence. Bharucha, for example, maintains that since he cannot 'see any performance on an exclusively pre-expressive level' (1993: 57) it does not exist, and that the 'anatomy of the actor is of no use until it is contextualized within an expressive framework' that 'cannot be separated from "culture, history, and style"' (1993: 57). All this without reference to the series of tapes Barba made at the 1980 Bonn ISTA with the Asian artists taking part in which he demonstrates the way in which similar pre-expressive elements are imbedded in their various cultural-based performance codes.[8]

Regardless of this criticism, Barba's focus on technique is in keeping with the interest in craft that has been a hallmark of Western performance since the latter part of the nineteenth and early years of the twentieth centuries. The concept of acting as a craft and the actor as an artist that can learn that craft from a teacher whose curriculum is based on a combination of experience and his own studies with his teacher(s) has dominated much of practical theatre discourse since Stanislavsky developed his system of acting in the early 1900s. A comprehensive history of the development of the modern Western actor hardly concerns us here, but it is no exaggeration to say that Barba has very consciously followed in the footsteps of those who went before him: Stanislavsky, Meyerhold, Copeau, Decroux, St Denis, and of course his mentor, Grotowski. However, as touched on earlier in the discussion of his formative years, Barba's path has travelled beyond the confines of Europe. These travels in the East coupled with his knowledge of the West has led him to realize a connection between cultural pluralism and the craft of the performer.

The connection lies in subtending culture. In keeping with Grotowski's notion of the *Via Negativa*, craft for Barba is not about accumulating skills.[9] It is concerned with discovering how to engender and project presence in every action on stage. The aim of craft for Barba is to master what Leonard Pronko calls 'deep structures' (1995: 73). Barba is not as interested in the scenic richness of Kabuki, the complex performance codes of Balinese dance, or the socio-historical context of Noh as he is in the presence of the performer that underscores all of them. The deep structures that this presence depends upon for Barba is possibly best understood in terms of Geertz's concept of the stratigraphic, that is, the notion that humankind is a composite of levels: biological, psychological, social, cultural, etc. These levels are somewhat like the layered skins of an

---

8 In this series of tapes, Barba conducts lecture/demonstrations with an unidentified Balinese dancer, the Odissi dancer Sanjukta Panigrahi, and Katsuko Azuma, a Nihon Buyo performer from Japan. Since these tapes identify what Barba calls the pre-expressive and demonstrate how it functions in different cultural performance forms, any criticism of the pre-expressive has to either take them up directly or address what they reveal about Barba's concept. These tapes are available through the Odin Teatret.

9 *Via Negativa* was a term used by Grotowski in his Poor Theatre period to describe what training was for him and his Polish Theatre Laboratory: a means of eradicating a performer's personal psycho-physical and vocal blocks rather than a system based on accumulating skills (Grotowski, 1969: 16–17).

onion which, though interrelated, can be peeled off to reveal ever more 'essential' layers of humanness (Geertz, 1973: 37). Barba's notion of craft calls for the peeling away of the various layers of codification, enculturation and personal expression in order to engage the basic energies of the biological body. His anatomical essentialism is based on the notion that we are all biologically equal. All bodies, regardless of their racial, ethnic or national origins, are fundamentally the same and hence have to use similar techniques to harness energy and project presence.

Unlike the focus Theatre Anthropology places on the biological layer of Geertz's stratigraph, Barba's relationships with Latin America and the exchanges in barter give greater emphasis to the socio-cultural and even political layers. Obviously Barba's teaching of performer techniques in Latin America draws upon his anatomical concerns with the pre-expressive. But as will be taken up in greater detail in the Latin American section later, the socio-cultural affinity between Barba and his Latin colleagues, as well as the political realities of making theatre in countries such as Cuba, Peru, Argentina and Chile is of greater significance than the biological in their contact. In barter, meanwhile, the entire emphasis is on socio-cultural exchange and, to a lesser extent, the political context within which the exchanges take place.

References

Barba, Eugenio (1988), 'Eurasian theatre', *The Drama Review*, Vol. 32, No. 3 (T119), Autumn: 126–30.

Barba, Eugenio (1988a), 'The way of refusal: the theatre's body-in-life', *New Theatre Quarterly*, Vol. 4, No. 16: 291–99.

Barba, Eugenio (1995), *The Paper Canoe: A Guide to Theatre Anthropolocy*. London and New York: Routledge.

Barba, Eugenio and Nicola Savarese (1991), *A Dictionary of Theatre Anthropology: The Secret Art of the Performer*. London and New York: Routledge.

Bhabha, Homi K (1994), *The Location of Culture*. London and New York: Routledge.

Bharucha, Rustom (1993), *Theatre and the World: Performance and the Politics of Culture*. London and New York: Routledge.

Burnham, Linda Frye (1991), 'Currents: the L.A. Festival, 1990: year one on the Pacific Rim', *The Drama Review*, Vol. 35, No. 3 (T131) Autumn: 108–17.

Carlson, Marvin (1990), 'Peter Brook's "The Mahabharata" and Ariane Mnouchkine's "L'Indiade" as examples of contemporary cross cultural theatre', in *The Dramatic Touch of Difference: Theatre, Own and Foreign*. Tobingen, Germany: Gunter Narr Verlag, pp. 49–56.

Clifford, James (1988), 'On Orientalism', in *The Predicament of Culture: Twentieth Century Ethnography, Literature, and Art*. Cambridge, MA: Harvard University Press, pp. 255–76.

De Marinis, Marco (1995), 'From pre-expressivity to the dramaturgy of the performer: an essay on *The Paper Canoe*', *Mime Journal*: Incorporated Knowledge: 114–56.

Geertz, Clifford (1973), *The Interpretation of Cultures*. New York: Basic Books.

Grotowski, Jerzy (1969), *Towards a Poor Theatre*. New York: Simon & Schuster.

Hall, Edward T. (1977), *Beyond Culture*. New York: Anchor Books.

Innes, Christopher (1981), *Holy Theatre: Ritual and the Avant-Garde*. Cambridge and New York: Cambridge University Press.

Livingstone, Robert Eric (1995), 'Decolonizing the theatre: Césaire, Serreau and the drama of negritude', in *Imperialism and Theatre: Essays on World Theatre, Drama and Performance*, ed. J. Ellen Gainor. London and New York: Routledge.

Pavis, Patrice (1992), *Theatre at the Crossroads of Culture*. London and New York: Routledge.

Phelan, Peggy (1991), 'Here and there', *The Drama Review*, Vol. 35, No. 3 (T131) Autumn: 118–27.

Pronko, Leonard (1995), 'Two Salomes and a Kabuki montage: on reading a dictionary of Theatre Anthropology', *Mime Journal*: Incorporated Knowledge: 70–81.

Schechner, Richard (1991), 'An intercultural primer', *American Theater*. Vol. 8, No. 7 (October): 28–31; 135–6.

Schechner, Richard and Willa Appel (eds) (1990), *By Means of Performance*. New York and Cambridge: Cambridge University Press.

Taylor, Diana (1991), 'Transculturating transculturation', in *Interculturalism and Performance*, ed. Bonnie Marranca and Gautam Dasgupta. New York: Performing Arts Journal Publications, pp. 60–74.

Watson, Ian (1995), *Towards a Third Theatre: Eugenio Barba and the Odin Teatret*. London and New York: Routledge.

Wirth, Andrzej (1991), 'Interculturalism and iconophilia in the new theatre', in *Interculturalism and Performance*, ed. Bonnie Marranca and Gautam Dasgupta. New York: Performing Arts Journal Publications, pp. 281–90.

ISTA and Theatre Anthropology

1

Staging Theatre Anthropology
Ian Watson

The International School of Theatre Anthropology (ISTA) is a most unusual organization because it is both an institution and an acronym for a conference while at the same time providing the empirical basis and rhetorical framework for Eugenio Barba's performance research. The institution, which Barba founded in 1979, is based at the *Nordisk Teaterlaboratorium* in Holstebro, Denmark and arranges conferences in conjunction with sponsors in different parts of the world. To date (2002) there have been eleven of these conferences (most often simply referred to by the same acronym as the organization, i.e., ISTA) since the first one in Bonn, Germany in 1980: Volterra, Italy – 1981; Blois and Malakoff, France – 1985; Holstebro, Denmark – 1986; Salento, Italy – 1987; Bologna, Italy – 1990; Brecon and Cardiff, Wales – 1992; Londrina, Brazil – 1994; Umeå, Sweden – 1995; Copenhagen, Denmark – 1996; Lisbon, Portugal, 1998; and Bielefeld, Germany – 2000.

Despite differences between these various ISTAs, most of them consisted of a three-part programme: a private workshop/research session for invited participants; a forum open to a larger public; and a series of barters as well as public performances for the general public by the artists attending the meeting.

The private, closed sessions have always been the most important part of ISTA. The variations in these sessions from one gathering to another are dependent upon the aims of the particular meeting, thematic considerations, and the perceived needs of the participants. The sessions usually consist of lecture/demonstrations, classes with various of the master performers attending the conference, seminars, and workshop/ rehearsals that explore the creation of intercultural performance texts. Barba dominates this part of every ISTA, leading or introducing and guiding each of the activities. Those invited to take part in this segment of the conference always include: seasoned artists with whom Barba is familiar (master performers from Asia, the Odin actors, and select theatre practitioners from the West); intellectuals (theatre scholars, scientists, and critics all headed by a small group of Italian theatre professors who have been among Barba's closest collaborators since his early days in the theatre); and young theatre artists just beginning their professional journey.

The open forums at ISTA usually last no longer than a few days and are primarily designed to allow those unable to attend the longer, closed meetings access to the ISTA research, Barba's ideas, and various scholars' thoughts on topics of related interest. These sessions, which like their closed counterpart, are dominated by Barba, most often take the form of lecture/demonstrations, a more conventional conference-type symposia, or a combination of both.[1]

Locations

ISTA is a multiplicity of locations. Apart from being the research site that is most often associated with it, ISTA is a geographic locale with shifting boundaries. These boundaries move outwards from the contained circle of the closed session to the more public, open forum, and eventually embrace the entire community through the performances and barters.

The closed session is, as Kirsten Hastrup points out, a social space (1996: 10): an environment in which people from various parts of the world with an interest in performance and/or Barba's ideas on it come together for a limited period of time. These people live, observe, discuss and share the experience of ISTA together collectively. Friendships are formed, ideas are generated, and frustrations are often aired through this informal social dimension. Informal or not, this aspect of ISTA does not entirely vanish at meeting's end. During the conference, the social dynamic is strongest because it provides a 'heated' centre of face-to-face social interaction. But following gatherings, many of those who have made meaningful contact continue a less intense dialogue via telephone,

1 For more detailed descriptions of ISTA see: Hastrup, 1996: and Watson, 1995: 149–73; 177–8.

mail, and/or e-mail. They establish an expanded social space based on a community of shared interests and technological possibilities.

It is also a pedagogical space. If nothing else, ISTA is a site of learning, especially for those who are attending it for the first time. The teaching sessions, lecture/demonstrations, the seminars and the work-shop/rehearsals are all educational opportunities for those willing to learn.

The research that is at the root of ISTA is based on a three-part model of universality, historicity and inscription. This model is dominated by concerns with the universal nature of performance, but these concerns are predicated upon an understanding of the body as a historical site as well as a site of cultural inscription.

As touched on earlier in 'Contexting Barba', Theatre Anthropology is solely concerned with what Barba terms the pre-expressive level of performance. His ISTA research has a two-part agenda. The first part is concerned with identifying and isolating the pre-expressive level of performance, which he maintains is common to all genres of theatre regardless of their cultural heritage. The second focuses on applying the pre-expressive to contemporary western theatre practice.

With his focus on the pre-expressive, Barba is ever conscious of the performer's body as a historical 'text' of sorts. The actor's training and experience privileges the corporal over the intellectual. The performer's knowledge is centred in the body because it is concerned with doing, display and exhibition. It is primarily an orally transmitted art. There are many important theoretical manuals and books on acting, especially those by the great masters and visionaries like Zeami, Stanislavsky, Artaud and Grotowski. But these books are only adjuncts to the performer's training with his teacher(s), his own work in the studio, and his experience on the stage.

The master artists who work with Barba at ISTA embody the histories of their forms. The Odissi dancer Sanjukta Panigrahi, one of Barba's original ISTA collaborators, carried the heritage of an ancient art form revived in her body. Her artistry was based on the teaching of her guru, Kelucharan Mahapatra, her ability to give physical form to the ancient carvings of temple dancers on the walls of the temples in Orissi, and the transformation of the Natyashastra's performance rules into the Odissi dance form. Kanichi Hanayagi, the *onnogata* and Nihon Buyo performer who has been involved with ISTA since the late 1980s, is, through his formal training with his masters from childhood, the product of a historical tradition with its roots in seventeenth century Japan. Similarly, more recent Western actors who have taken part in ISTA, like Thomas Leabhart and Gennadi Bogdanov, have a historical dimension that is pertinent to

Barba's research. Leabhart studied with and continues to perform pieces created for him by the founder of corporal mime, Etienne Decroux; while Bogdanov, who both teaches Meyerholdian biomechanics and uses it to create performances, traces his heritage to Meyerhold himself through his study of biomechanics with, Nikolai Kustov, one of Meyerhold's pupils.[2] How presence is encoded into these historical stage bodies is part of Barba's research interest at ISTA.

Interwoven with the acknowledgement of the performer's body as a historical confluence is the notion that it is also a site of authentic cultural inscriptions. These inscriptions are encoded into the bodies of the actors through years of training and performance experience. And, even though, as critics such as Rustom Bharucha (1993: 54–67) and Phillip Zarrilli (1988) rightly point out, these inscriptions are not Barba's focus at ISTA, they are an important factor in his research. This is because he maintains that the codified forms of performance he examines at ISTA have the universal pre-expressive principles imbedded in them. Thus, one of ISTA's main concerns over the years has been to investigate the pre-expressive principles that underlie the narratives of cultural and historical inscription in each of the performance traditions represented at the various conferences.

Author/authoritarian

All of the formal research at ISTA is generated by one man, Barba. As I have pointed out elsewhere, Barba maintains that ISTA is predicated upon the understanding that those who come to it do so in order to be confronted with what interests him (Watson, 1995: 170). This interest is centred on the operative level of performance and appeals to the moral high ground of universality. Barba focuses on what is common to all performance, he examines the level of performance that erases difference through an emphasis on the anatomical. Cultural differences are subtended by biology at ISTA and in Theatre Anthropology, the body of knowledge it is founded upon. The problem is that the shades of authoritarianism which pervade meetings dominated by the ideas of its organizer, the inclusion of Asian performers in what at least appears to be the subservient roles of 'objects of study' by the 'wise' Western intellectuals, and the socio-political interplay of domination and submission that both

---

2 Leabhart first attended the 1994 ISTA in Londrina, Brazil. He has since become an important member of Barba's ISTA team. Bogdanov only took part in the Copenhagen ISTA. A pupil of his, Ralf Raüker, gave a demonstration of biomechanics at the Umeå ISTA.

of these hint at, imply a universal space in which the ghosts of colonialism play no small part.

Despite the number of eminently qualified people at every ISTA and the potential for collective research and enquiry this affords, the discursive space in formal settings is limited at gatherings. Homi Bhabha's notion of an 'in-between' space separating cultures that is an area of negotiation, debate and compromise (1994: 22) is essentially a decided space at ISTA. Even during the symposia segment of the open session, those who present papers are usually not asked to address questions about Theatre Anthropology. Barba invites them to talk on topics he suggests that are related though not directly pertinent to Theatre Anthropology. Typical examples include the paper presented by the Italian anthropologist Piergiorgio Giacchè at the symposium on 'Semiology of Performance and Theatre Anthropology' during the Salento ISTA which discussed his survey of local Salento theatre audiences, a paper by Fernando de Toro, a Chilean scholar based in Canada, at the same ISTA which provided a basic overview of theatre semiotics, and the presentation on the historical relationships among performance, comedy, and politics in the United States by Ron Jenkins at the Bologna ISTA symposium, 'Performing Techniques and Historiography'.[3] As Zarrilli discusses in his critique of the 1986 ISTA in Holstebro, one cannot talk of a discourse on Theatre Anthropology at ISTA since ISTA's research is essentially monovocal (Zarrilli, 1988).[4]

The nearest one comes to discursive research at ISTA is when Barba allows master performers who are attending the conference for the first time to conduct their own lecture/demonstrations. There are usually very few of these lecture/demonstrations at any one ISTA since most of the master performers are permanent members of Barba's ISTA staff who are present at every gathering. The 1996 Copenhagen meeting was unusual in this regard, however, because, apart from lecture/demonstrations by many of those who had worked at previous conferences, it included lecture/demonstrations by five performers who had not been to ISTA

3   The first academic symposium organized as part of ISTA was for the Salento conference in 1987. The one-day symposium, entitled 'Semiology of Performance and Theatre Anthropology', included papers by Monique Borie, Marco De Marinis, Fernando de Toro, Piergiorgio Giacchè, Patrice Pavis, Jean-Marie Pradier, Franco Ruffini and Ferdinando Taviani. Most ISTAs since then have included similar symposia. For details see: Hastrup, 1996: 210–18.

4   A distinction needs to be made between the discursive natures of ISTA and Theatre Anthropology. ISTA is monovocal, but Theatre Anthropology is not. The latter is dominated by Barba through his writings and pre-eminent position at ISTA. Nevertheless, volumes such as this, and the section on ISTA in my own *Towards a Third Theatre* (1995: 149–73) and *The Performers' Village* edited by Kirsten Hastrup (1996) continue to broaden the discursive nature of Theatre Anthropology.

previously: one each by Gennadi Bogdanov (the Russian biomechanics expert mentioned earlier), Carolyn Carlson (a modern dancer and choreographer trained in the United States now based in Paris), Stina Ekblad (one of Sweden's leading actresses), Steve Paxton (a well-known modern dancer and choreographer from the United States), and Stephen Piers (a principal dancer with the Royal Danish Ballet).

Barba usually discusses or works with performers following their lecture/demonstrations. For those who have attended several ISTAs, these sessions with the perennial Asian masters and western performers are somewhat predictable and are clearly intended more as pedagogical exercises for those attending ISTA for the first time than research sessions. But this is less obvious when he works with new performers like Bogdanov. Following the latter's lecture/demonstration in Copenhagen, Barba questioned him extensively about the nature of biomechanics while he also asked Bogdanov to repeat many parts of the exercises he had shown. Barba, who no doubt had seen Bogdanov's work prior to the lecture/demonstration, was clearly not as familiar with it as with the Asian forms he has been studying at ISTA for many years. Yet, despite what appeared to be a genuine exploration of Bogdanov's technique, Barba never explained the purpose of his questions, did not suggest they had provided information that either confirmed or contradicted his theory of the pre-expressive, and did not allow others to question him during the session. This monovocal research model, which relegated participants to the role of mute observers, was repeated, with slight variations, for each of the ISTA neophyte masters in Copenhagen.

The lack of dialogue at ISTA has been a source of complaint among participants since at least the 1986 meeting where the debate became so acrimonious that it almost threatened the gathering altogether.[5] But Barba and others closely involved with organizing and planning ISTA, are well aware of this criticism and do little, if anything to address it. Why? One explanation lies in Barba's creative style. As his entire professional history confirms, he is an autocratic director who favours the pedagogy of experience over discussion. In describing his own attempts to understand the meaning of theatre in the context of the cultural plurality that he has chosen to work in, for example, he clearly states his preference for action over verbal discourse, 'I repeat to myself the words which for thirty years I have whispered to my actors: "What you have to do, you have to do. And don't ask, don't ask"' (1994: 113). If, as Barba and his closest colleagues maintain, one of ISTA's aims is to develop a 'new way of seeing'

---

5   For a brief description of the 1986 Holstebro ISTA and the contention surrounding it see: Watson, 1995: 159–61.

(Taviani in Watson, 1995: 172), then, even at the expense of being misunderstood, he suggests an autodidactic posture of learning to observe by observing rather than by augmenting observations with constructive discussion.[6]

An even less easily supported, but related explanation, suggested by the anthropologist Hastrup who has followed Barba's work in recent years, is that 'explicitness kills experience' (1996: 13). In other words, to talk about something somehow or other destroys it. Barba may well endorse an element of this, since it is a dictum one often hears in the training, workshop, or rehearsal studios where corporal enquiry is understandably favoured over cerebral deliberation. But its relevance to what claims to be a scientific gathering is suspect. Rather than providing a justification for Barba's posture, Hastrup's suggestion raises another question: why invite humanist scholars and intellectuals to ISTA at all if there is to be little or no opportunity for discussion? Certainly they can depart with their observations and conclusions gleaned either in isolation or in casual conversations with fellow participants outside of the formal programme, but they are not afforded the opportunity to contribute anything to ISTA's research during the conference proper. All too often, those to whom discussion is a vital part of their enquiry process are ignored or silenced at ISTA.

This silencing and the accompanying lack of explication has the ring of mystery and unshared secrets to it. Barba's authoritarian posture and negation of formal discourse establishes a dual-level power structure at ISTA. The most obvious and overt structure is the one in which Barba is leader and everyone else is a follower. In this structural dynamic, he is the acknowledged organizer and official director of the conference, he is the chief guru among a select group of master teachers, and he is the dominant presence in all activities. There is also a parallel covert structure linked to the importance of silence at ISTA. Barba positions himself as the owner of a knowledge that is neither explained fully nor is open to discussion. It is a mystery that only he, as the leader, and a select few of his closest colleagues, have access to. This mythologizing, coupled with ISTA's authorial posturing, cuts across the generally accepted notion of scientific discovery being open to question and verification by others.

---

6   It should be noted that attempts have been made to encourage a dialogue of sorts within the formal ISTA programme from time to time. In Brazil, for example, there were sessions entitled 'Gardens' that were essentially break-out seminars in which participants, guided by leaders chosen by Barba, discussed aspects of ISTA's research among themselves. However, there has never been any direct investigation of Asian or western performers in the formal ISTA programme by anyone other than Barba.

A related problem at ISTA is the hierarchical nature of conferences. Hastrup identifies a concentric hierarchy consisting of four distinct groups with Barba as its centre: what she terms the 'Council of Elders', a group of Italian theatre professors who have followed Barba's work since the late 1960s and early 1970s and are his closest intellectual colleagues. These are the 'Nobility', or master performers from Asia and the West who are ISTA's major pedagogues; the 'Jesters' who comprise the experienced intellectuals, critics, scientists and performers who bring expertise to their observations and any possible discussions; and what she calls the 'waterbearers', the lowercase of which betrays their (lack of?) importance to the ISTA equation as neophyte theatre practitioners or students who often form the bulk of participants but whose voices are rarely heard (1996: 12–15).

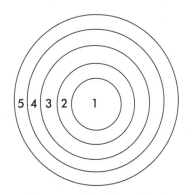

1 Barba – the 'heated centre'
2 Council of Elders
3 Nobility
4 Jesters
5 waterbearers

1 The concentric hierarchy at ISTA

Hastrup's characterization of this hierarchy in concentric terms unintentionally depicts the relationships of discourse within what she calls the 'ISTA family'. As already discussed, there is little or no public discourse at ISTA, but there is a great deal of private contact among different layers of the hierarchy. Those closest to Barba have greatest access to him while those furthest away have little or no contact with the leader of ISTA. Contact with Barba aside, however, there is informal dialogue across and between Hastrup's concentric boundaries. These dialogues, in which elders meet nobles, jesters, and even on occasion waterbearers, are predicated upon hierarchies of professional experience, knowledge of theatre anthropology, and even personal characteristics such as degrees of shyness and one's willingness to attempt social interaction in a foreign language.

The 'other'

Barba has been criticized for what might best be characterized as mystifying the 'other'. This criticism is partly based on Barba's lack of concern for the socio-historical context of the Asian performance forms he examines at ISTA. His focus on what subtends culture rather than cultural inscription and the context from which it springs, leaves him open to the charge of essentializing the East, of exoticizing rather than explicating difference. This, combined with his authorial voice, which implies a division between the dominant and submissive, revives the ghosts of imperialism in any relationship with Asia and insinuates a bipolar difference of self and other.

There is an irony of sorts in this criticism since Barba is ideologically committed to the erasure of otherness. Theatre Anthropology is concerned with the transcultural, with what is common among performers from different cultures. It is unconcerned with what divides performers into East and West, them and us. Merely choosing to compare Oriental and Occidental performance genres, without examining the historical and/or cultural framework of either, does not necessarily exoticize the most unfamiliar. Barba is committed to a detailed and thorough analysis of technique without cultural favour. He scrutinizes western performance as thoroughly as he does Odissi dance or Kabuki. Theatre Anthropology is concerned with demystifying the performer's quality of presence without regard to the cultural origins of his or her performance form.

A further irony with regard to otherness and performance is that, despite the fact that the concept of otherness in post-colonial discourse is born of those critical of Eurocentric bias, it smacks of the same Eurocentrism that marked the colonial mindset it is intended to address. Our contemporary notion of cultural otherness owes a great deal to anthropology, a Eurocentric discipline based upon subjective examination and objective explanation of 'other' cultures.[7] This interpretive model of cultural relations reaffirms the socio-political bias of colonialism: the Europeanized centre of power and knowledge as self and all else as other. But, otherness is a trope on cultural relativity and has a shifting locus; it is a cognitive frame generated by ethnocentrism rather than Eurocentrism. A great part of the book *Theatre and the World: Performance and the Politics of Culture* by the Indian theatre director and scholar Rustom Barucha (1993), for example, in which he uses Indian culture and theatre as a referent from which to criticize exploitation of it by the 'other' Euro-

---

7   For a thorough examination of the relationship between anthropology and
    otherness see: Fabian, 1983.

American cultures, is predicated upon this relativity. Similarly, critics who argue that the Asian performers at ISTA are others from Barba's perspective, have to also admit that Barba and his Odin actors are the others from Panigrahi and her musicians' Odissi, Indian point of view.

The construction of otherness implies a lack of agency on the part of the other, suggesting that the minority culture is entirely subject to the dominant in relationships between them. The reality is, as Fernando Ortiz's concept of the neocultural, discussed in 'Contexting Barba', insinuates, more complex. Ortiz argues that cultural interaction is a dialectic of sorts in which original cultures subsume, adapt, and/or incorporate cultural fragments each from the other with the potential of becoming creolized versions of their original selves (Taylor, 1991: 61–2). Creolization, or what Ortiz prefers to call a neoculture, is the consummate relationship between self and other. But, even if the relationship is far from its dialectical conclusion, each culture can appropriate elements of the other. Even if a minority culture is not an equal partner in a cultural relationship, it is as capable of adopting elements from the dominant culture as the latter is of exploiting the former. Traditional performers such as Panigrahi and Katsuko Azuma, a Japanese Nihon Buyo master who was a leading pedagogue during ISTA's formative years, for instance, credit their ISTA experiences with giving them greater insight into their own forms, helping them to understand other performance genres, and assisting them in the teaching of students (Panigrahi in Skeel, 1994: 114–15; Azuma in Skeel, 1994: 126; Azuma, 1986; Panigrahi, 1986).

Even though otherness does not deny agency, the constructions of power that underlie cultural contact and exchange have implications for Barba and for cultural relations in general. In most meaningful negotiation between cultures, power structures are inextricably linked to otherness, to issues of the majority versus the minority, of the dominant versus the subaltern, and/or control versus submission. These bipolarities are the product of the lack of equality in cultural relations and one would be naive to suggest that they do not play a part in Barba's creative work and research. As touched on earlier, Barba has been criticized by respected scholars like Patrice Pavis and Rustom Bharucha of appropriating material from other cultures without due regard to the socio-historical context of the material (Bharucha, 1993: 54–67, 240–5; Pavis, 1992: 160–82).[8] Cultural appropriation raises questions of theft, loss and the diluting of authenticity. But, as Fred Turner argues, this notion of appropriation is

---

8 Pavis seems to want to both criticize and not criticize Barba. He first accuses Barba of cultural appropriation then, because he feels that the term appropriation has ramifications of imperialism, corrects himself and characterizes Barba's methodology as one of 're-elaboration' (1992: 161).

based on a false analogy between cultural and industrial goods. If the latter are sold and shipped elsewhere, they no longer exist where they originated. Cultural goods, on the other hand, are like ideas, they can travel and be adapted by another while also remaining intact at their origin (Turner, 1991: 260–2).

Turner's argument maybe somewhat simplistic, especially in the light of Ortiz's concept of the neocultural, but it is pertinent to Barba's practice. As discussed in 'Contexting Barba', for instance, Barba incorporates material from other cultures into his productions; directly as in the case of *Teatrum Mundi* or *The Million*, or indirectly as in most of the productions based on thematic sources from other cultures. In both instances, he is unconcerned with the source cultures: they merely provide points of departure or fragments of performance for his productions. But in neither instance is anything taken from the source culture that in any way damages the latter. The source culture retains its authenticity with what Xiao-mei Chen terms its 'intrinsic core' intact (1995: 9). Barba is not a cultural anthropologist seeking an encyclopedic understanding of a particular society; he is an artist and researcher whose inspiration is rooted in cultural pluralism. Similarly, Theatre Anthropology and ISTA draw heavily on a variety of traditional performance cultures, but the transculturalism they are predicated upon does not expropriate material at the expense of these cultures. Despite their ISTA experiences and the insights it has afforded them, Panigrahi and Azuma, for example, maintain that it has had no effect on their traditional performances (Panigrahi, 1986; Azuma, 1986).

Staging Theatre Anthropology

Elsewhere, I laid out a five-part research model followed at most ISTAs: prior to a particular conference, a theme is chosen and a research methodology decided upon; this research invariably leads to findings that are, in turn, tested; following their testing, these findings are applied by performers or scholars in their work outside of ISTA (Watson, 1995: 165–6). Unfortunately, this model fails to take recent developments at ISTA into account. During the first eight to ten years, Barba's ISTA research was primarily concerned with exploring performance principles that underlie the pre-expressive. This research culminated in the English language version of the *Dictionary of Theatre Anthropology* (Barba and Savarese, 1991).[9] Subsequent ISTAs have shifted the focus from research

---

9   *The Dictionary of Theatre Anthropology* has been published in a number of
    languages, including Italian, French, Spanish, Portuguese and Serbian. The Italian
    version, *Anatomia Del Teatro*, (Casa Usher, Milan and Florence, 1983), The French

to using a variety of performance forms to confirm what is already accepted fact by Barba and his closest colleagues. The most recent performance genres that have been introduced into ISTA, such as the Brazilian Candomblé, Leabhart's corporal mime (both making their first appearances at the 1994 Londrina conference), and Bogdanov's biomechanics (in the 1996 Copenhagen meeting),[10] have not been examined in the same way that the Asian forms were in the earlier ISTAs, with Barba meticulously dissecting the performers' scores in search of the elusive nature of stage presence. They have instead been displayed in relatively brief lecture/demonstrations as tacit confirmation that presence is the product of pre-expressive principles which function across cultures. This tendency to confirmation is further compounded by the fact that many of the same artists appear at every ISTA. These artists rarely repeat material in research sessions but, the very fact that Theatre Anthropology's findings are largely based on studies that include them, could lead one to question how much significant research is taking place.

There has been a paradigmatic shift at ISTA from the deductive to the inductive. The more recent meetings have seen the conventional scientific research model, that has its origins in an exploration of what is not known, overturned in favour of verifying what is accepted fact. It could be argued that Barba is staging Theatre Anthropology at ISTA. If so, he is staging his knowledge for participants who, as mentioned earlier, are denied the space to question it.

Putting the thorny issue of verification aside for the moment, what Barba is doing in staging theatre anthropology is transforming a mental construct into an observable fact. He is co-opting a strategy from the hard sciences. But Theatre Anthropology is not a hard science. Its aim is to uncover what Barba himself terms, 'bits of good advice' (Barba and Savarese, 1991: 8). Theatre Anthropology is a created body of theory and practice, one man's attempt to explain the phenomena of stage presence. It is not a discipline attempting to uncover natural laws.

Barba is the nucleus of Theatre Anthropology. He positions himself as both its author and authority. He 'discovered' Theatre Anthropology,

---

Anatomie de L'Acteur (co-published by Bouffonneries Contrastes, Cazilhac, Zeami Libri, Rome and Odin Teatret Forlag, 1985), and the Spanish edition, *El Arte Secreto Del Actor* (Escenologia, Mexico City, 1990), all preceded the English version. But all of these, most especially the earlier Italian and French editions, are less comprehensive and complete than the definitive 1991 English edition.

10 Gennadi Bogdanov, the Russian master teacher of biomechanics, conducted a lengthy workshop/demonstration which was part of the official programme at the Copenhagen ISTA in 1996. As mentioned in note 2, above, biomechanics made an impromptu appearance once prior to that at ISTA when a pupil of Bogdanov's, Ralf Raüker, gave a demonstration of the technique at the Umeå gathering in 1995.

he developed its concepts, language, rhetoric, applications and its theoretical premises. He is also at the centre of the research that verifies it. In addition, he is the chief organizer and leader of every ISTA who, even though not responsible for fund raising in most instances, decides the theme, designs the programme, chooses who will be invited, and who will be given the opportunity to address participants. In short, Theatre Anthropology is so dominated by one man that it is in danger of being labelled a hermetic hegemony.

Intellectuals are displaced in the formal programme at ISTA since there is no space for discussion. They are less displaced but equally 'silenced' in their published ruminations on the latter. The locus of all published material on Theatre Anthropology is Barba's ideas. Scholars either tacitly support Barba's conceptual framework by either attempting to explain it or elaborate upon it (this represents the majority of publications including, among others: Hastrup, 1996; Skeel, 1994; Pezin, 1986; Pezin, 1982; and Ruffini, 1981), fewer examine Theatre Anthropology's basic premises with a healthy scepticism (Pavis 1996; De Marinis, 1995), and an even smaller group attack Barba's ideas and/or personal style (Bharucha, 1993: 54–67; Zarrilli, 1988; Munk, 1986). None that I am familiar with takes Barba's notion of Theatre Anthropology as a point of departure for further study of contemporary performance practice.[11] Barba is the measure of all things.

Barba's contact with the artists of ISTA is equally based on a paradigm in which knowledge is a metonym for power. This contact is probably best characterized by what Rey Chow identifies as a 'master discourse/native informant relationship' (1993: 33). The artists are confident in the (native) cultural inscriptions they bring to ISTA but, as artists such as Panigrahi and Azuma attest, in working with Barba they discovered anatomical principles underlying their creative work that they were previously unaware of. Barba's knowledge combined with the 'active information' the artists bring to ISTA allows him to 'reveal' the pre-expressive principles embedded in their performance scores to them. In one very real sense, he 'knows' more about their performance forms than they do. And as Edward Said notes, 'to have such knowledge of such a thing is to dominate it, to have authority over it' (1979: 32).

---

11 Theatre Anthropology may remain Barba's domain in contemporary performance analysis, but there have been attempts by at least two Italian theatre historians, Ferdinando Taviani and Franco Ruffini, who have worked closely with Barba for many years to reassess aspects of theatre history in the light of Barba's ideas. Taviani has done this with regard to commedia dell'arte and Henry Irving's acting style particularly (1991), and Ruffini has made a similar study of Stanislavski's actor training system (1991).

Despite arguably questionable ethics in the configurations of power that are at the heart of Theatre Anthropology and ISTA, Barba claims the moral high ground. In his book, *The Paper Canoe*, he states that 'Theatre Anthropology does not give advice on ethics, it is the premise of ethics' (1995: 39). These ethics are inextricably linked to craft. It is the performer's moral obligation to be 'present' on stage at all times and this presence is rooted in the pre-expressive principles that are the focus of Theatre Anthropology's concerns. Barba does not address critics such as Bharucha who have attacked him as a neocolonialist for exploiting other cultures (1995, 1993) because he does not recognize such criticism as valid. He is unconcerned with cultural appropriation/expropriation. His focus is on a transcultural craft of performance with its roots in anatomical similarity, not on what marks cultural identity.

The focus on craft in Theatre Anthropology is the source of some confusion because, even though Theatre Anthropology is as much directed at those who analyse performance as it is at those who perform, its rhetoric is firmly rooted in the workshop/rehearsal studio rather than in that of the academy or the sciences.[12] In *The Paper Canoe* Barba characterizes Theatre Anthropology as being a 'pragmatic science' which is 'a study of the performer and for the performer (1995: 13). The scepticism of scholars such as Barucha, Pavis and De Marinis about the whole notion of the pre-expressive only confirms this pragmatic bias (Pavis, 1996; De Marinis, 1995: 127–34; Bharucha, 1993: 57–61). The pre-expressive maybe useful for the Barba trained performer, but as Barucha points out, it is difficult, if not impossible, for the scholar to separate the expressive performance codes from what Barba maintains are the universal principles underlying them (1993: 57–61). As Stanislavsky, Grotowski and most acting programmes confirm, performer-centred systems of analysis and training are invaluable tools for the actor. But, the implications embedded in the word anthropology, coupled with Barba's claim that Theatre Anthropology 'becomes useful when it makes the creative process accessible to scholars' (1995: 13), insinuate much more. Unfortunately, the confusion sewn among scholars by the central principles of Theatre Anthropology only serves to highlight a lack of conceptual and linguistic precision. This lack of precision makes the transition from a performer-centred body of knowledge to a field of study on a par with disciplines such as cultural or physical anthropology difficult.

Yet everything is in keeping with the nature of the man who is at the centre of Theatre Anthropology and ISTA. He is a charismatic, authoritar-

---

12   For a thorough description and discussion of this rhetoric see Barba and Savarese, 1991; and Watson, 1995: 149–73.

ian figure who virtually single-handedly has guided an insignificant tiny group of neophyte actors far from the centres of cultural power to a place of importance in Europe's theatrical history. He has developed a body of theory that contexts his and the Odin Teatret's place in the Euro-American independent group theatre movement; and he has transformed a personal need to understand the nature of acting into a transcultural examination of the art of performance. Even though he is obsessed with a collective art form, he is a very private man who has never betrayed his creative calling by moving into the mainstream or commercial worlds of the theatre. Rather than move from what many would see as the periphery to centre-stage, Barba has theorized his location. Regardless of his many publications, his world is essentially one of private research on the margins of culture to be shared by a select few. This, combined with his obsessive determination and autocratic style, has had important implications for Theatre Anthropology. He dominates it and defines its boundaries.

There is, however, an inherent contradiction between the limited boundaries he has established for the field, the pre-expressive level of performance, and the implications of a broad, if not encyclopedic, scope in identifying it as a form of anthropology. This contradiction reflects a tension that is at the root of much of Barba's work: that between the director's hands-on, subjective concern with the acting process in the workshop/rehearsal setting and the intellectual's desire to objectify and globalize that process.

Barba's global inclinations place Theatre Anthropology in much the same position as that of sociology and anthropology during the early part of the twentieth century: a nascent discipline with the potential to become an established body of knowledge supported by a wide array of both practical and theoretical scholarship. Theatre Anthropology could become a field of enquiry that informs a broad range of performance analysis. Unfortunately, its limited focus on the pre-expressive, combined with the elitist nature of ISTA, in which collective research and meaningful dialogue are all but ignored, is severely hampering its potential. If Barba's global instincts are to win out over the discourse of his practice, Theatre Anthropology has to broaden its concerns beyond that of the pre-expressive. It has to include, among other things, studies of the socio-cultural contexts of performances, examinations of the relationship between presence and the historio-cultural inscriptions of particular performance forms, and investigations of the cultural influences on the reception of presence. Such an expansion would provide scholars of performance with a means of analysis worthy of the name anthropology. If, instead, Barba's directorial instincts win out, I fear that Theatre Anthropology will not survive its author. That would be a shame and theatre's loss.

References

Azuma, Katsuko (1986), Interview with the author. Nordisk Teaterlaboratorium, Holstebro, Denmark, 20 September.

Barba, Eugenio (1994), 'The steps on the river bank', *The Drama Review*, Vol. 38, No. 4 (T144) Winter: 107–19.

Barba, Eugenio (1995), *The Paper Canoe: A Guide to Theatre Anthropology*. London and New York: Routledge.

Barba, Eugenio and Nicola Savarese (1991), *A Dictionary of Theatre Anthropology: The Secret Art of the Performer*. London and New York: Routledge.

Bhabha, Homi K. (1994), *The Location of Culture*. London and New York: Routledge.

Bharucha, Rustom (1993), *Theatre and the World: Performance and the Politics of Culture*. London and New York: Routledge.

Chen, Xiao-mei (1995), *Occidentalism: a Theory of Counter-Discourse in Post-Mao China*. New York: Oxford University Press.

Chow, Rey (1993), 'Against the lures of diaspora: minority discourse, Chinese women, and intellectual hegemony', in *Gender and Sexuality in Twentieth Century Chinese Literature*, ed. Tonglin Lu. Albany: State University of New York Press, pp. 23–45.

De Marinis, Marco (1995), 'From pre-expressivity to the dramaturgy of the performer: an essay on *The Paper Canoe*', *Mime Journal*: Incorporated Knowledge: 114–56.

Fabian, Johannes (1983), *Time and the Other: How Anthropology Makes its Objects*. New York: Columbia University Press.

Hastrup, Kirsten (ed.) (1996), *The Performers' Village: Times, Techniques and Theories at ISTA*. Graasten, Denmark: Drama.

Munk, Erika (1986), 'The rites of women', *Performing Arts Journal*, Vol. 10, No. 2: 35–42.

Panigrahi, Sanjukta (1986), Interview with the author. Nordisk Teaterlaboratorium, Holstebro, Denmark, 20 September.

Pavis, Patrice (1992), *Theatre at the Crossroads of Culture*. London and New York: Routledge.

Pavis, Patrice (1996), 'A canoe adrift?' unpublished manuscript.

Pezin, Patrick (ed.) (1982), *Bouffonneries* (France), No. 4. Entire issue devoted to Theatre Anthropology.

Pezin, Patrick (ed.) (1986), *Bouffonneries* (France), No. 15/1. Entire issue devoted to Theatre Anthropology.

Ruffini, Franco (1981), *La scuola degli attori*. Milan: La Casa Usher.

Ruffini, Franco (1991), 'Stanislavski's "System"', in *A Dictionary of Theatre Anthropology: the Secret Art of the Performer* by Eugenio Barba and Nicola Savarese. London and New York: Routledge.

Said, Edward W. (1993), *Orientalism*. New York: Vintage Books.

Skeel, Rina (ed.) (1994), *The Tradition of ISTA*. Londrina, Brazil: FILO (International Festival of Londrina) and Universidade Estadual de Londrina.

Taviani, Ferdinando (1991), 'Energetic language', in *A Dictionary of Theatre Anthropology: the Secret Art of the Performer* by Eugenio Barba and Nicola Savarese. London and New York: Routledge.

Taylor, Diana (1991), 'Transculturating transculturation' in *Interculturalism and Performance*, ed. Bonnie Marranca and Gautam Dasgupta. New York: Performing Arts Journal Publications.

Turner, Fred (1991), 'The universal solvent: mediations on the marriage of world cultures', in *Interculturalism and Performance*, ed. Bonnie Marranca and Gautam Dasgupta. New York: Performing Arts Journal Publications.

Watson, Ian (1995), *Towards a Third Theatre: Eugenio Barba and the Odin Teatret*. London and New York: Routledge.

Zarrilli, Phillip (1988), 'For whom is the "invisible" not visible? Reflections on representation in the work of Eugenio Barba', *The Drama Review* 32 (T117): 95–106.

2

Transcultural dialogue: lecture/demonstrations at ISTA

Nicola Savarese

When Barba and his company the Odin Teatret first began touring outside of Scandinavia in the late 1960s and early 1970s, they were drawn to Barba's homeland, Italy. The fledgling company attracted the attention of a group of young Italian theatre scholars just beginning their careers in the academy. This group, that included Claudio Meldolesi, Franco Ruffini, Fabrizio Cruciani, Ugo Volli, Ferdinando Taviani and Nicola Savarese, has remained a touchstone of sorts for Barba throughout his career. It is this group of professors and critics who have provided much of the intellectual stimulus and a critical eye to his artistic and research endeavours over the intervening years. Two of these, Taviani and Savarese, have played particularly significant roles in Barba's career. Taviani, a professor of theatre at L'Aquila University near Rome, has become the Odin's unofficial historian, having written a book and numerous articles on the company's development over the years. He also acts as a dramaturg on many of Barba's Odin productions. Savarese, on the other hand, a professor of theatre at the University of Rome Tre in Rome and a performer in his own right, is one of Europe's leading experts on Asian and Eurasian theatres. He played a major role in the formation of ISTA and continues to be a senior adviser to Barba on all matters concerning the organization. In addition to being part of the scientific team at the first ISTAs, Savarese documented them, suggested avenues of investigation to Barba, and, in collaboration with Barba, compiled *A Dictionary of Theatre Anthropology: The Secret Art of the Performer*, published in English by Routledge (1991). No-one knows ISTA or Barba's intercultural research methodology better than Savarese. (Ian Watson)

Being a theatre scholar who has taken part in every International School of Theatre Anthropology (ISTA) gathering since the organization was founded in 1980, I consider ISTA to be a privileged place where I have had the opportunity of expanding my experience and knowledge of theatre through encounters with masters from a variety of European and Asian performance traditions.

One of the most interesting aspects of ISTA, for me, has always been the balance between the technical nature of the research at conferences and the individualization of each research project. My first and most enduring impression of ISTA is that of attending an anatomy class during which one sees the simultaneous dissection of the actor and the *mise-en-scène*, the artist and his/her technique, as well as the differences between practitioners and scholars. Leaving aside ISTA's findings, which are numerous,[1] I believe that the scientific approach we have adopted has paid dividends because it has given us access to the smallest details of the theatre world; it has allowed us to stop when needed, as well as to go forwards and backwards over performance fragments with the aid of both Eastern and Western theatre masters from diverse cultural backgrounds. This empirical approach is rare in theatre studies, which is far too often diluted by either the scholar's geographical or temporal distance from what he is studying.

Another salient aspect of ISTA, in my opinion, is the transcultural dialogues that it promotes through the multiplicity of performance traditions that are at the centre of every gathering. These dialogues are predicated upon Eugenio Barba's notion of 'professional identity' in which he privileges training, craftsmanship, and practical experience over national identity, political and religious beliefs, or individuated personality. Despite the practical application of findings made at ISTA, the discourse it has generated, or the questions it has raised about performance, the dialogue among the practitioners and scholars from different cultures who comprise the core of each and every conference is ISTA's most relevant political accomplishment, and its most fecund achievement, from a scientific point of view. This dialogue, between students and teachers, directors and actors, and between researchers of practice and theoreticians, has given birth to 'a new way of seeing' and has allowed us to understand some of the most hidden aspects of performance technique.

Having its origins in Barba's own keen observations of performance, ISTA might even be characterized as a 'school of the gaze'. Even though every ISTA is comprised of actors who belong to very diverse cultural tra-

---

1 These findings are discussed at length in Barba (1995) and Barba and Savarese (1991), two books that I regard as essential to any study of Theatre Anthropology.

ditions, their traditions share common principles of scenic behaviour which, during research sessions, are the objects of that gaze. Performers and scholars alike focus on these principles in an attempt to understand the nature of presence and, in the case of the former, to identify and appropriate the principles for their own creative work.

This is how, following sixteen years of public sessions and publications, the value of Theatre Anthropology is beginning to be recognized. The value centres on Theatre Anthropology's notion of 'recurring principles' which have proved to be invaluable tools for understanding the role of technique in conveying presence on stage, and for reassessing theatre and its history in the light of these techniques. For me, as a theatre historian, the latter is one of Theatre Anthropology's major contributions: the rereading of theatre history within the context of a transcultural diffusion of performative techniques and the transmission of these techniques, not only from one generation to the next, but also from one culture to another.[2]

Despite its success, I still encounter sceptics who question ISTA's research. Those who have doubts and raise questions are an invaluable and necessary part of any scientific enterprise. They are the ones who generate dialectics and plumb the depths of the researcher's gaze. What bothers me is that many of the questions raised by these sceptics are the same: is not looking for common principles among different theatrical traditions a universalist temptation or, even worse, an ethnocentric one? Moreover, how is it possible to study these principles within various performative traditions without examining their socio-cultural context?

Since Barba himself has addressed these questions at length elsewhere, it would be repetitive to do so again here (Barba, 1995: 36–49). But to be fair to the sceptics, there is some justification for their confusion because, even though most of them are aware of ISTA's findings, few know anything of its closed activities. Yet it is during these latter sessions that most of ISTA's work is done. It is here that one learns to understand a research process that does not offer solutions and answers, but continues to formulate questions and generate doubt. In short, some scholars commit the same kind of mistake about ISTA and Theatre Anthropology that many critics make about theatrical performance: they only look at the product (i.e., the results) without considering the creative processes

---

2   The result of my historical research in this vein is the book *Teatro e spettacolo tra Oriente e Occidente,* Roma and Bari: Laterza (1995), which deals with the complex relationships between the theatres of Europe and Asia from Ancient Greece to the present day.

involved in producing that product. Analysing the creative process identifies methodological mistakes and identifies areas of further research.

For the sake of clarity, we at ISTA have, on certain occasions, omitted from our published findings 'all the work, the network of doubts, the wrong experiences, the long road to clarity, as well as the comings and goings of the research which precede and underlie the results' (Barba and Savarese, 1983: 11). On other occasions, I have found that, even though many essays and documents about ISTA have been widely disseminated in numerous languages, it is not easy to trace the sources of findings back to the closed research sessions at ISTA. This is especially true of those sources that contain their own contradictions: the mobility of the school; the mixture of recognized teachers and self-taught pupils; the lack of a hierarchic distinction between pedagogues and students; the contributions of multiples cultures through the artists' techniques and individual stories; ignoring false distinctions among forms such as dance, mime and pantomime; learning how to see while learning how to learn. Yet, ironically, it is these very contradictions which make ISTA one of the most interesting and atypical pedagogical experiences.

Contradictions aside, the major source of misunderstandings about Theatre Anthropology is the lack of knowledge of ISTA's scientific agenda. For this reason, I would like to concentrate on what it is that confirms Theatre Anthropology as an empirical, pragmatic, and operative science.

Let us return to the question of transcultural dialogue that I touched on earlier. How are the dialogues conducted during ISTA's public sessions? This question, which prompts us to reflect on the dialogues themselves rather than on the results they achieve, is central to an understanding of how it is possible for masters from different performance traditions to hold a dialogue among themselves without either addressing their individual cultural contexts or rushing to conclusions about the nature of interculturalism.

The dialogues are rooted in a paradox: instead of engaging in a search for answers, they are concerned with participants generating questions. As an American industrialist, whose name escapes me, once wrote, 'One does not need exceptional intelligence to understand that an answer is wrong, but one needs a fairly creative mind to appreciate that a question is incorrect'. Although true, this paradox does not explain how dialogue, that is, the process of questions and answers, functions at ISTA.

Dialogue is usually thought of as an alternating discourse between two or more people, be it a quiet debate or an animated discussion, a violent dispute, or an endless series of controversies. But it is difficult to imagine teachers, students, directors, performers, musicians, scholars, critics and professors from different cultures and traditions being able to sit around a table engaged in a meaningful dialogue about the nuances of performance. The primary obstacle to such a dialogue is differences in language. ISTA's public sessions are a virtual Babel of languages. Participants come from many different countries with few, if any, sharing a single common language (other than a greater or lesser command of English) and a great percentage of those attending the meetings having to rely on translations that inevitably lack the richness of the original language. But differences in national languages are far from ISTA's only linguistic difficulty. Most of those attending also have a specialized language specific to their profession. Even though theatre knows few national boundaries, those who work in it tend to have jargons that relate solely to their genre of theatre. Similarly, scholars have discipline-specific terminology and research methods.

There are, of course, different types of discussions at ISTA: one speaks, converses, argues, and simply chats with fellow participants. Some of these encounters are positive, because they generate a worthwhile exchange of information, while others, which remain at the level of rhetorical exercises or degenerate into academic confrontations built around prejudices, are less valuable. However, even though the so called 'normal' forms of dialogue do exist at ISTA, they are rarely a means of acquiring further knowledge. I recall, for instance, the misunderstandings at the 1986 ISTA which focused on the female role in different cultures. Some participants questioned the programme as well as the nature of the debate. This was because the meeting was described in the official literature as an 'International Congress' but, following traditional ISTA practice, little time was devoted to discussing the theme of the meeting, as would normally be done at a more conventional congress. In hindsight, the term congress was probably ill-advised and the notion of dialogue, as it relates to ISTA, could have been explained more clearly.

The etymology of dialogue encompasses a dual transaction, one in which there is an exchange of words, the other in which the 'logos flows' but without alternating speech acts between protagonists. The latter is pertinent to ISTA. As a scholar, I have had the opportunity to talk to master performers at ISTA on various occasions. During these meetings, I posed many professional and private questions. I often asked them to repeat words or expressions, even demonstrate physical postures, attitudes and movements from their performance forms so that I could gather information and take photographs for my own work.[3] But these

---

3   This was particularly true during the early sessions of ISTA when I was preparing the first edition of *A Dictionary of Theatre Anthropology*, which appeared in Italian (Barba and Savarese, 1983).

private conversations are but a small part of my contact with these masters. Most of the time I, like the majority of the participants at ISTA, attend their lecture/demonstrations rather than engage in 'dialogue' with the masters. I 'listen' without intervening in the dialogues they conduct among themselves and with their students. These lecture/demonstration are 'mute dialogues' in which we participants witness the making of theatre at its most delicate moment: its creation.

There are various types of lecture/demonstrations at ISTA. These range from those that focus on physical and/or vocal training to others centred on performance techniques such as the codification of physical actions or particular forms of improvisation. These demonstrations raise many interrelated questions such as: What are the basic postures of a particular form? What does codification consist of? How is energy manifested, and how is it structured gesturally?

The lecture/demonstrations at ISTA are entirely the responsibility of the master performers involved. Rather than shaping them the way a theatre director might, Barba functions both as a catalyst who ensures the artists' freedom to present what they wish and as the first witness who is an intermediary for other participants. Barba does not ask specific questions of the performers at the outset, nor does he request a particular technique. He rather poses the performer a question or suggests something that forces him to reflect as he works. This strategy prompts the performer to leave the stable ground of familiar technique and explore uncertain waters in the way only a master can.

The lecture/demonstrations allow the master performers to not only direct the gaze of spectators, but to also reflect upon their own art. Some of the lecture/demonstrations begin with an 'inner-dialogue' prior to the masters engaging in a public dialogue with others. This inner-dialogue is a reflective interrogation of sorts between the masters and their tradition or between the masters and their professional experience. It is only later, following a number of lecture/demonstrations by artists from different performance traditions, that a true dialogue, which compares similarities and differences, can take place.

The nature of the dialogues at ISTA only serves to emphasize how unique a setting the latter provides for theatre research. ISTA brings together artists from different performance cultures around the world with scholars, researchers and neophyte theatre workers in a single forum. It also privileges exchange, confrontation and negotiation over 'results', that is, unlike most research institutes, it is research-centred rather than findings-driven.

This concern with research is nowhere more evident than in Barba's ongoing interest in the first day of a performer's training, which he believes contains the ethical and pedagogical nucleus of every artistic discipline. Following the 1986 Holstebro ISTA, Barba has repeatedly asked the master performers during ISTA meetings to recreate their first day of training as an artist.

There have been different reactions to this proposal. Most of the Eastern artists have had few problems remembering their first day of training. A number of them have shown how they sat in front of their guru to copy his physical actions and demonstrated the difficulty they had in maintaining simple positions of the head, eyes, arms, hands and torso during the initial exercises. Other masters, especially those from the West, have not been able to remember the first day exactly. But all have been able to demonstrate a generic sense of the exercises done at the beginning of their training.

The most valuable aspect of these particular lecture/demonstrations has been not so much that the masters have been able to recreate a historically significant event, that is, the transmission of performance knowledge, but that in doing so they have drawn attention to the duality involved in the transmission. This duality, of first observing the teacher then attempting to repeat precisely what he did, requires developing the skill of 'knowing how to look' even prior to 'knowing how to do'. The seeds of Theatre Anthropology lie here.

Anthropology is an 'encounter between knowledges' in which the aim is to explain the 'other' culture in one's own cultural terms. This explanation is, of course, predicated upon the fact that 'the entire tradition of anthropological thought and its research methodology is the product of an enculturation that is much broader in scope than the "science" of anthropology itself' (Giacchè, 1995). The lecture/demonstrations at ISTA are an 'encounter between knowledges' in which the tools of a western, enculturated 'science', Theatre Anthropology, are used to explain performance forms from different parts of the world. At ISTA, however, the degree of encultural 'contamination' is minimized. This is because, the master artists show their physical scores, training, and repeat corporal techniques from their traditions rather than merely providing verbal explanations that, for courtesy's sake, invariably favour the observers' culture. By starting from the deepest knowledge of one's own artistic culture, as only a master can, performers convey 'deep' meanings and knowledge without mediating them through explanations of the historical and/or cultural context from which they spring. In other words, the more a master artist submerges herself in her own culture through performance at ISTA, the closer she will come to being an transcultural vehicle, a vector of her own personal and particular culture.

This is why the lecture/demonstrations at ISTA are transcultural dialogues. They do not negotiate a common ground with the observer beforehand. They do not end in the intermediate space of a conversation aimed at eliminating difference by translating them for spectators (the intercultural approach) and/or by combining various of them (cultural syncretism). They provoke instead reactions and reflection by presenting unmediated authentic performance fragments without considering the home cultures of either participants or their fellow artists (i.e., the transcultural).

I have looked for similar transcultural movements in the past; but it is rare to find situations analogous to the ISTA lecture/demonstrations in theatre history, not because there were none, but because there is little information about them. However, despite the lack of documentation, there are a few well-known events from the past that might be compared to the lecture/demonstrations. Brecht's attendance at the 1935 demonstration by the great Peking Opera performer Mei Langfang in Moscow, for instance, was the 'mute dialogue' that lead to Brecht's theory of 'alienation'.[4] In a similar vein, the encounters in Tokyo between Jean-Louis Barrault and Hisao Kanze, one of Japan's greatest post-War Noh actors, in 1960 and 1978 spring to mind. During these meetings, the unforgettable interpreter of Baptiste and the Noh actor exchanged their work techniques in public with few words spoken between them. As Barrault himself puts it, in silence '... *nous étions tous deux nous passant nos trucs. Nous étions heureux*' [we were passing our tricks to each other. We were happy] (1961: 87).

The reactions of Asian artists to lecture/demonstrations by European actors are less known. One such encounter, between Ennosuke II (a great Kabuki performer) and the Russian Ballet during the former's 1919 European tour was documented. Following a London performance of the ballet, Ennosuke II arranged to meet Karsavina and Massine, the young directors of the company. Ennosuke II writes that during the meeting, which consisted of the reciprocal presentation of several dance pieces followed by the exchange of a few essential words of explanation, he discovered that Japanese dance is essentially *horizontal* while its European classical counterpart is based on *verticality* (Azzaroni, 1988: 15–17).[5]

---

4 Brecht's famous essay 'Alienation effects in Chinese acting' first appeared in English in the London-based magazine *Life and Letters* in 1936. It was subsequently included in John Willet's *Brecht on Theatre*, New York: Hill & Wang (1964), pp. 91–9.

5 Even though this incident is described by the Kabuki actor Gunji Yasunori in Azzaroni, 1988: 15–17, it originally appeared in Ichikawa Ennosuke II's *Ennosuke Zuihitsu*, Tokyo: Nhonshoso, 1937.

These essentially non-verbal transcultural exchanges are based on two inter-related factors, observation and performance. The observer learns about the other through witnessing fragments of a performance, while the other's primary means of communication is performance – a performance that is firmly rooted in a deep knowledge of his particular theatre form.

This type of exchange raises questions of emic and etic borders because it blurs the line between the observer and the observed. The anthropological convention of the observer watching, annotating and analysing the observed's behaviour is challenged by the barter-like dynamic of these transcultural dialogues. The dialogues call for an inter-active transaction in which the self and other often exchange roles. Equally, the observer in attempting to explain what is being observed, frequently challenges and engages the subject's psycho-emotional reality by trying to understand his or her internal performative process.

This blurring of the emic and etic revisits the question of whether it is possible to study the creative processes of actors from cultures other than one's own without examining the historical and social context of the performance forms involved. It is, provided the scholar/observer is prepared to participate fully in both the creative and scientific processes by reflecting upon his own personal experience *illic et nunc,* that is, by becoming involved in the process rather than remaining an outsider observing an objectified other. That is why it is normal at ISTA to see scholars attempting the acting exercises proposed by teachers, just as it is common to find other scholars observing these exercises rather than participating in them directly. These are two, often interchangeable, attitudes during which there is 'deep' dialogue with the teachers because it happens without words. After all, history tells us that the most significant dialogues have been written by one person.

(Translated from Italian by Susana Epstein.)

A version of this chapter first appeared in *The Tradition of ISTA* (1994) edited by Rina Skeel. This was a volume of essays published by the International Festival of Londrina and the Universidade Estadual de Londrina on the occasion of the 8th session of ISTA held in Londrina, Brazil.

References

Azzaroni, G. (1988), *Dentro il mondo del Kabuki*. Bologna: CLUEB.

Barba, Eugenio (1995), *The Paper Canoe: A Guide to Theatre Anthropology*. London and New York: Routledge.

Barba, Eugenio and Nicola Savarese (1983), *Anatomia Del Teatro*. Milan and Florence: Casa Usher.

Barba, Eugenio and Nicola Savarese (1991), *A Dictionary of Theatre Anthropology: The Secret Art of the Performer*. London and New York: Routledge.

Barrault, Jean-Louis (1961), *Journal de bord. Japon, Israel, Grèce, Yougoslavie.* Paris: Julliard, p. 87.

Giacchè, Piergiorgio (1992), 'Una equazione fra antropologia e teatro', a paper presented at the Theatre Sociology Congress in Lisbon (this essay was later published in *Teatro e storia*, Annali 17, 1995).

3

Actor as *refusenik*: Theatre Anthropology, semiotics and the paradoxical work of the body
Nigel Stewart

'Theatre', Eugenio Barba has said, 'is a possibility of shaping revolt'. Barba has touched upon this belief in writing (1988: 299), and he professed it with considerable passion at the conclusion of the seventh public session of the International School of Theatre Anthropology (ISTA), held in Brecon and Cardiff in April 1992.[1] In this exploration of the particular possibilities which Theatre Anthropology creates for revolt, I consider Barba's direction of a work-in-progress at the Brecon ISTA in terms of Derrida's and Kristeva's theories of the sign. Integral to this is an analysis of the relation between *bios* (the 'pre-expressive' work of the body) and *logos* (the 'expressive' meanings which that work can produce). The relation between the *bios* and *logos* is of fundamental importance not just toTheatre Anthropology, but to a general understanding of the body in performance.

---

1 Directed by Barba and hosted by the Centre for Performance Research (CPR), the 'Brecon ISTA' was held in two parts – a practical exploration called *Working on Performances East and West* at Christ College, Brecon (4–10 April) and a conference called *Fictive Bodies, Dilated Minds, Hidden Dances* at Chapter Arts Centre, Cardiff (10–11 April).

Pre-expressivity

At ISTA the most palpable object of study is the *physical score* (a precise and repeatable sequence of actions performed by the body or voice). The physical score is the material of dramaturgy: the montage, '"weaving", ... or work of actions' (Barba and Savarese, 1991: 68ff, 241).[2] From this dramaturgy, the largest unit, the *mise-en-scène*, is composed.

ISTA limits its research to the physical scores of European and Asian forms of theatre which are governed by systematic rules of physical behaviour (Barba and Savarese 1991: 6–7). These rules do not relate to the 'complex of stereotypes, of automatic behaviour models' (Barba 1988: 294) with which a person is *encultured* and upon which movement in daily life is based. On the contrary, the behavioural rules which ISTA studies are extra-daily. They are specific to the theatrical tradition into which the performer is *accultured*. They are the basis of a 'codified virtuosity built up during apprenticeship' (Elsass, Pradier and Savarese, 1987: 6).

These extra-daily rules of behaviour function in two interdependent ways. First, they function semiotically. A physical score has a semantic dimension. Put simply, it *expresses* meaning. According to the conventional Saussurean model, an action can be understood as a sense image (or signifier) that is 'indissolubly linked with an internalised mental representation or concept' (Leach, 1976: 17), or signified, of some kind of original event (or referent). This link is made by the particular personal, cultural or artistic codes within the performance tradition into which the performer has been accultured and which dictate how actions can be meaningfully selected and combined into the physical score. However, if signifier and signified together constitute a sign that points to or, alternatively, substitutes for the referent, this referent is itself a sign. Physical scores, then, are no different from other signifying systems in that they exist within an ever-expanding world of semiosis in which sign points to or substitutes for sign in *infinitum progressum*.[3] A physical score, then, has this semiotic or *expressive* capacity.

Second, the extra-daily rules of Eurasian theatre function somatically. They affect weight, balance, the shape of the spinal column, and so on. A physical score thus also has a physiological or biological dimension. According to Theatre Anthropology, these rules encode five 'recurrent and transcultural principles': altered balance, dynamic opposition, sub-

---

2 This volume, with more than 600 illustrations, presents the results of ISTA's research between 1980 and 1990.
3 See Umberto Eco, 'Social life as a sign system', in David Robey (ed.), *Structuralism: an Introduction* (Oxford: Clarendon, 1973), p. 57.

stitution (or equivalence), reduction (or absorption), and consistent inconsistency (or coherent incoherence) (Barba and Savarese, 1991: 5).

According to Theatre Anthropology, an arabesque in ballet, an *aragoto* position in Japanese Kabuki, the *déséquilibre* of Decroux mime, or the *tribangi* pose of Indian Odissi, are all culturally specific manifestations of the first 'law', *altered balance* (Barba, 1995: 16–22; Barba and Savarese, 1991: 34–53). These asymmetrical configurations alter the centre of gravity, displace the spinal column and consequently place the body in a state of disequilibrium (Barba and Savarese, 1991: 232). In order to reach a new balance, the body's righting reflexes compel different body parts to extend in opposing directions, engaging antagonistic muscles and traversing the body with counterbalancing lines of force. As muscular activity is both increased and focused, the body is placed in a dynamic not static state.

The first 'pragmatic law' (*altered balance*) thus also implicates the second law (*dynamic opposition*) (Barba, 1995: 22–5). But this second law also governs the directions that the body takes sequentially as well as simultaneously. For example, the 'anticipation/action/reaction' principle in cartoon animation (Barba and Savarese, 1991: 176), or the *otkaz/pozyl/stojka* phases of the Meyerholdian acting cycle, or the travel paths codified for the entrances of different characters in Chinese Opera (1991: 178), are all examples in which an action begins with a refusal: the performer, in other words, starts a gestural or travel path in the opposite direction to where the path will finally lead.

The parts of the body which extend in dynamically opposing directions within an altered state of balance do not *imitate*, but *substitute* for those parts that would be engaged in daily life, setting up an equivalent system (Barba, 1995: 30–2). For instance, in order to push a heavy object forwards in daily life the back leg and the arms are exerted. However, when this activity is mimed in the *belle courbe* of Decroux mime the arms (held towards forward-middle) might 'imitate' a forward push, but effort is really directed down the front leg. Accordingly, in this 'extra-daily' technique, the front leg *substitutes* for, or is an equivalent to, the arms and back leg of the 'daily' technique (Barba and Savarese, 1991: 96–7). Similarly, when a bow and arrow are mimed in Odissi, a sudden forward propulsion of the torso substitutes metonymically for the flight of the arrow (1991: 98–9). In these and many other instances this third principle, 'equivalence, which is the opposite of imitation, reproduces reality by means of another system' (1991: 96).

If the performer is obliged to find a substitute, then this is because of the absence or omission of the object which would normally be pulled or pushed (the heavy object, the bow, etc.). As a result of this omission and the system of equivalence, energy is not dispersed, but is *reduced*, absorbed or retained, and thus intensified. This operation of reduction constitutes the fourth 'pragmatic law':

> the compression, into restricted movements, of the same energy which would be used to accomplish a much larger and heavier action. For example: engaging the whole body in the action of lighting a cigarette, as if one was lifting a heavy box and not a little match or nodding with the chin and leaving the mouth slightly ajar with the same force that would be used to bite. Working in this way reveals a quality of energy which makes the performer's entire body come [a]live, even in immobility. (Barba, 1995: 25–30; Barba and Savarese, 1991: 15)

Whereas the body in daily life is organized to produce maximum effect from minimum effort, the de luxe balances, dynamic oppositions, reductions and substitutions which characterize extra-daily technique are marked, from the perspective of daily life, by a 'strenuous artificiality and waste of energy' (Barba, 1986: 119). However, from the perspective of scenic life these laws dilate energy. In this respect the extra-daily body is *inconsistent* with the daily body. Moreover, extra-daily technique also makes use of *incoherent* or contradictory combinations of elements: 'one may talk of dynamic immobility, maximal energy consumption through minimal movement, being expressive in spite of oneself. One may also employ the concept of "being decided", which is an active passive form: dynamic immobility' (Christoffersen, 1989: 51). Yet extra-daily technique promises a difference in potential. Incoherence gathers its own *coherence* when 'the actor can transform ... inconsistency into a new culture of the body through practice and training ... by a process of innervation and by the development of new [neuro]muscular reflexes' (Barba, 1986: 119). 'Coherent incoherence' (or 'consistent inconsistency') is, then, the fifth and final 'pragmatic law'. It suggests that the efficacy of an extra-daily technique depends upon the degree to which, through patient practice, it has been acculturated as a way of thinking and behaving in a performance situation.

These five principles account for *scenic bios* (the energy or 'presence' of the performer) and thus for a physical score's somatic or *pre-expressive* capacity. Theatre Anthropology is principally the study of pre-expressivity – the 'common competence' (Barker, Hoff, Pradier, Ruffini and Yamaguchi, 1990: 2) of Eurasian theatre. My contention, however, is that Theatre Anthropology is at its best when it demonstrates the dynamic bond between the pre-expressive and expressive dimensions of the body in performance. Specifically, Theatre Anthropology shows, through the application of the laws of pre-expressivity, not just how an action can 'develop in unexpected ways or to conclude in a way which is opposite to how it began' (Barba and Savarese, 1991: 56), but in how complex meanings develop as a result. And, as I shall elucidate, this places *logos* (sign, meaning) and *bios* (soma, force) in a radically new relation.

The underscore

Since the Bologna ISTA recognized that 'pre-expressivity has its foundation in mental as well as sensor-motor rules which are integrated with the performer' (Barker *et al.*, 1990: 2), the Brecon ISTA properly investigated the interior logic of performance. The question can be put in various ways. What *is* the nature of the correspondence between mental and sensor-motor rules? If there is a common material basis to the *texts* (weaves of physical action) from different forms, are there analogous notions of *subtext*? If we can compare *physical scores*, can we also compare the *underscores* which performers use to justify their extra-daily behaviour? Above all, how does the pre-expressive work on physical action as a physiological event affect the performer's expressive work on physical action as a semantic event?

The methodology employed at the Brecon ISTA compares with the approaches taken at the Salento[4] and the Bologna ISTAs.[5] Exceptional performers from different cultures were gathered.[6] Seven groups of observers, made up of paying participants and ISTA's (mostly) Italian research team, wrote scenarios on the theme of the *refusenik* – 'an individual who does not follow the norms, opinions or doctrines of authority' (Centre for Performance Research, 1992), the person who embodies paradox (from *para*, 'beside', and doxa, 'opinion' or 'dogma'), the outsider: the one who shapes revolt.

Each scenario was edited down to a fragment or 'diamond' by Barba, and each performer created a physical score based on one of the seven 'diamonds'. The performers then organized themselves into working groups within which basic interactions between individual physical scores were built. Barba montaged this material, primarily considering the pre-expressive efficacy of the performers' work by modifying their

4   See Elsass *et al.*, 1987: 6; also Pavis, 1989: 38. This latter article was reprinted (without photographs) in Patrice Pavis, *Theatre at the Crossroads of Culture* (London and New York: Routledge, 1992), pp. 160–83.
5   See Barker *et al.*, 1990: 4.
6   The performers at Brecon included seven actors and two musicians from Odin Teatret, Odissi performer Sanjukta Panigrahi and her four musicians, *onnogata* performer Kanichi Hanayagi with translator and Kabuki specialist Mark Oshima, and four performers from the Balinese Dharma Shanti Company.

material according to the five 'pragmatic laws'. From this work a provisional *mise-en-scène* (called *The Seven Diamonds of Brecon*) emerged and the research topic (the 'underscore') was investigated. The findings contributed to the general understanding of Theatre Anthropology.

The burnt bride rises

The example of the development of two interrelated episodes should be sufficient to illustrate this methodology, which was intended to exemplify Barba's strategy as a director, and to simplify into three categories the many definitions of underscore proposed by participants throughout the week in response to the work they saw. These categories are based on a provisional typology which Patrice Pavis, a member of ISTA's research team, proposed at the end of the Brecon sessions.

One indicative working group consisted of Sanjukta Panigrahi and Odin performers Julia Varley and Iben Nagel Rasmussen. Varley used the first mode of underscore – the muscular memory of a physical response to a stimulus. She chose a simple element from the third 'diamond' (*a book*). From this she derived the idea of working with an actual piece of paper. Her process involved displacement: from flapping the paper, she loosely shook her hands; from scrunching the paper in one hand, she gathered her torso and grimaced; and so on, until she had built a sequence of different physical actions (signifiers), each one underscored by the exact mental correspondent (signified) of the original action with the paper (referent).

The second category which emerged was the performer whose underscore consists of a personal or cultural association. Rasmussen, for example, built a score by re-enacting a personal association of the first 'diamond' (*a speaking corpse*). She began flat on her back, covering herself in a large shawl which slipped off as she gradually rose, her body then delicately poised, left hand fluttering, only the whites of her eyes exposed. Here the underscore would be the 'inner film' of impressions from the analogous event.

Panigrahi represents the third type – the performer, typically from an Asian tradition, who works from a 'repertoire of codified expressive functions'[7] to build a narrative. With her immense and precise vocabulary of movement (2000 combinations of *mudras* or hand gestures, 60 basic postures, 180 basic steps, and so on), Panigrahi elaborated a story in gesture based on the fourth 'diamond' (*a queen who takes off her clothes and meditates in silence*). Here the underscore is the sequence of semantic units or

---

7   Patrice Pavis's definition offered during work on 10 April 1992.

signifieds which, *via* the code of the theatrical tradition (Odissi), corre-
sponds to the sequence of vehicle units or signifiers (e.g. the *mudras*).

Yet what Barba sought to make clear was not the expressive underscore but the pre-expressive quality of this physical material. Controver-
sially, he had Panigrahi and Varley wrap themselves in shawls so that their
'anecdotes' – Panigrahi's Odissi *mudras* and Varley's personality traits –
would be omitted (Barba and Savarese, 1991: 191). This drew attention to
impulses in their torsos, the material basis of the 'anecdotes' or 'literature'
of the original actions (Barba and Savarese 1991: 97). Similarly, Varley
was asked to clarify the *dynamic opposition* of an action with which she
passed the rising body of Rasmussen, so that she moved backwards and
away before forwards. Simultaneously, she was required to *reduce* and
focalize her grimace into a wrinkling in the nose, synchronized with the
very point at which Rasmussen's shawl fell off. Barba's attention to technique had thus begun to produce an unintended expressive content:
mourner smells corpse.

The interaction between Panigrahi, Rasmussen and Varley was interwoven with another episode constructed from an even more elaborate
process of substitution and reduction. Removing I Ketut Suteja from the
work he had devised with the other Balinese performers, Barba asked him
to perform his score whilst kneeling and holding two arbitrarily chosen
objects – a football in one hand and a knife in the other. Barba's purpose
was to erase those actions which he specified as the most 'anecdotal', the
most 'Balinese' – such as complex oscillations in the fingers of hands bent
back at ninety degrees – in order to expose pre-expressive impulses in
Suteja's trunk and face. The impression began to emerge of what the Balinese would describe as a refined, *manis* (soft) character: graceful, boyish,
gentle, excited.

But Suteja's 'anecdote' began to return. Further measures were called
for: the football was replaced by the *head* of Odin performer Tina Nielsen
(who had already developed a score based on the seventh 'diamond', *a
wall of books*), whilst the knife was replaced by her right wrist, and this
wrist, as the devising process matured, by a lighted match. As the match
was produced by a hand still retaining a residual vibration of the Balinese
hand movements, Rasmussen, from the other side of the space, shook a
piece of paper in her 'fluttering' hand; meanwhile, the prone Nielsen, her
head still in the hand of Suteja, sang a haunting Danish folk song while
she performed a highly reduced version of her score.

The pre-expressive work had formed an unpremeditated elaboration
of the sixth 'diamond' (*a dead woman reappears to the husband who has
burnt her*): a young woman (Nielsen), perhaps a bride, sings gracefully as
she is tenderly set on fire by her husband (Suteja); simultaneously,

mourners in cloaks (Varley, Panigrahi) notice her charred corpse (Rasmussen) rise from its shroud.

Once the image of the lighted match and the shaking paper had been established, it was soon reused several times in other episodes and contexts – a *leitmotif*, so to speak! For example, at the conclusion of one episode, Odin performer Hisako Miura was asked to produce, with sleight of hand, a match over a pile of books that had been abruptly dropped from a height. In a duet between Kanichi Hanayagi and Odin performer Torgeir Wethal (recycling material developed at the Bologna ISTA), Wethal was directed to hurriedly shake and drop a piece of paper handed to him by Hanayagi, as if it had burnt him (a condensation of match and paper).

Force and meaning

The Brecon ISTA demonstrated that Theatre Anthropology's attention to the somatic qualities of the physical score has decisive semiotic consequences. The most decisive consequence is the gap that opens up between what the performer *presents* through her or his physical score and what the performer *intends* through her or his underscore. This gap between presentation and intention, score and underscore, can be fruitfully compared with Derrida's discussion of Freud's general theory of perception and memory. In the traditional model the conscious perceives an event as it occurs and then stores it as a memory. Freud's model is different: an event causes an excitation in the neurological system, but the force leaves no mark on the perceptual neurones which receive it since they offer no electro-chemical resistance.

> Other neurones, which would oppose contact-barriers to the quantity of excitation, would thus retain the printed trace. … This is the first representation, the first staging of memory … in the sense of visual depiction, and … theatrical performance. (Derrida, 1978: 201)

It is only *later* that these re-presentations selectively accede to consciousness: 'the "perceived" may be read only in the past, beneath perception and after it' (Derrida, 1978: 224): 'we are the eternal latecomers to the "now" of our experience' (Harland, 1987: 14).

For Derrida, the actual physical pathway (track, furrow, trace, groove) of lowered electro-chemical resistance is the signifier. This identifies 'the force which runs throughout the mental world with the force which runs throughout the material world' (Harland, 1987: 153). This, indeed, is Derrida's vision of arche-writing and Artaud's vision of spatial poetry (Artaud, 1974: 25–7, 55): writing not as written or spoken words (still less as inward signifieds willed and intended by a mind) but as non-phonetic picto-hieroglyphic marks (Derrida, 1978: 218) operating *independently of and prior to consciousness*.

This is homologous with the process witnessed at Brecon. Barba, according to the premises of Theatre Anthropology, no more treated the body as a supplement to or expression of the will and intention of the performer (the traditional model) than Derrida treats the unconscious as a supplement to the conscious. In both cases the priority is reversed. In the evolution of the physical score, the performer did have an event 'in mind' (Varley's flapping paper, Rasmussen's personal association) but this event, according to Derrida, would have 'always already' been a *reproduced* event by the time it was perceived (1978: 211). Moreover, this event was no more than a pretext for the body's further and unforeseeable reproduction of it to the spectator. Within each action, the performer's thought (signified) of the original event (referent) excited *extensor* muscles – but the accultured pre-expressive properties of the performer's body made certain that they were dialectically resisted by *flexor* muscles.[8] This resistance ensured that (1) any intended movement was displaced into what appeared as an abstract picto-hieroglyphic mark (signifier) in space and (2) that this mark could be remembered. It was only with the repetition of the mark that it began to suggest meanings in excess of those originally intended. As in Freud's model, meaning was 'not *sent* but only *received*' (Harland, 1987: 132).

The Brecon ISTA therefore demonstrated that in creative work there is always a gap – indeed, an *aporia* – between what the performer intends and what the performer presents. By modulating the performer's action according to the laws of pre-expressivity, Barba only increased this gap, thus contesting the liberal humanist and expressive realist assumption that actions in performance are to be understood simply 'in the sense of what someone means them to mean' (1987: 126),[9] and that the spectator merely interprets what the actor intends in an hierarchy of interpretation (actor interprets director, director interprets writer).

Barba's erasure of the performer's score demonstrated a loyalty through a kind of betrayal, 'if to betray is at once to denature … but also to … manifest the foundation of force' (Derrida, 1978: 236). And with the manifestation of force came the revelation of unconscious meaning from behind the conscious anecdote. Through the work on pre-expressivity the body materialized the Derridean-Freudian unconscious. With the body's 'weave of actions' and the brain's 'weave of pure traces … meaning and

8   See Barba, 1986: 118.
9   Compare Catherine Belsey, *Critical Practice* (London, Methuen, 1980), pp. 7–14.

force are united' (1978: 211). At ISTA the *signifying* process, is nothing less than a *somatic* process, a *work of the body*.

Intertextuality and différance

But if *logos* (meaning) was restored to *bios* (force), *logos* was radically dis-orientated. The work of the body left in its wake a density of paradoxical imagery. Paradox was displayed in two respects – in what Kristeva would call *intertextuality* and in what Derrida would call *différance*. First, the metamorphosis of material and the relocation of scores into contexts unintended by the performer and unforeseen by the director, and the recycling of material from earlier performances, demonstrated that the ISTA *mise-en-scène* is not so much a text as 'a *permutation of texts*, an intertextuality: in the space of the given text, several utterances, *taken from other texts*, intersect and neutralize one another' (my emphasis) (Kristeva, 1980: 36).

Thus, within the emerging gap between intention and presentation, paradox was located between the meanings which the physical score had gathered for the performer within the interior scene of the underscore and the very different meanings which that physical score had when jux-taposed with other physical scores within the *mise-en-scène*. If the final image cluster in the above example made reference to the sixth 'diamond', it was made up of physical scores each of which related to entirely differ-ent 'diamonds' (Panigrahi basing hers on the fourth 'diamond', Varley on the third, and so on). Because of Varley's proximity to Rasmussen, a meaning to an action from Varley's score was suggested to us (mourner smells corpse) but the difference of her underscore (scrunching a piece of paper, and by then *much* else besides) was *also* suggested, immediately destabilizing the more apparent meaning.

Second, paradox was displayed within the *mise-en-scène* itself. If the said image cluster made reference to the sixth 'diamond', it was, on closer inspection, equally a 'knot'[10] of signifieds which refused a governing sense. It did this by fusing opposites: *tenderness* (Suteja) with *murder* (Suteja) and *disgust* (Varley/Panigrahi), and *dying* (Nielsen) with *rising* (Rasmussen). Since these meanings were co-present, they could not be seen to simply and statically exclude each other. On the contrary, this was a demonstration of thinking *through* opposites (Barba and Savarese, 1991: 58-61), especially in the co-habitation of diametric meanings within the one body of Suteja – a semantic condition which resembles the

---

10 A term used frequently by Barba. See Pound's principle of the 'vortex' in Peter Jones (ed.), *Imagist Poetry* (Harmondsworth: Penguin, 1972), p. 39.

somatic state of *dynamic opposition*. There was an *element of the same in the difference*, a palpable restless flow from one meaning into its opposite. This is close to Derrida's notion of *différance*: [11] a state in which meaning is always *differentiated* (tenderness and murder are opposite) but always *differed* (*tenderness* spills over into *murder* and *vice versa*). Within *The Seven Diamonds of Brecon*, then, the signified was placed in crisis, not a stop but a starting point for another meaning, and therefore not a signified at all but another signifier. Indeed, the dissemination of visual and aural material (especially the lighted match and paper) was closer to music – the art of the signifier alone – than, say, to mainstream theatre where convention will delimit a field of possible signifieds.

The manifestation, through the work on pre-expressivity, of unconscious paradoxical meanings through the body of the performer, irrespective of her or his intentions, has two critical implications which are interrelated. First, the performer's sense of self is reorientated. Not only did the gap between intention and presentation problematize the notion of a free and autonomous self, origin and keeper of meaning, but the performer's identity and integrity was seen to reside in the pre-expressive capacity of her or his tradition rather than in the personal or cultural meanings which that tradition expresses.

Identity and revolt

At Brecon this was a contentious issue. If 'identity is the way in which one organizes those features that one perceives as characteristic of oneself' (Elsass, Pradier and Savarese, 1987: 4), and if the Eurasian performer's extra-daily accultured body places physical features (e.g. fingers and hands) in the highest state of organization (Panigrahi's *mudras*, Suteja's alacritous digital micro-actions, and so on), the corollary is that tradition and technique are a function of identity, the means of 'autodefinition' (1987: 4). For the Eurasian performer, then, personal identity is an issue of professional identity within a cultural tradition. It follows that to erase features of this tradition is to challenge – some would say deface – the performer's identity and the culture which he or she represents.

Nonetheless, through this disorientation the performer is obliged to grasp her or his *idem*: 'an axis ... which orients him to life's circumstances, oppositions, and obstacles' (Barba, 1987: 1). This axis is the material body. The performer is thus stimulated to discover her or his body-as-country and 'body-in-life ... his personal motor, the internal temperature' (Barba, 1988: 299).

---

11 See Alan Bass in Harland, 1987: 138; Derrida, 1978: xvi.

The second implication is that this body-in-life shapes a way of revolt. Within a sign-system, the sign is fixed and stable (signifier is bound to signified, both point to a single referent). At the centre of this stability is the signified which betokens '"the Law" ... an inward rational principle [which] serves to control and take charge of outward material things' (Harland, 1987: 146), 'the major constraint affecting any social practice' (Kristeva, 1975: 47). The major constraint within the capitalist system of exchange, for example, is 'the general equivalent or sign of the [body's] work invested in the exchanged object' (Kristeva, 1973: 35) – namely, money.

But at ISTA there is no such system of exchange. Work is understood as 'the intermediate phase between energy and the specific movement of a force' (Ruffini in Barba and Savarese, 1991: 241) which, as I have argued, always already carries unpremeditated paradoxical meanings. So at ISTA it is not the stable sign which constrains the value of movement and work but pre-expressivity or '"matter" *qua* movement and work' which 'precedes, determines and decentres the sign' (Kristeva, 1973: 36).

In the making of the ISTA *mise-en-scène*, meaning is neither controlled within a cultural signifying system nor seen to be supplanted by some purely 'natural' animal essence. Rather meaning is *disseminated* by an outward material and heterogeneous *somatic-semiotic* process, operating dynamically and independently beyond the authorial control of either director or performer, which transgresses the sign's systematicity (Kristeva, 1975: 48, 51, 54). Such dispersal of meaning beyond a sign system can only appear, within the terms of that system, as 'waste' (Harland, 1987: 148; Barba, 1986: 267; Kristeva, 1975: 52).

The Eurasian performer's bio-physiological picto-hieroglyphic marks in space exceed, in a 'waste' of intertextuality and *différance*, conscious signification or 'socially instituted socially controlled meaning' (Harland, 1987: 168): 'polyvalent and multi-determined, [it] adheres to a logic exceeding that of codified discourse ... fully coming into being only in the margins of recognized culture' (Kristeva, 1980: 65).

It is here that the two implications of the body's manifestation of paradoxical meanings rejoin each other. For if the signifying body-in-life is a way of revolt against inward law and rational principle it is equally a revolt against the 'semiotic logic of the sociality in which the (speaking, historical) subject is embedded' (Kristeva, 1975: 48). The Eurasian performer's identity, then, is one of creative asociality (Barba, 1986: 199). The signifying work of the body creates paradox which is *para-doxa*. This is what Barba cites as resistance against ideological uniformity (Barba, 1988: 299). This is what Artaud understood as revolt (Artaud, 1974: 7, 77). This is the actor as *refusenik*.

The Seven Diamonds of Brecon demonstrated one solution – unsettling and productive – to the problems inherent in any interaction between cultures: the identities of performers East and West were experimentally displaced, but in each other's direction (Pavis, 1989: 49-54). At the same time, the materiality and heterogeneity of the bodily signifiers opposed translation (Derrida, 1978: 210; Kristeva, 1975: 53) and thus eschewed cultural syncretism. *The Seven Diamonds of Brecon*, like prior ISTA *mise-en-scènes*, was liminal, hovering curiously *between* traditions, a site of paradox and revolt, a place in which identity was lost and strangely found.

A version of this chapter first appeared in *New Theatre Quarterly* (1993), Vol. IX, No. 36.

References

Artaud, Antonin (1974), 'The theatre and its double', in *Collected Works*, Vol. IV, trans. Victor Corti. London: Calder & Boyars, pp. 1–110.

Barba, Eugenio (1986), *Beyond the Floating Islands*. New York: Performing Arts Journal Publications.

Barba, Eugenio (1987), 'Anthropological theatre', unpublished paper, Bahía Blanca, Argentina: The Third Theatre Gathering, International Encounter on Anthropological Theatre, p. 1 (this article is published in the appendix of Chapter 14).

Barba, Eugenio (1988), 'The way of refusal', *New Theatre Quarterly*. Vol. IV, No. 16.

Barba, Eugenio (1995), *The Paper Canoe: A Guide to Theatre Anthropology*. London and New York: Routledge.

Barba, Eugenio and Nicola Savarese (1991), *A Dictionary of Theatre Anthropology: the Secret Art of the Performer*. London and New York: Routledge.

Barker, Clive, Frank Hoff, Jean-Marie Pradier, Franco Ruffini and Masao Yamaguchi. (1990), 'Sixth ISTA Public Session, The University of Eurasian Theatre: Bolognia, Italy', unpublished report. Holstebro, Denmark: Nordisk Teaterlaboratorium.

Centre for Performance Research (1992), unpublished letter, 26 February.

Christoffersen Erik Exe (1989), 'The presence radiated by the actor-dancer', *Nordic Theatre Studies*, Vol. II, No. 3 (Munksgard): 49–52.

Derrida, Jacques (1978), *Writing and Difference*, trans. Alan Bass. London: Routledge.

Elsass, Peter, Jean Marie-Pradier and Nicola Savarese (1987), 'Fifth Public Session of ISTA: Salento, Italy', unpublished report. Holstebro, Denmark: Nordisk Teaterlaboratorium.

Harland, Richard (1987), *Superstructuralism: the Philosophy of Structuralism and Post-Structuralism*. London: Methuen.

Kristeva, Julia (1973), 'The semiotic activity', *Screen*, Vol. XIV, Nos 1–2 (Spring–Summer: 25–39).

Kristeva, Julia (1975), 'The system and the speaking subject', in *The Tell-Tale Sign*, (ed.) Thomas Sebeok. Lisse, Netherlands: Peter de Ridder Press, pp. 47–55.

Kristeva, Julia (1980), *Desire in Language: a Semiotic Approach to Literature and Art*, (ed.) Leon S. Roudiez. Oxford: Blackwell.

Leach, Edmund (1976), *Culture and Communication: the Logic by which Symbols are Connected*. Cambridge: Cambridge University Press.

Pavis, Patrice (1989), 'Dancing with Faust: a semiotician's reflections on Barba's intercultural mise en scene', *The Drama Review*, Vol. 33, No. 3 (T123) Autumn: 37–7.

Finding equilibrium in disequilibrium: the impact of ISTA on its Balinese participants

I Nyoman Catra and Ron Jenkins

I Nyoman Catra is a Balinese dancer and musician who has been a member of Barba's artistic staff at many ISTAs. Ron Jenkins, Artistic Director and Chair of Theatre at Wesleyan University, has conducted research into Balinese perform-ance for over twenty years and has attended ISTA on numerous occasions where he has worked extensively with the Balinese troupes involved. This is the first time that an Asian artist who has taken part in ISTA has written about the expe-rience. (Ian Watson)

As a Balinese actor/teacher/choreographer and an American scholar/ teacher/director who for years have been coming together at The Inter-national School of Theatre Anthropology (ISTA) from opposite sides of the world, the two of us are still in the process of discovering the impact that ISTA has had on our work. ISTA has given us a common ground and a frame of reference that is fundamental to the three-year collaboration that we undertook in the mid-1990s at Emerson College in the United States, with the support of the Asian Cultural Council of the Rockefeller Brothers Fund, and that we now continue at Wesleyan University. The first seeds of our cross-cultural experiments were planted at the Salento ISTA in 1987 and the Bologna ISTA in 1990. I Made Bandem, the direc-tor of Bali's National Institute of the Arts (STSI) in Denpasar, who has been working with Eugenio Barba since 1977, encouraged us to plan a long-term project together that would help pave the way for the creation of a cross-cultural theatre programme at STSI to complement its already outstanding programme in traditional Balinese performance. It is difficult to generalize about Theatre Anthropology's influence upon the international cross-current of theatrical fertilization, but the specific case of our ongoing collaboration and its roots in Barba's work might cast light on the practical implications of ISTA that continue to germinate even after the sessions have ended.

Dynamic equilibrium: preservation and evolution of traditional performance technique (I Nyoman Catra)

The National Institute of the Arts in Bali, where I teach, is dedicated to preserving Balinese traditional culture while working to create a new culture. The question is, where will this new culture come from, inside Bali, or outside? The answer is both, and it is my experience at ISTA in conjunction with the guidance of I Made Bandem, who has also spent many years at ISTA, that helps me to understand how this is possible. At ISTA, traditional Balinese performance encounters the performance of other cultures in a mosaic pattern that is created by Eugenio Barba. From my position inside this mosaic, it is possible for me to see the elements that Balinese performance shares with other performance forms as well as the elements that make it different.

In America, I am continuing to investigate these similarities and differences, using the model of exploration I learned at ISTA. In Salento, Barba asked us to use traditional performance techniques to bring to life the western story of Faust. In America, I am using traditional performance techniques to bring to life other western classics like *The Bacchae* by Euripides and Shakespeare's *The Tempest.* In Bologna, Barba asked me to work on stage with the Japanese performer Kanichi Hanayagi to create a dialogue that transcended our different languages and techniques. In America, I have been creating dialogues with Chinese performers that go beyond our differences in technique and language. In America, as in ISTA, I am trying to discover how to stretch my traditional technique into something new while at the same time preserving it.

There is the system of work at ISTA that is like a mosaic. It gives me the opportunity to think about traditions and techniques from other cultures. At ISTA, there is an interaction between the performance languages of one culture and another culture. Whether it is body language, vocal language, gestural language or the language of singing, there is a thread that connects them all and enables them to communicate with one another. This is because they all share common elements. For instance, in singing there is always the resource of the voice that moves up and down the scale. The emotions, colours and textures of the voices are the same, and so are the melodies. The style in which these elements are used is different in the different traditions, but I hear a harmony that links them together. Eugenio finds this harmony by asking all of us to show him things. He never tells us what to show him, he just asks us to keep showing him things, until he finds the elements of our work that can be joined together and which fit in harmony with the work of the other artists. This is the mosaic process that leads to the creation of the *Teatrum Mundi* at ISTA.

During the Bologna ISTA, Eugenio asked me to perform a scene with Kanichi, who is Japanese. He wanted us to interact using dialogue, singing, or gestures. We combined all these languages. The theme was to have an argument. Eugenio asked us to begin by arguing about the days of the week. We didn't just say Monday, Tuesday, Wednesday, etc. We had to keep changing the vocal dynamics to create the fight. We moved from melodic patterns to sharp changes in rhythm. We didn't know the meaning of each other's words, but we could understand each other perfectly by listening to the basic qualities of each other's voice. We could call and respond to each other because we understood the feeling and the dynamics that were being communicated in the raw elements of our performance languages.

Even though the scene was about arguing, and we never agreed about anything, there was a harmony in the scene that came from our common understanding of performance language. It was our small mosaic inside the big mosaic of *Teatrum Mundi*. Each of us put in tiles of different shapes and colours, some Japanese and some Balinese, but we knew that they would fit together. We created a condition of dynamic equilibrium that kept the performance alive. Different elements are presented in opposition to one another, and the tension between them balances each other out. It is a technique that is very important in Balinese painting and religion. In Bali, we believe that human beings are always balanced between the world of the gods and the world of the demons and that they are always trying to find equilibrium between good and evil. The lines and dynamics of Balinese painting reflect this condition of dynamic equilibrium, as do the movements in our choreography where the muscles of the body are always moving in opposition to each other. In the scene with Kanichi, I could understand that this principle of dynamic equilibrium was part of his technique as well, and what kept our performance alive while we argued on stage together was our instinctive understanding that we had to use the non-verbal languages of our performance techniques to maintain a dynamic equilibrium between our two characters in their battle.

In the cross-cultural performance experiments I have made in America, I have continued to explore the dynamic equilibrium of performance languages and technique. For a production of *The Bacchae,* I used the character of Rangda to portray the aspect of Agave that is possessed when she kills her son Pentheus. The unbearable contradictions that lead a mother to kill her own son can be expressed in the wild irrationality of the Balinese Rangda whose voice moves back and forth from the highest pitch of wild shrieking to the deepest guttural laughter. Rangda is an embodiment of evil and death that is inextricably linked to qualities of good and rebirth. The dynamic equilibrium between positive and negative forces of heaven and hell is embodied in her voice, her mask, and her dance. Rangda has performed in many ISTA productions of *Teatrum Mundi*, and her presence in *The Bacchae* is a further step in her evolution into a character that speaks to the world beyond Bali. Euripides' play involves a tradition of religious trance dancing and possession, and Rangda also belongs to a tradition of trance, dance and possession in Bali. Perhaps the performance techniques of Rangda, based on patterns of paradox and contradiction, can offer some understanding of the lost theatrical techniques of the ancient Greeks, who also used masks, dance and music to give form to stories of paradox and contradiction.

In another play I worked with Chinese traditional artists to stage a story from the epic Chinese novel *Journey to the West*. I played the monkey king and a Chinese actress played the monk who tries to keep the energetic monkey under control during their pilgrimage. Even though she sang in Chinese and I spoke in Balinese, we used the non-verbal languages of our techniques to create tension and harmony in the scene. The monkey was running away from the monk who was trying to punish him, but they needed each other, and worked together as a team. The spiritual energy of the monk was opposite but complementary to the animal energy of the monkey.

Something happened to the languages of our performance techniques in America that was different from ISTA. The languages began to change and evolve, until we were both working together in a style that had something in it that was both Chinese and Balinese. Instead of putting the techniques together side by side in a mosaic, we were placing them on top of one another like overlapping transparencies, creating a new form that was neither completely Balinese or Chinese, but something appropriate to the classic text we were working on. This is part of the evolution of performance language that is also important to us in Bali. At the same time that we want to preserve our traditions, we want them to keep evolving so that our performance language does not become so rigid and inflexible that it cannot meet the demands of new work from other cultures that we want to perform in Bali. We want to make our own versions of non-Balinese plays that will show how Balinese performance techniques can enrich texts like *Journey to the West* or even Shakespeare and Euripides. Our experience at ISTA helps us to see that we are part of the world of intercultural performance. It plants the seeds for ideas and performance experiments that will help us preserve the integrity of our performance language at the same time that we allow it to grow into new forms that are part of the natural evolution of our culture. This tension between change and tradition in our stage techniques is another level of dynamic equilibrium that ISTA helps us to understand. But we must go back home to Bali in order to explore and develop it.

'Nothing of him that doth fade, but doth suffer a sea change.' (Ron Jenkins)

As I watch I Nyoman Catra grapple with the physicality of language in a rehearsal of Shakespeare's *The Tempest*, I cannot help but see it as the encounter of two great performance traditions. The precise physical and vocal technique of Elizabethan actors has not been passed down through an unbroken chain of masters and apprentices, so we can only conjecture as to the vocal rhythms and physical gestures used by Shakespeare's players at the Globe. Balinese technique, on the other hand, has been passed down from master to student for centuries, and Catra is the embodiment of that technique at its most radiant. When he sings the song of Caliban aching to be free, his body erupts in rhythmic pulses of liberation that are inseparable from the language.

In this rehearsal, an inheritor of the Balinese tradition, armed with the secrets of his ancestors, grapples with the ghost of an Elizabethan actor who once spoke those same lines. It is a startling struggle that forces an observer to re-evaluate both traditions, but neither artist is diminished. In the words of Ariel, sung in this rehearsal by Desak Made Suarti Laksmi, also a great Balinese traditional artist: 'nothing of him that doth fade, but doth suffer a sea change, into something rich and strange'. Catra does not lose the essence of his technique, but allows it to be transformed by the encounter with the world of Shakespeare's text into something new and unique. From Catra's perspective, the fit between Balinese performance and Shakespeare goes deeper than technique. The Balinese philosophy of Hindu-Buddhism mirrors the Elizabethan vision of a chain of being that links the world of man to the worlds of heaven and hell. To say that 'we are the stuff that dreams are made of' is a reinforcement of the Eastern concept of illusion or *maya*. The message of Ariel's song that describes the evolution of a shipwrecked corpse's eyes and bones into pearls and coral is in harmony with Balinese views of reincarnation and animism. What Western actor could identify so deeply with the themes of Shakespeare's play? To a modern western sensibility, the song is fantastical poetry. To Laksmi, it conforms to her instinctive vision of the universe, and she conveys its naturalness with the graceful Balinese melody she has composed to go with it. It is a tune that makes it easy to accept Ferdinand's confusing the music with the sound of the sea and the wind. As Laksmi sings her fingers tremble like palm leaves quivering in a sea breeze.

Catra and Laksmi would not be wrestling with the ghosts of Shakespeare if they had not been exposed to the cross-cultural experiments at ISTA. Repeated contact with performers from all over the world has whetted their artistic curiosity. They want to stretch their techniques in ways that will enable their tradition to evolve. They cherish their tradition, but they also see it as something in a constant state of living evolution, not something dead to be preserved in a rigid museum-like state. Their encounter with ISTA and western theatre is stabilizing as well as change-inducing. Questions asked by Barba at ISTA and the western students that they teach, force the Balinese to analyse and articulate principles of their own technique that they had simply taken for granted when they worked in isolation.

Catra, for example, has begun to dissect the dynamic qualities of Balinese movement patterns in response to western questioners who want to know why Balinese choreography always appears to be so aggressive. He found the clue in a conversation with a painter who showed him the difference between a 'leaning line' (diagonal) and a straight line. Catra realized that when he is on stage his body is always in the position of a leaning line and is being pulled by his muscles in two directions simultaneously. Because of this quality, which is so instinctive to any performer trained in Balinese technique that few of them would be conscious enough of the pattern to mention it, the Balinese actor is in a constant state of paradox. His muscles are struggling against one another internally even when the body is motionless, giving a dynamic quality to stillness. The 'leaning line' principle dictates that a body is always moving in two directions simultaneously, searching for equilibrium while in perpetual disequilibrium. According to Catra the actor must always *mencari keseimbangan di dalam ke tidak seimbangan* (search for balance where there is no balance).

The physical presence of the Balinese actor, constantly searching for equilibrium in a state of disequilibrium, mirrors the condition of great theatrical situations and texts, where dramatic tension is continually heightened by unresolved conflict. Shakespeare's plays certainly fall into this category, full of language that bristles with action, paradox, and contradiction. What actor is better prepared to embody that text than one who knows the secret of encoding the conflict between equilibrium and disequilibrium into his flesh. When Catra plays Caliban, his physical presence is both gloriously free and hopelessly enslaved, and it is the tension between these states that makes him riveting to watch. His movements are both bestial and angelic, again mirroring the contradictions in Shakespeare's text. Catra's body is an ideogram that conveys the paradox of Caliban's character in a muscular cluster of physical brush strokes. The Balinese performer's technical ability to convey complex meanings through the body has always astonished western observers who are accustomed to a more intellectualized verbal style of acting.

When Artaud first saw Balinese performers in the 1930s, he called them 'animated hieroglyphs', and imagined their bodies as ideograms conveying physicalized layers of metaphysical meanings: 'These three dimensional hieroglyphs are in turn brocaded with a certain number of gestures – mysterious signs which correspond to some unknown, fabulous and obscure reality which we here in the occident have completely repressed' (Artaud, 1958: 61).

The most interesting word in Artaud's description is the last: 'repressed'. It suggests the possibility that western performances might once have been imbued with these highly charged ideograms, but that our actors have lost the secrets required for expressing the metaphysical language of the body. The heightened poetry of *The Tempest*, with its invocations of the spiritual world, seems to cry out for these living hieroglyphs, as do the texts of other great western classics that modern actors struggle to resurrect. The ancient Greeks, performing in the temple of Dionysus, most certainly choreographed the choruses of Aeschylus and Euripides with dancing hieroglyphs charged with a spirituality echoed by today's Balinese temple dancers. Catra has tried his hand at *The Bacchae* as well, attempting to capture the irrational passions of Agave in the leaping shrieks of the Balinese demon widow Rangda.

As Catra and Laksmi endeavour to express the paradoxical qualities of western classics with the paradoxical techniques of their traditional performing arts, they themselves are in a state of paradox. They are trying to maintain their traditions at the same time that they want to reinvent them. This is a state to which they were introduced at ISTA, which thrives on this same contradiction. Neither of them is disturbed by this contradiction. On the contrary, it seems to invigorate them with a sense of challenge. Like the Balinese actor who incorporates the 'leaning line' into every action on stage, Catra, Laksmi, and the STSI director Bandem are perpetually poised between the old world of Balinese tradition and the new world of Western innovation. It is a position in which they are continuously searching for equilibrium in a world of disequilibrium, and they would not have it any other way.

References

Artaud, Antonin (1958), *The Theatre and its Double*, trans. Mary Caroline Richards. New York: Grove Press.

5

Odissi and the ISTA dance: an interview with Sanjukta Panigrahi

Ron Jenkins and Ian Watson

Sanjukta Panigrahi, along with her guru Kelucharan Mahapatra, is credited with reviving the all but extinct Odissi dance, an ancient Indian performance form from Orissa state. Odissi is a solo form that combines music, song and a style of dance that includes a rich choreography with *mudra* hand gestures, similar to those in other Indian genres such as Kathakali, and pantomimic movement to convey complex narratives of love, personal sacrifice, and humankind's relations to the gods. Panigrahi, along with her husband Raghunath who conducted the musicians and sang the songs accompanying the dances, was one of the leading exponents of the form. She gained an international reputation both as a dancer as well as an ambassador for classical Indian dance on her many tours through Asia, Europe, the United States, and Australia. When he was organizing the first ISTA in 1980, Barba asked Panigrahi to join him in his research endeavours. She subsequently became one of his closest ISTA collaborators and worked at every ISTA until her untimely death in 1997.

This interview is a compilation of two interviews. The first, by Ian Watson, was conducted at the 4th ISTA conference in Holstebro, Denmark in 1986. The second interview by Ron Jenkins, was made during the 9th ISTA meeting in Umeå, Sweden. Panigrahi rarely granted interviews and in these two she discusses similar things from time to time and at others touches on items she has not talked of previously. For this reason, I thought it most efficient and informative to combine the interviews. (Ian Watson)

IAN WATSON How did you first become involved with ISTA?

SANJUKTA PANIGRAHI In 1977 I was invited to several festivals in Germany and France. Holstebro organized an Indian festival around the same time and I was asked to perform. I had a brief meeting with Eugenio in Holstebro and I was fascinated by some of his ideas. I don't remember what exactly now, it was so long ago. Some time later I received a letter from him asking me if I could collaborate with him on a new experiment he was organizing. It has always been my desire to know something new, to invent or experiment. So I said, yes, I will collaborate. We had the first ISTA meeting in Bonn, in 1980. Actually, I was a little afraid because I was not acquainted with this kind of work. At first I thought that I had made a mistake by coming because I was being asked questions I could not answer. I was very upset. You see, in India we start learning dance when we are four or five years old. You don't know what your body is, you cannot feel your body, you don't know your mind. You learn from a guru, I won't call him a teacher, he is a guru ... a master teacher. You just follow him like a parrot, you imitate what he does. You do not understand the meaning of the dance, where you are bending, where you are taking the stress, or where the tensions are in your body. You merely repeat the same positions exactly every time you do them. You follow as if you were blind. We call it *guru-shishya parampara*, to hand down from teacher to pupil. It has been like this for ages. We do not ask our teachers how much tension here? How much this should bend? We just follow.

IW What did you do in the early, formative ISTAs?

SP The focus at the first ISTA in Bonn was on training. We pedagogues taught initial exercises from our forms, how to mould the body, and about discipline.

IW You were teaching a dance as you would in India?

SP No. I was teaching the exercises we do before the dance starts. We have exercises for strengthening all parts of the body: the toes, heels, then the whole leg, the chest, the spine, the head, even eye exercises. These exercises are used prior to all dances. At the second ISTA in Volterra in 1981, it was somewhat different. We were divided into four groups. Every group was a family and the pedagogues were the parents of the various families. In my group we did exercises with music, how to hear the music and implement exercises from it. I realized in ISTA that you feel less tired when you do exercises to music. Following these exercises we did some training on different kinds of standing and sitting positions.

IW These are all positions taken from Odissi dance?

sp   Yes, but they are used in other forms as well. In Volterra, Eugenio also suggested that we teach our folk dances to participants as a form of relaxation. In doing this we worked on contact in the dances. We also worked on positions and the changing of positions, how to develop choreography and a little about dramaturgy also. In the third ISTA in France [1985] we mainly talked about our forms because the entire meeting was only seven days long. Each morning everybody was doing exercises, and we talked about our training. In the evening we gave performances. We also discussed how to narrate a story and how to choreograph it.

iw   Do you think that ISTA has affected you in any way?

sp   Let me tell you a little of my personal history with ISTA. When I first worked with Eugenio I was often confused about things. When he told me to do something, I would do the opposite. If it was something that was not part of my form, I would draw a total blank. I was often upset, and sometimes he was also upset. One day after working with Eugenio I was very angry. I returned to my room and I said to my husband, 'I don't know why he wants me to try these things.' My husband asked me, 'But why didn't you try it, why didn't you at least explore it and see what was there?' I began thinking about what my husband said, and slowly I started to understand and accept Eugenio's suggestions. To understand my initial reactions you must realize that in India when you attain a certain level of performance and you are recognized as a famous dancer, no one dares offer suggestions to you. So, the first time it happened to me it was a shock. My attitude changed entirely after that. I was willing to try things. I was willing to explore ideas and see where they would lead me. Prior to ISTA I was not open to suggestions. This openness has helped me a great deal.

ron jenkins   How?

sp   It has helped me with my teaching. When I first came to ISTA, Eugenio asked me questions like, 'When you are in such and such a position, how much do you bend, how much tension is involved?' As I said earlier, I didn't understand his questions at first, but they gradually began to make sense as I reflected on exactly what my body was doing during the dance. I found I could feel each part of my body. I could define the role each part played in the formation of the dance. When we began working with other cultures I was a little wary because I did not want to go out of my tradition. It was only later that I became secure in the knowledge that I could work with artists from other cultures without loosing my artistic identity. Gradually I grew up with the ISTA techniques and I could feel my limbs, my body … and it also helped my teaching in India.

RJ   How did it help your teaching?

SP   Students today are very clever. They can see much more than my generation could. We did not have television when we learned. We didn't have tape recorders. Now they have modern gadgets that enhance their perception. Nowadays they ask, 'If we keep our left leg in this position is it correct?' You have to answer them very correctly, otherwise they feel shaky about you and their training. So ISTA's way of defining and analysing the body has helped me in teaching.

RJ   Your students ask you the same questions now that Eugenio asked you in ISTA's formative days?

SP   Yes.

RJ   Has ISTA changed the way that you perform?

SP   No, not at all.

RJ   Here at ISTA you invent new things without compromising your artistic identity. Do you also invent new things in India when you perform?

SP   Yes, otherwise the dance becomes stagnant. All Indian classical dance is free to invent. We are allowed to improvise, we are allowed to make innovations, but there is a rule: you have to keep to the principles, codes and techniques prescribed in the ancient treatises and families. As long as you remain faithful to that rule you can invent. In India there are two aspects to dance, pure dance, *nritti*, and narrative dance, *nritya*. Narrative dance entails a great deal of facial expression. We say in India that this use of the face is difficult because it is where the artist's individuality comes to the fore. Pure dance, on the other hand, involves rigour and technique so that the dance becomes virtually automatic. We say that the dancer has two masters: one says that you practice your technique very vigorously, the other says that you forget your technique. But what is the meaning of forgetting your technique? You practise so hard that it comes to you automatically. You don't think of your technique. If you think of your technique you cannot take the spectator beyond it, you remain in the technique. But there is a world beyond technique where you can take your spectator.

RJ   Is the way in which you invent how to tell stories influenced by your ISTA experience?

SP   No I don't think so. My body and mind have been trained rigorously from early childhood. This training has shaped my expression and it is so much a part of me that it is very hard to change. When I invent, I naturally think in a very traditional Indian way. This is because it is in my body, it is in my mind, it is in my thoughts.

RJ   What about when you have to improvise with a performer from another culture here at ISTA? What happens when you improvise with Augusto Omolú, the *Orixá* dancer from Brazil, or Kanichi Hanayagi, the Kabuki master, neither of whom have been shaped by your training?

SP   At first it was strange for me, I was not used to it. But gradually I became accustomed to it and learned to appreciate its value. As Tom Leabhart [a Decroux trained mime who is currently one of Barba's ISTA pedagogues] was saying yesterday in his talk about Decroux, you don't have to stare at a person with two eyes wide open to know their movements. You can, after having worked with them for a time, feel their movements, where the turn is coming, and you can react to your partner's actions. With enough experience, you know how to respect a person's quality while at the same time retaining your own.

RJ   Can you be more specific about what you mean by 'quality?'

SP   The shape, flow and intensity of movement that one's body senses rather than sees.

RJ   But what qualities does your body sense from a 'foreign' culture? And how do you respond to these qualities in terms of your own cultural heritage?

SP   The turns, the movements, and the use of the space. You have to respect the design and use of the space, the ups and downs. But my responses are always coloured by being an Indian; my expression is inevitably Indian.

RJ   But what, for example, is the difference between the way you and Augusto make designs in space?

SP   Augusto repeats actions. Once we have completed a formation, we don't repeat it. When we have completed a pattern of movements, we move on to another pattern and only when it is complete can we return to the first pattern. In this repetition, however, the space is often used differently. The hand and body gestures can be wider, more expansive, for instance, with diagonal movement in the space.

RJ   Have you noticed anything different about the other performance cultures here at ISTA?

SP   The Balinese use space much the same way that we do.

RJ   What about the Japanese?

SP   Much the same.

RJ   So it was Augusto's movement design and use of space that was most difficult for you to adjust to?

SP   Yes, because it is more circular and repetitive.

RJ   Are there any differences between your use of space and the Japanese or Balinese?

SP   The Japanese are more internal. They don't exhibit their movement.

They use all the power that we display but, as Katsuko Azuma [a Japanese Nihon Buyo performer who was a pedagogue at the early ISTAs] once told me, they contain the power within. In India we are extroverts, more like the Balinese.

RJ   The Balinese display their feelings in their movements and use of space?

SP   Yes.

RJ   Are there any differences between you and the Balinese?

SP   We do not share all of the same movements, though they make a similar difference between narrative and pure dance. But they tell the stories in their own way, sometimes using a fan and often using hand gestures that are different from ours. The formation of the body is also different, especially the shoulders.

RJ   Do the ideograms that Eugenio has been talking about in the morning sessions, the notion of painting in space with your body in the vein of Japanese calligraphy, make sense to you [this question refers to a session conducted at the ISTA in Sweden]?

SP   Yesterday when he asked me to make an ideogram of digging under the surface, I did it, but it was very difficult. I understood a little better when he asked me to show the way of walking in Odissi dance, especially when he got me to repeat it slowly to demonstrate that there are eight different things involved: one, you are keeping your weight on the balls of your feet; two you are going on your toes; three, you are making a circle; four, you are moving on your heel; five, you are turning the foot; six, you are putting the foot flat; seven, you bring your back foot forward; and, eight, you again have your weight on the balls of your feet. I began to question, are there eight parts to the walk or not? And I realized that there are. So, when I returned to the exercise of digging under the surface, instead of just doing it without thinking in terms of parts of an ideogram, of how many actions are involved, I began to deconstruct it. I broke it into ten parts and this helped me repeat the action accurately.

RJ   Do you ever use that idea of breaking actions down into ideograms when you make your own work in India?

SP   I haven't up to now.

RJ   Do you think that you will?

SP   Yes, because it is helpful.

RJ   You said earlier that you never lose your artistic identity at ISTA. What is your identity as a performer?

SP   From childhood people have said that I appear to be a strong-willed person and that I project this strength when I am on stage. In India I am identified as a solo performer and my specialty is playing different characters during the telling of one story. My repertory primarily consists of narrative dances with as many as four, five, or even six characters, all of which I project differently with different body movements and expressions.

RJ And when you change from one character to another, how do you do it?

SP With movement and with expression. I really cannot tell you. I have to show you. It involves a mental adjustment, which is a spontaneous reaction that is the product of many years of training and practice. When you are playing a queen you have to feel like a queen then, when you become an old person, you have to feel like an old person. If you don't take on these feelings, you are not able to project.

RJ What happens in the moment of change?

SP When you know your technique, when you are at ease with your technique and you are no longer struggling to control it, then the feelings come automatically.

RJ And in that moment of change, does the movement or the feeling come first? Do you feel like a queen before you move as one or does the movement lead to you feeling like a queen?

SP At the point of change I feel like a queen; then the movement comes automatically.

RJ Given how many years you have been involved with ISTA, is there anything that is still difficult for you at these meetings?

SP Teaching is always a challenge. When I am asked to teach somebody at ISTA, my first thought is: they don't know India or its traditions, they have not seen them. How can I put the seed of India in these students in five days when this type of training takes many years? What can I do to make them at least feel something of what the dance is about?

RJ Just the essence?

SP The essence. In India a teacher working with a new pupil works for months at a time, but at ISTA you cannot. In India there is no compromise. Of course you are not teaching students the dance here, but even giving the sense of it is difficult.

RJ So it has to be a compromise at ISTA?

SP Yes.

RJ Do you make different choices at times? Did you make a different choice at this ISTA from the previous one, for example?

SP Yes.

RJ What's the difference?

SP A different choice of body movements.

RJ Why did you make such a change?

SP   Sometimes the basic things of my dance are the same, such as the square position of the body, the basic walk, or the *tribangi* [an ubiquitous Odissi dance position in which the head, spine, and legs are bent in different directions suggesting a gentle 'S' shape]. They are always the same. But I construct some body exercises differently because I like to do that. I like to invent exercises while retaining the principles of the form.

RJ   Do you invent new body exercises in India also?

SP   Yes. In India we do it in a different way because we know the students individually. For some students all exercises are the same, but differences in students prompts different special exercises. We know who needs what. There are some students, for example, whose backs are not straight, so we ask them to go to the wall and to move up and down the wall so that they know what it is to have their back straight while they move.

RJ   Are there any exercises that you invented at ISTA because they are better for western bodies to learn eastern techniques?

SP   No.

RJ   Have you tried the wall exercise at ISTA, for instance?

SP   I don't have time at ISTA to use it. Here I just try to explain the logic of the dance because it is not so simple to get into the body so quickly. The students at ISTA understand the logic, the principles; they can then use them in their own way. They don't have to study the dance.

RJ   When you try to explain ISTA to people in India who have never been here how do you describe it?

SP   People are very curious about ISTA in India. When they ask me about it I say that we don't only perform. We do have some performances, but really the focus is on technical and special work, that is, on analysing your body and feeling your body, knowing your movements while being sure of your art and yourself.

RJ   If you could change anything at ISTA, do something differently, introduce something new, what would it be?

SP   I have not thought about it.

RJ   Think about it for a second.

SP   Ask me later. If you ask me without warning, I cannot tell you.

RJ   You mean that ISTA is so perfect that you cannot think of anything you would change?

SP   There must be new ideas. You cannot say that there is something ultimate. There is always something new. You can never have perfection. An artist strives for perfection her whole life and then at the end of her career she thinks that she has yet to do something, yet to learn something, yet to go somewhere. So it is a never-ending process. I don't think it will end. You always get something new, a new thought and you try to learn it. I always say that we are students for our whole life and when we see something new, somebody doing something that offers a better way than your own, you try to learn it.

Interculturalism and the individual performer: an interview with the Odin actress Roberta Carreri

Ian Watson

Roberta Carreri has been a member of the Odin Teatret since 1974. She, like her Odin colleagues, has studied a variety of performance forms from different cultures and is a member of the pedagogical staff at the International School of Theatre Anthropology (ISTA). The interview took place on 25 January 1993 when Carreri was in New York to perform and conduct a workshop. This interview first appeared in *The Performers' Village: Times, Techniques and Theories at ISTA* (Graasten, Denmark: Drama, 1996), edited by Kirsten Hastrup.

IAN WATSON The opening and closing dance in your work demonstration, *Traces in the Snow*, incorporates a number of different Asian performance forms. It includes the Japanese *jo-ha-kyu*, components of Balinese dance/drama and others. What is the significance of combining these for you?

ROBERTA CARRERI I had been working at the Odin for six years and had already developed my personal training when Eugenio organized the first ISTA conference in Bonn, Germany in 1980. He invited me to the conference and I met the Japanese, Indian, Balinese and Chinese theatres. I spent two weeks at ISTA, where I was in a very privileged situation because, in addition to the morning sessions in which everyone worked with the Asian masters, I received extra lessons from the Japanese teacher, Katsuko Azuma – a Nihon Buyo master [Nihon Buyo is a Japanese dance form that has its origins in Kabuki], and the Indian Odissi dancer, Sanjukta Panigrahi. I worked with Katsuko most. She spent two or three hours every afternoon just with me, teaching me the Kabuki 'Lion Dance'. Oriental masters teach the postures as well as the physical patterns of the dance, and there was this simple posture, the standing posture which is the beginning of the 'Lion Dance', that has been a key to much of my subsequent work. This posture made me feel my body from inside. I always had the experience of feeling what my arms and legs were doing when I danced: they filled the space with energy. But, I was focused on the surface of my body, I was never really conscious of what was happening inside my body, I was unaware of what I now call the 'in-tension', that is, the inner tension of the body. The *jo-ha-kyu* she taught me was also very important for my understanding of 'in-tension' because of the body posture it calls for, the walk this body posture leads to, and the need to create an inner resistance to counter forward motion. Then I had the experience with Sanjukta who, contrary to Katsuko's teaching which emphasized a rigidly straight spinal column, cut the line of my body. In the Odissi, my spine was like a snake, zig-zagging from one side to the other. My experiences in the Japanese and Indian theatres were very different, but what I discovered in being exposed to them was territories of my body that I didn't know, territories that I was not aware of.

IW What do you mean by 'territories of the body?'

RC Compare the body to a continent, with rivers, mountains and plains inside which there are gold, emeralds, diamonds, even oil. To discover the continent's inner wealth you have to explore under the earth, dig mines. It's been a geological work finding this part inside myself. How to feel the body from inside, which is very different from learning how to do a split or how to leap in a dance where your major concerns are if you are doing it right and how your body looks in the space. My geological self is not like this, it is concerned with inside not outside.

IW What is the difference between your 'geological self' and the Stanislavskian psychological approach to theatre which is also concerned with the inside?

RC It is another inside, I think. Mine is physiological. It is a series of tensions between different muscles in the body which I can reproduce at any time without engaging psychological memory. It is a physical memory, and it is very concrete: merely moving two parts of the body and keeping the eyes on a specific point while the head is tilted forward a little, for example, changes my normal everyday presence without requiring any psychological adjustment on my part.

IW This simple tilting and the line you talk of in the spine, is that just copying, just reproducing what the masters taught you?

RC Yes.

IW That's all it's doing?

RC In the beginning, yes. But then it's mine. Now it's mine. In the beginning it's reproducing and that's why it's interesting, because me, as a western person – I would never discover this for myself. When I ask students in workshops to find actions, they invariably reproduce what they are used to doing in normal life. So I have a lot of introductory work to do with them before we can begin to explore the nature of actions. Everyone has a body culture which is a product of socialization. We are born into a particular culture from which after about one year of life we learn how to walk, we learn how to take food and how to eat, we learn how to speak and so on. But as we learn these things, our behaviour becomes more and more limited. And when an actor who has not met other cultures improvises, what he does is reproduce a series of cliches of behaviour based on his enculturation.[1] Despite what people say about the creativity of improvisation, I have very seldom seen an actor improvise something truly original. Unless we have a very precise task, even we Odin actors, who have been working with improvisation for many years, reproduce our clichés when we improvise. I have found tricks for myself which help: when you improvise you imagine the point of a knife being forced into your back, for instance, or a tiny piece of broken glass in your shoe. The eastern masters have a very precise body knowledge which makes these tricks superfluous. They have rules that allow them to find these feelings from inside: physical feelings from inside your body that we are not usually aware of in our cultures. My contact with these performers helped me meet these other parts of my body. Things which are the product of hundreds and hundreds of years of culture which I would never have found alone in my one short life.

IW Are there other specific Asian performers who have influenced your work as much as Katsuko and Sanjukta have?

RC Natsuko Ajima, a Butoh dancer, and Kazuo Ohno [one of the founders of Butoh] as well.

IW But Butoh is a modern Asian form. It doesn't have the traditional history of Kabuki, Nihon Buyo, or Odissi dance.

---

1   Carreri is using the word enculturation in the way Barba defines it. Enculture is an obsolete word, which the Webster's dictionary defines as 'lack or neglect of cultivation'. Barba's use of the term is somewhat different. He describes the encultured body as one which has absorbed the cultural body patterns of its particular culture. As Barba puts it: 'Each one of us is an incultured body. We use a daily body technique which derives from the culture in which we have been born, from our family environments, from our work' (1989: 312).

RC Oh, but it has the core, which is the old core. You cannot forget the origins of Butoh. Butoh's founders, who were trained as modern dancers in post-war Japan, wanted to get back to their traditional cultural roots. When I studied with Natsuko, I discovered that the first walk she taught me had the same body rules in it as the Noh dances. Not only that, in Butoh, as in the Noh, it is often the ghost of a character which is on stage. The only thing that I found very different is the work with the eyes, this was its biggest challenge for me. In Butoh you dance with the eyes out of focus, you relax your eyes so that you see nothing and you see everything, you go inside yourself and there you are in your own world and you dance. The other big secret that Kazuo Ohno shared with me came in a conversation one day when he explained that, 'In western culture, this is dance,' and he made a wonderful, typical ballet jump. 'But,' he said, 'this is not real dance. Real dance is not what happens outside the body, it's what happens inside the body. There is where the real dance is.' And you can see it wherever, you can see it in music, you can see it in dance, in theatre, there are people that are dancing inside. There are people that are the music and there are people that are making music. Those that make music are earning their salary. Those that are dancing the music, they are the real artists. They are the people that make the audience dance with them.

IW In describing this you are really touching on a balance between technical skill and performance in which it is difficult to isolate and/or quantify either factor. One's skills maybe the foundation of 'dancing the music', but they alone are not sufficient, these skills are only part of an equation that includes performance itself. As difficult as it is to separate them, I would like to try and discuss skills separate from performance in order to better understand the intercultural roots of your work. Let's begin with the source of skills: training. At the Odin you spend a great deal of time on training. Most of you continue to train more or less daily, even though you've been with the company many years. This training is individual-based, with each of you developing his or her own training. It seems to me that there are a number of factors influencing your particular training: your early years at the Odin when you studied with the older actors from the group and Eugenio, your years of experience in performing as well as developing your own training, and your studies of Nihon Buyo, Odissi dance, Butoh, etc. Putting the other influences aside for the moment, how have your studies of performance forms from other cultures informed your training and development as an actress?

RC So we come back to the first question, which I now realize I didn't answer. When I came back from ISTA, I was fascinated by the work of the Japanese, Indian, Chinese and Balinese. So what I did in my training was to imitate them, imitate their extraordinary way of moving the body in space. I had this training which was twenty minutes of Japanese walks, then twenty minute of Indian postures, followed by twenty minutes of different Balinese walks.

IW You also studied with the Balinese?

RC No, but I observed them and had an affinity with what I saw ... . I really felt it. The focus in the eyes, the tension in the shoulders and in the body, I felt that I could imitate it. And that's exactly what I did. I imitated what I had seen the Balinese performers do, with the shoulders and elbows high up and the tension in the torso. I would never have done this spontaneously, I would never have found a reason to. But when I did it physically and I focused my eyes, then a very specific and special kind of power arose in my body. I found the same straight line from the coccyx to the top of my head that I had experienced in the Japanese theatre. The legs were bent, there was this tension from my coccyx to the top of my head, and then when I raised my shoulders and elbows as well as focused my eyes, I experienced my body becoming like a lamp that makes light. I felt that it was present, I felt a stream of energy.

IW You were conscious of this stream of energy?

RC Yes, of course. I felt the stream of energy as if it were electricity. I worked with this for months, then I became pregnant and some other things, personal, professional things, happened and ... well, life kept going. Eugenio continued organizing ISTAs and in 1987 I was invited to take part in the Salento conference where I once again met the world of ISTA.

IW You had not been to an ISTA between 1980 and 1987?

RC I was at the 1986 Holstebro conference, but it was not practical. It consisted of lecture/demonstrations mostly and the people of the Odin were involved primarily in organization. But in '87 I attended as an actress, and I began thinking how I could combine my Bonn experience with what had happened in the meantime. I chose a very western piece of music, 'Heart Attack and Vine' by Tom Waits, something more western than that I could not find. Then I tried putting my experiences with the different kinds of dance to this music.

IW It's strange that you should chose that piece of music to work with because in many ways it is a product of a culture other than your own. You are an Italian living in Denmark, not a North American with roots in the Blues. What is the connection to Waits and the Blues for you?

RC I like it. It makes me want to dance. Not only that, he has a very sensual voice. In Holstebro we have a fine library with an enormous amount of records from all over the world and when I run a workshop, I ask my students to go and find a new piece of music every day from the library that they want to share with others. So each day I am bombarded with eight or more pieces of music which are absolutely different, harmonies from Mongolia, chants from Africa, Tom Waits, Jazz like Keith Jarrett, very different, Satie, Philip Glass, who knows! This exposure to music from different cultures opened my ears in something the same way that experiencing different performance cultures opened my body.

IW In choosing to put fragments and adaptations of theatre forms you had learned at ISTA to Waits's music, you were really creating a performance. But what about the training? The work you have done with the Asian masters and your subsequent development of it is in your body, it is part of what Phillip Zarrilli would call 'in-body knowledge' (1984). How does this in-body knowledge influence your training?

RC It influenced me most directly when I was first trying to do what I had learned from the Asian teachers. It influenced me for a long time. Eventually, I centred much of my training on developing the Japanese walk. In addition to the sense of the inside I mentioned earlier, this helped me move away from the linear nature of the walk and explore its potential for various kinds of circular movements. In the past few years, I have been working more and more with breath and energy. Many people who have seen this work say, 'You are doing t'ai chi'. But it is not t'ai chi. The centred presence that I found in working on the Japanese walk is also in t'ai chi. It is the in-tension in the spinal column that I talked about before. And you should remember that the spinal cord doesn't end in the neck, it ends in the eyes. The eyes are the last vertebra. If you lower your eyes, you have one tension in your head, if you raise them, a different tension. I have been working a lot with presence, a still, centred presence inside my body. I let my legs and arms take me around in the space while I focus on this presence. I have been working more and more on the connections between my breathing and my actions: how the breathing in or breathing out affect my action; how I can make a very powerful action soft; how a rushed movement can be powerful without being harsh; how to be aggressive while being subtle and soft, like a mean cat.

IW   This kind of training is far removed from merely reproducing the Asian forms you studied. It is an elaboration of the basic introductory work you've done with them. It's as if you've used what you've learned from them as a point of departure for your training, and that what you learned remains as a memory that continues to inform the present. But what about productions? Since actors' improvisations are the major source of material for productions at the Odin, what shapes the actors would seem to be an important factor in them. Is this true? What influence has your contact with other performance cultures had on these improvisations and the productions they generate?

RC   A lot. For example, in the last production [the Odin production *Talabot*] I had a whole dance that had its roots in my experience with Brazilian Candomblé. The Candomblé dance is based on a specific way of moving your spine in snake-like waves with a movement that starts from your coccyx and goes up to your eyes. It all began when Eugenio asked us to improvise to some music. The music prompted a very precise movement in my body that I recognized as the dance of *Oshala*, which is one of the African Gods I learned about in Brazil.

IW   But the music was not Brazilian?

RC   Oh, no, it was not Brazilian at all. It was a ballad improvised by Jan Ferslev [an Odin performer who is primarily a musician and composer]. And from the initial impulse other movements came, but they were inspired by … . I have the feeling that my body has an intelligence of its own. Something like Grotowski [Jerzy Grotowski, the Polish experimental theatre director and researcher into ritual performance techniques, who Barba worked closely with in the early 1960s] said: 'The body does not have memory, it is memory.' I think that there are some people who have a very developed physical intelligence, memory you can call it.

IW   Would it be fair to say that the intercultural influences on your production work are indirect rather than direct? Let me explain. A direct intercultural influence would be one in which a production in one culture incorporates the form of one or more performance genres from another culture. Maurice Béjart for example, created a ballet in the mid-80s using this approach. He took a well known Kabuki play, *Chushingura* (The Treasury of Loyal Retainers) by Takeda Izumo, Miyoshi Shoraku, and Namiki Senryu, used Kabuki-like costumes, various Kabuki movement patterns, and commissioned a score that combined Kabuki instruments and traditional ballet music. With these components he created a major work for the Tokyo Ballet, a world-class Japanese company that normally dances European classical ballet pieces. The Kabuki elements were obvious in what was essentially a modern ballet. The intercultural is more indirect in your work. You begin with identifiable cultural forms but, through your training and improvisations, you explore, experiment and elaborate what you begin with to create something distinctive. Excluding your dance in *Traces in the Snow*, which is meant to openly display its intercultural elements, I could not come up to you after a performance and say that part was Kabuki, the other section was taken from Noh, etc.

RC I would say exactly the opposite. I would say that they work indirectly because they only use the form. I take it directly because I take the core and then I change the form. Béjart takes the form, but what about the core? The core doesn't interest him. He has the story, the costumes, everything; but do the performers convey the presence of the Kabuki? What is the core of theatre if not the presence of the performer? You can produce the presence of the actor in many different ways, of course, but eastern theatre has taught me to find it physically. This means working with precise parts of my body to activate streams of energy. There are different ways, but I can do it anywhere or anytime because it calls for a physical precision I can master, rather than conjuring up a past psychological moment that is much more difficult to reproduce at will. My body has knowledge. If you know something, you cannot pretend that you do not know it, you cannot. Once you know it, you know it. Once I have learned something with my body, which means that it took me months, it took me years to master it. When I find it, I have it. Whatever I do, I cannot forget what I know. If you say get up from that chair theatrically, of course I will find a way of getting up from the chair that is theatrical, and of course I will not think, 'Now I am using an Odissi *tribangi*' [a basic posture of the form]. I do not think that, but my body will do it.

IW Each of the Odin actors, particularly the ones who have been with Eugenio for many years, have similar stories to your own: they have been exposed to different cultural forms and have developed their own training. What you have is a group of individuals whose professional interests and training are in some ways quite different. Despite these differences, every two to three years this group meets in the rehearsal room to create a production together, a production that will have its genesis in improvisations. Since the emphasis in the early stage of rehearsals at the Odin is on individual improvisations, the initial stock of improvisations is, in your case, the product of your past experiences, multicultural interests, training, and response to the themes you are working on. But, as Eugenio begins to create what he calls his montage, that is, construct scenes, he brings the separate improvisations together. You have to work together. Given your very different professional histories, how do your various experiences and the way in which each of you has elaborated them relate? Do you appear as unrelated figures in space, with no contact between you, or are you able to integrate your training and individual development into a cohesive whole?

RC We have different experiences. Torgeir [Torgeir Wethal, one of the founding members of the Odin who is still an actor in company], had been with the Odin for ten years when I joined the group. He stopped training shortly after I arrived. The training during the first decade was so brutal that he didn't want to train any more. Iben [Iben Nagel Rasmussen who has been an active member of the group since 1966] came eight years before me. She and another colleague had developed a personal training, a language which was their own. When I came, I just learned what Torgeir and Iben knew; they taught me. Then I began elaborating my own training. My elaborations were inspired by other cultures. First, in the winter of 1979, I met the Brazilian masters, the Candomblé dancers I told you about. Then I met the eastern masters. I was fertile soil, I was very open to these influences because I was hungry for inspiration. These meetings helped me develop my own training. But, the training is one thing, the work on performance is something else. The training allows me to develop my physical intelligence, my body memory. When I make an improvisation I don't think about looking Japanese or looking Balinese or anything, that is out of my mind. Yet it is in my body. This means that when I do something, whether I recognize it or not, it has to do with my training and what inspired the training. But I am doing it as an Italian woman who lives in Denmark and is a member of the Odin Teatret. So I will not walk like a Japanese Kabuki performer. I will not take the outside elements, what is visible. I will not walk like a Balinese in the improvisation. Everything is chewed and digested, it has gone into my blood, into my body, and it comes out like Roberta. Our initial improvisations are created individually; then we memorize them, much like a dancer learns a piece of choreography. But Eugenio is the one who makes the montage, that means that he chooses which performer's actions go with which actions of his or her colleague. He removes what doesn't fit. The result is something of a genesis, because it goes through the head of Eugenio. So all my work with the Japanese masters is suddenly galaxies ago. It is still there, but it is invisible.

IW So there is no conscious attempt, on your part at least, to make a performance which displays the multicultural roots of your training in performance?

RC This is a difficult question to answer because in my one-woman piece, *Judith*, my meeting with the Butoh world is quite present, even if it is re-elaborated. The material is not the same as it was in the beginning because Eugenio changed things during rehearsals. Nevertheless, it's there. But I don't do it to show what I know, for the sake of display. That's not it. The work with the Butoh people and their techniques helped me find something very deep inside myself that allowed me to express myself, many layers of myself, and that I express in spite of myself ... for example, I didn't know how I appeared in *Judith* until I saw the first photographs, I didn't know my eyes were crossed for one section of the piece until I saw the pictures, I didn't know that.

IW You talk constantly about Roberta and Roberta's experiences, but what is the relationship between Roberta expressing this inner self and character?

RC This is a very tricky question. You know that I am not an actress. I am a performer.

IW What distinction do you make between the two?

RC I am not playing a character. I am giving a name to myself on stage, and this is very different. In *Judith*, you could have called me Lady Macbeth, you could have called me Salome, Magdalena, whatever. And, provided you do not listen to the text, which provides a context for the character, you can see *Judith* and justify anyone of these choices.

IW But isn't that partly tied up with how you create performance texts at the Odin? You had developed much of your physical score for *Judith* long before Eugenio suggested the Judith story. You could have taken almost the same score, the same physical pattern of characterization and told the story of Lady Macbeth or Salome.

RC With a few changes, yes.

IW You don't think of character in psychological terms?

RC No, not really. If I say I am Antigone, for example, I have to think about who Antigone was, when she lived, and so on. Of course I know all those things, but I do not take them into consideration when I make my improvisations.

IW Is that what you did when you played Antigone in *Oxyrhincus Evangeliet* [a 1985 Odin production]?

RC Something like that. I don't know if I am supposed to say this, but half of my score in *Oxyrhincus* was created by working with a chair and a big tube, not the usual improvisations. I only made one normal improvisation for *Oxyrhincus*, the rest was physical work. Then, I put on a costume, sang while I was doing it and, if one had read the programme and knew about my brother Polynices, who was also in the production, it was clear that I must be Antigone. I call my one-woman piece *Judith*, but most of the material in it was not created with the thought that I want to behave as Judith would have behaved. It comes from other pictures. Eugenio never gives a theme for an improvisation which has something to do with the scene that he is working on, otherwise the temptation to illustrate the story is too great.

IW And this improvisation, as well as the images that underlie it, remain with the actor into the production?

RC You have to be flexible. Eugenio changes things, changes parts of the improvisation as he builds the montage. But what underlies the improvisation remains, he never touches that.

IW So even though you do not concern yourself with the psychological nature of character, there is a subtext of sorts. A tension in performance between what underlies the performer's score and the context of the role he or she is playing?

RC The scene in *Traces in the Snow*, in which the young warrior comes into the throne room to face the king who wants to sentence him to death, is a good example. One way to do it would have been to come storming in and kneel down in front of the king, as it might happen in life, another is the way I do it. I have a score that was developed out of an improvisation for something totally different. The actions fit the scene, but I have a different set of images that effect my physical behaviour. By working with these images I give to the character of this noble warrior another depth that makes him more real. You cannot avoid being aware of context, but you must be careful not to let it absorb your first improvisation's score and images. This, of course, leads to a third thing, the moment of performance: first there is the improvisation and the images that prompted it; then the context these are placed in; and the third part is the performance itself. You, the actor, in the moment. And this I cannot analyse, I cannot think about it when I am doing it because I am absorbed in the moment. I am taken by the stream, and what happens in me during the performance I cannot speak about because I have no memory of it.

IW What Mihaly Csikszentmihalyi calls flow [1975], when you are one with what you are doing. In those moments in the theatre, what is there is the sum total of all your experience and the influences in your training: the Kabuki, the Butoh, the Odissi … .

RC I don't think about that.

IW No, but as you say, when you get up from the chair, you don't think about the *tribangi*, but it's there because it's in your body memory.

RC You can see it, but I cannot. If I jump out of myself, I can see it …

IW You're talking about being conscious of it. I'm talking about it being there whether you are conscious of it or not.

RC I am what I am, and what I am is the sum total of what I have been living. It is the result of all my life experiences, including my childhood education, my pregnancy, my first love experience. It is the result of all those things together. And, of my meeting with the Kabuki, the Brazilians, the Balinese. It's the result of all this. So I am in that moment all those things. Yet, not quite all these things. I am only what I have kept of them. When you read a book there are only four or five sentences that you keep. These are the four or five sentences that you have chosen which are different from the sentences that another might choose … and this choice is you.

References

Barba, Eugenio (1989), 'The fiction of duality', *New Theatre Quarterly*. Vol. 5, No. 20: 311–14.

Csikszentmihalyi, Mihaly (1975), 'A theoretical model for enjoyment', in *Beyond Boredom and Anxiety*. San Francisco: Jossey-Bass, pp. 35–54.

Zarrilli, Phillip (1984), 'Doing the exercises: the transmission of in-body performance knowledge in a traditional martial art', *Asian Theatre Journal*. Vol. 1, No. 2: 1–31.

1 Sanjukta Panigrahi (standing) and Katsuko Azuma, a Nihon Buyo performer,
   rehearsing a version of Goethe's *Faust* at the 5th ISTA, Salento, Italy (1987)

2 Eugenio Barba (left) rehearsing with *Teatrum Mundi* ensemble at the 11th ISTA, Portugal (1998)

3 A barter in a parking lot in a suburb of Bahía Blanca, Argentina, between local people and groups attending the Third Theatre gathering (1987)

4   The Odin Teatret performing at a barter in a pirson in Milan, Italy (1996)

5   Eugenio Barba conducting a workshop at *Reencuentro Ayacucho '88*, the Third
    Theatre gathering in Huampaní, Peru (1988)

6 The Odin Teatret in Ayacucho, Peru during the Third Theatre gathering,
Reencuentro Ayacucho '88

7 The barter outside a Peruvian village near Ayacucho in 1978 (see Chapter 16,
page 259)

Barter: performance as cultural exchange

7

The dynamics of barter
Ian Watson

Webster's Dictionary defines barter as an action: 'to trade by exchange of commodities rather than by the use of money'. The dictionary views barter as a verb; Barba, and others like him who have embraced theatrical barter, view it as a noun. A theatrical barter is an event in which actions are the currency of exchange, performances of songs and dances, displays of training exercises and techniques, even fragments from full-length plays are transformed into commodities in barter. But, unlike an economic barter, in which the emphasis is on commerce, the focus in theatrical barter is on the traders and how they interact. Those who meet to exchange and the dynamics of that exchange are far more important than what is exchanged in the barter as noun.

Economic barter is invariably associated with primitive societies which, for one reason or another, do not have a stable currency exchange system in place. In these societies, goods and services are privileged over attempts to transpose the latter's worth into coins and paper. Theatrical barter is predicated upon this model. Contemporary theatre is, by necessity, cast in economic terms: performances are exchanged for money. They must be, if for no other reasons than to defray production costs and to at least give the impression of following the accepted business practice of paying those involved. But a number of companies bent on challenging the boundaries of theatre and conventional economic models have experimented with barter. These barters, in which cultural products are the commodities of exchange, have been attempted by leading experimentalists such as Peter Brook who, during his three-month African trip with the International Centre for Theatre Research in late 1972 and early 1973, explored exchanges with the local communities they encountered, Poland's Gardzienice which has traded their work for traditional performance material in the villages of Eastern Poland since the 1970s, and Eugenio Barba.

Apart from challenging the conventional economic view of theatre, barter provides some valuable insights into performance dynamics and prompts questions about the theatre's role in cultural relations. The insights and questions are nowhere better explored than in Barba's work. This is because, apart from helping to formulate an understanding of the relationship between barter and theatre through employing barter in his theatre practice for almost thirty years, he has also questioned its nature and implications in his writings.

Barter

As touched on earlier, in Barba's notion of barter, coined in the early 1970s, one group of people performs for another and, rather than the second group paying money, it performs for the first. A scene from a play is exchanged for a traditional song, a display of acrobatics for a folk dance, a poem for a monologue, etc.

Barba and his Holstebro-based theatre group, the Odin Teatret, have mounted barters in a variety of settings and among many different communities ranging from rural villages in Wales and Brittany to the Yanomami Indians in Amazonian Venezuela, from small towns in Europe, Latin America and Asia to major cities like Montevideo, Bologna and Paris.

Even though there are exceptions, most barters are typical of the one Barba organized in Bahía Blanca, Argentina as part of the 1987 International Group Theatre Gathering. In this barter, many of the groups from the gathering worked together in the grounds of a large housing complex in a neighbourhood on the outskirts of the city. All of these groups began their performances simultaneously in different parts of the grounds, and gradually moved toward a parking lot at one end of the complex. The various audiences followed the performers to the parking lot where each theatre group presented a short performance. These presentations were followed by artists from the local community who had prepared an array of folk dances, traditional and popular songs, as well as a recital of original poetry to entertain both the visitors and their neighbours.

The basic model aside, every barter has elements that are unique to it. As mentioned in 'Contexting Barba', the barter between the Odin and the Candombe performers from the black community of Montevideo a few weeks prior to the Bahía Blanca meeting combined the Odin actors and local Candombe dancers, drummers, and singers into a single performance rather than having Barba's colleagues and the Candombe artists perform separately. A barter in the Danish village of Tvis in 1992 included a procession through the village, an exchange of performances in the local hall, and a communal meal prepared by the villagers. The Danish anthropologist, Mette Bovin, has even used barter in her fieldwork in Upper Volta, West Africa (renamed Burkina Faso following the 1984 revolution). This fieldwork, conducted in 1982 with the Odin actress Roberta Carreri and the technique she calls 'provocation anthropology' which allowed her to witness local performance material, are described later in this volume by Bovin herself.

Regardless of which form they take, barters are a point of meeting between cultures. In every barter one community meets another through the exchange of cultural products and, provocation anthropology aside, these products are not as important as the process of exchange itself.

Role shifts and communities

The conventional relationship between actors and spectators in western theatre is passive; that is, the audience is presented with a prepared cultural product in which they rarely take an active part.[1] Barter, on the other hand, invokes a participatory model in which not only the audience becomes part of the action, but, in doing so, it engenders a structural instability in the performer/spectator relationship. The three major structural components of barter – the professional actors, members of the local community who perform, and those from the community who are its audience – shift roles during the event; and, in the most successful of barters, these roles all but dissolve entirely.

The professional actors in the Bahía Blanca barter, for example, were performers during the first part of the event. Later, as they watched the

1   There have been attempts, particularly in avant-garde theatre, to transform this traditional actor/audience relationship. The Living Theatre and Richard Schechner's Performance Group, for instance, experimented with audience participation in productions such as the Living Theatre's *Paradise Now* and Schechner's *Dionysus in '69*. But these experiments generally influenced the qualitative rather than the structural nature of the performer/audience contact because the alterations in the relationship were only partial and/or temporary. The spectators who chose to watch rather than participate remained within the conventional audience/cultural product paradigm. Even those who chose to take part in the action were only allowed to do so in the segments of the *mise-en-scène* prepared for improvisation with the audience. This latter group merely shifted back and forth between their conventional role and being part of the cultural product itself.

local singers and dancers, they became spectators; and, with the formal part of the barter drawing to a close, the division of roles blurred when their hosts encouraged the actors to join them in their dances and songs while, under the guidance of several of the actors, some people from the neighbourhood attempted to imitate what the professionals had done.

Similarly, the community performers shifted from being audience to the various presentations by the groups to being actors. While in the latter part of the barter they were protagonists in the dissolution of roles, because it was they who either encouraged the members of the theatre groups to join them or were the most curious to learn from the professionals.

Those from Bahía Blanca who remained as spectators throughout the event were a special kind of audience. Since the barter was mounted as a meeting that involved the local community, those who did not perform had a vested interest in the presentations by their neighbours. The local artists represented the neighbourhood, their songs and dances were what Erving Goffman might have termed the community's face.[2] A face which was even further loaded by the fact that much of what they presented to the 'foreigners' was traditional material with deep socio-historical roots in the community. Their community was on display, so the entire neighbourhood had an invested relationship with their performers. The local people who only watched were spectators to the professional actors, but they became active observers when their friends performed because they were part of what was presented. They moved from the ludic mode of the conventional theatre audience to witnesses of an exchange in which they had a stake; they were the barter's *invested community*.

Following the completion of the presentations, the divisions between spectators and performers became unclear as both groups mingled together. The spectators congratulated 'their' performers, talked with the professional actors about what they had done, discussed the latter's props and admired their costumes. Some even joined the local performers who were teaching songs and dances to the actors from the International Gathering.

Sociologically speaking, the third stage of the barter was the most interesting because it not only involved a shift in roles but also something akin to what Victor Turner calls spontaneous communitas, that is, 'a

2 Goffman defines face as '… an image of self delineated in terms of approved social attributes – albeit an image that others may share, as when a person makes a good showing for his profession or religion by making a good showing for himself' (1967: 5). This definition focuses on individual behaviour, but in the case of barter, the entire community's face is presented through its representatives.

direct, immediate and total confrontation of human identities' (1982: 47–8). It is not so much that the individuated roles of 'foreign actor', 'local performer', and 'community spectator' ceased to exist during this latter phase, but that they were only a backdrop to a foregrounded liminality in which the common experience of the *'barter community'* took precedence over everything else. The structural system of social organization, with its hierarchical earned and/or assigned roles, was irrelevant in the barter community. The barter was a meeting of cultures in which the barter community subsumed the separate, homogenous cultures involved through performance and personal contact. One's role in whatever theatre group he or she belonged to, or one's social status in Bahía Blanca was irrelevant; this was '… a "moment in and out of time," and in and out of secular social structure, which reveal[ed], however fleetingly, some recognition (…) of a generalized social bond …' (Turner, 1969: 96).

The barter community is the mark of a successful barter because the communitas that characterizes it is its intended conclusion. The initial, formalized performative phases of a barter are catalysts to the unstructured exchange of communitas and the inversion of roles it generates. Even in the most successful of barters, however, the community is temporary. It can last a relatively short time, as it did in Bahía Blanca, with the unstructured conversation and random exchanges of performance material lasting no more than thirty minutes before the professional groups began packing their props and costumes while the majority of local people returned to their apartments for supper; or it can be extended, as it was during the meal in Tvis, when villagers and their visitors shared food and conversation for several hours following the last performance of the barter. The barter community is a temporary 'coming-together' that dissolves as participants return to their homes and their normative social roles.

Barter as narrative

The event narrative

Much as a conventional theatre performance is a complex interweaving of what semioticians call texts, barters include an interplay of aural (verbal, musical, sound effects, etc.) and visual (physical action, set design, costumes, etc.) texts. But, unlike conventional theatre, barter does not have its origins in a literary or dramatic text. In the vein of experimental theatre directors like Joe Chaikin, Richard Schechner and Barba himself, barters are a mixture of improvisation and fixed scores in which the performance text takes precedence over its literary counterpart. Barters consist of fragments of rehearsed performances arranged together in a structure reminiscent of the vaudeville show in which a series of unrelated acts, with little or no causal connection between them, are strung together as an entertainment. Even the individual 'acts' in a barter are rarely the product of a literary text. This is because the professional actors' contributions invariably have their roots either in the improvisation techniques of the Odin and other groups like it or, in the instances when Barba's colleagues from the East take part in barters, in the oral traditions of Asia; while the host performers usually present material that typifies their community or popular songs that they have learned either from other singers or from recordings. The professional performers in the Tvis barter, for instance, included Barba's longtime International School of Theatre Anthropology (ISTA) colleague, Sanjukta Panigrahi, dancing a piece from her traditional Odissi dance repertory, an elegant ballroom dance on stilts by the Italian group Tascabile di Bergamo, a parade and selection of Peruvian dances by Lima's Yuyachkani, as well as a song by one of the Odin actresses from the company's 1988 production *Talabot*. The local community replied with, among other things, a performance of traditional trumpet music by a group of hunters, a demonstration of training by the local girls' handball team and a game played by young male and female scouts with a sheet and ball, both of which were accompanied by music, a well-known Danish antiwar song presented by a group of young women, as well as folk dances from the Tvis area.[3]

The various textual components of a barter, the aural and visual elements of the individual acts, the relationships between these performance fragments, and the developmental arc of the entire barter from beginning to end are what could be described as the *'event narrative'*. Unlike the individual performance fragments, which are usually rehearsed and have fixed scores, the event narrative is a once only performance that is not repeatable. It begins with the gathering of people through a parade or some other similar invitation, proceeds into the sharing of performances as contact is made between the professional performers and the local community, then, if the barter is successful, moves into a less structured exchange with the formation of the barter community. Marking the completion of a barter's event narrative is difficult, however. This is because, unlike its theatrical counterpart in which the ending of the production is

---

3 Aesthetic theories aside, the favouring of the performance text over its literary counterpart as a point of departure for barter has cultural and practical exigencies. Language can present a problem for barters since they are frequently performed in countries and/or regions in which the actors and their hosts do not share a common tongue.

usually clearly indicated, barters, as already noted, tend to dissolve gradually rather than terminate abruptly.

Another important feature of the barter's event narrative is its degree of flexibility. Even though the individual performance fragments within it are fixed, the overall presentation is essentially improvised. Aside from the basic chronological structure of gathering, contact through the exchange of performance, and the formation of the barter community, the event narrative is flexible enough to tolerate changes and interjections without fundamentally affecting its dynamics. Since it is neither plot-based nor is there a causal relationship between the performance pieces in a barter, the order of the latter can be altered with little or no influence on a barter's outcome. Speeches can be inserted into a barter without unduly affecting its course, as was done in the Montevideo Candombe/Odin meeting when a local black leader stopped the collective dancing during the latter phase of the barter to address the performers and spectators; and barters provide a space for individuals to inject and/or remove themselves from the event (such as the shyer children who moved in and out of the local folk dances during the Bahía Blanca barter, or the members of the audience that Yuyachkani cajoled into performing Peruvian traditional dances during their Tvis presentation) without hindering its outcome.

The socio-cultural narrative

In addition to the event narrative, there is a duality of socio-cultural narratives associated with barter, one concerned with process, the other with structure. Despite its reliance on improvisation, barter is essentially authorial. It has a clear intention which is the product of various wills: Barba's initially, then those of his performers, and, in most instances, also those of the host community. Barter is designed to bring different cultures together through performance. Some barters may be more successful than others in inducing a barter community but, at least at the level of intention, the socio-cultural narrative supersedes its performance counterpart because barter is predicated upon efficacy rather than aesthetics.

Process aside, barters' intentions are imbedded in their very structure. In keeping with Aristotle's distinction between epic poetry and theatre (1961: 49–51), barters do not merely narrate cultural dialogue, they embrace mimeses and play it out. In every barter, there is an instrumental action in which two cultures meet, but that meeting is also a performed action. Barter is an orchestrated performance in which the entire event is a socio-theatrical metaphor of its intentions, which are to induce contact and an exchange between different cultures. These intentions are the very structural dynamic of barter itself.

Space

Geography and space are at the root source of barter. This is because barter's genesis lies in the Odin's temporary change of location in the early 1970s. As I described in *Towards a Third Theatre* (Watson, 1995: 22–3), barters (as well as the company's street theatre work) were developed in direct response to the climate and nature of life in southern Italy. Prior to Barba and his colleagues training and rehearsing in the Carpignano region of Italy in 1974, the company's preparatory work and research had all been done in Scandinavia. The climate of northern Europe, with its temperate, short summers and long, cold winters, directed the company's work indoors. By contrast, the warmth and long days of the southern Mediterranean beckoned the actors to train in the open. This liberation of space, combined with the curiosity of the local people about the strangers who had come to live in their midst, led to the Odin performers demonstrating their physical and vocal training for the villagers. These demonstrations took place in public spaces such as town squares and, in response to them, the townspeople sang their traditional songs and presented regional dances. A meeting point between two very different cultures, that of professional actors from modern Europe's group theatre movement and the heritage of southern Italian village life with its roots in antiquity, presented Barba with a model that he has incorporated into his work ever since.

The use of performance as a means of cultural contact not only had its beginnings in a move from northern to southern Europe, it also reversed the vectors of location in Barba's work. His studio-type theatre, which constituted the Odin's entire repertory prior to 1974 and continues to be the major thrust of the company, is best characterized spatially by Marvin Carlson's notion of the modern 'pilgrimage theatre' (1996: 85). Citing Ariane Mnouchkine's Théâtre du Soleil, based at the Chateau de Vincennes in an outer suburb of Paris, as an example, Carlson describes pilgrimage theatres as those that call for travel to remote places associated with a particular artist or ensemble of reputation in which the travelling is part of the experience. Barba and his company have always remained at the margins of the world's cultural capitals and witnessing their productions invariably involves lengthy travel on the part of the audience. The Odin's home is in Denmark, one of Europe's smaller, northern countries, many hours travel even by aeroplane from centres such as Paris, London or Rome; not content with national isolation, Barba's theatre is in Holstebro, a town of little more than 30,000 people in Western Jutland, far from Denmark's major cities; and to add yet one more layer to the Odin's marginalization, its theatre and training complex are on the very edge of Holstebro, several miles from the town centre.

When the company tours, which it does for much of the year, it invariably performs in theatres that reflect its home location. These theatres are most often far from the fashionable suburbs or cultural hubs of the cities or towns where they are located because they are the headquarters of groups similar to the Odin. Generally speaking, to see Barba's studio productions in Europe or in Latin America, the two parts of the world where he and his colleagues most often perform, one has to be prepared to travel far from the bright lights of midtown.[4]

These pilgrimages are in stark contrast to Barba's barter (and street theatre) performances. In barter, the audience no longer travels to the theatre, the theatre comes to it. Location ceases to be defined by the periphery since barters take place at the social hubs and confluences of the cities, towns or villages where people live, work, relax, and gather. The journey is reversed: the pilgrims are no longer the audience, they are the performers. This reversal highlights how important an understanding of spatial dynamics is to any investigation of barter.

Location and space are fluid in barter. Somewhat in the vein of street theatre, a barter must attract its audience, direct the latter's attention, and establish its performance space. In the Bahía Blanca barter, for instance, the various groups began performing in different parts of the neighbourhood, then, once they had gathered an audience, moved in procession toward the car park that had been chosen as the main site for the barter, taking their spectators with them. On arriving in the car park, several of the performers took on comic personas, reminiscent of early silent films, and, with a combination of humour, gesture and pantomime, directed the spectators into a semi-circle that defined both the playing and audience spaces.

---

4   When the company performed in Paris during the 1985 French ISTA, for instance, it did so in Malakoff, an outer suburb, rather than in the heart of the city. Similarly, during its Brazilian tour in 1994, the company performed in the southern part of the country in Londrina rather than in centres such as Rio de Janeiro or São Paulo. When the group travelled to New York in 1984, it was to perform at La Mama in the East Village not in the theatre district of midtown.
  A telling irony of the Odin's notion of location and use of space was evident during its 1987 tour of Argentina. Tour organizers had arranged for the company to perform at the Cervantes Theatre in the capital, Buenos Aires. The Cervantes is one of Buenos Aires' major theatres located in the downtown area of the city. On arriving at the theatre, the company discovered that it was an ornate opera theatre with boxes, rows of velvet seats, and an Italianate sloping stage with grooves set into it for large flats to be slid in and out for scene changes. Unable to perform their production on a sloping stage, Barba asked that all the seats in the orchestra be removed and that the boxes around the theatre be closed off. The company then constructed their set in the orchestra area and performed their entire Buenos Aires' run in it. Even when at the cultural centre, Barba manages to relocate himself at the margins.

A similar format is often used in barters held indoors, such as the one in Tvis, which began with a single parade through the village that moved to the local community hall. Inside the hall, tables had been set up around an open area at one end of the room in front of the stage for a meal that was to follow the performance. This area and the raised stage behind it became the main centres of action during the barter.

Even though there are almost as many subtle variations on this model as there are barters, these and all barters entail a three-part process in relation to space. This process is: gathering and directing the audience to the main performance area, establishing and maintaining spatial boundaries before and during the barter, and dissolution of the space as the barter community is formed. The gathering and directing phase of the barter is marked by movement toward the main performance area, by a lack of clearly demarcated audience and performer spaces due to the porous relationship between performers and spectators as they intermingle during the parade, and by a 'heated' area of performance activity centred on the performers themselves.

This lack of defined space is indicative of the barter proper also. Most barters establish a performance space around which the audience gathers and the 'heated center' of performance activity is more clearly defined than it is during the introductory parade. Nevertheless, the space is rarely architectural (i.e., defined by auditorium seating and/or a raised stage), and it is easily and often 'invaded' by spectators during the barter – as by the children in the Bahía Blanca barter, mentioned earlier, who were either unaware of performance conventions or chose to rebel against them.

Just as the final phase of a successful barter culminates in the fading of the formal separation between spectators and performers, it is also marked by the dissolution of spatial divisions. In the barter community there is no stage, nor is there an auditorium. There is a shared space in which cultures meet. During the communal meal that concluded the Tvis barter, for example, the space became a place in which a meal and conversation were shared. This informal sharing, or social performance, was prompted by the more theatre-like segment of the barter. But, the roles and divisions of space that were necessary to the theatrical part of the barter were replaced by the barter community. Performers, audience, stage, and auditorium became somewhat meaningless terms, at least until the meal was over and all had begun to make their way home.

The performers in a barter are cartographers of space. They 'map' their sites of performance within the larger confines of the city, town, or village by first moving along a specific pathway then by defining the boundaries of the performance space proper with their actions. They are existential inscribers of performance territory, and in keeping with the existential, the inscriptions are readily dissolved. Unlike architectural markers that call for an earthquake or the wrecker's hammer for dissolution, their existential counterparts disappear with the transition from performer to member of the barter community.

Barter maps invariably begin in the streets and move toward a social node, or what Carlson terms an urban confluence (1989: 10–11), such as a park, plaza, car park or community hall. These maps usurp architecturally delineated spaces by transforming them from functional environments defined by social usage to what Joseph Roach would call ludic spaces (1992: 172). They become sites in which the virtual, playful, and imaginative takes precedence over the functional. No longer defined entirely by buildings, sidewalks or streets, the spaces are fluid. They are defined by the actors and the spectators who move through them and the unpredictable reigns. Anything can happen: costumed singers may appear on the balconies of vacant buildings serenading those below (as in the Montevideo barter); a fire-eater surrounded by giant bird-like figures on stilts might suddenly command the space (as happened in the Bahía Blanca barter); or the beginning of a barter could be announced by a solo trumpeter dressed in a top hat, starched white shirt, and dress black pants on a rooftop with a fanfare following which he rappels down the side of the building into the crowd (which it was in Montevideo).

As playful as these ludic spaces are, they are complex matrices in which important items are displayed and shared. At their most basic, each barter site is a geographic space which has varying degrees of functional and symbolic significance for the host culture. The Montevideo barter, for instance, in which the Odin joined with performers of Uruguay's most readily recognizable black performance form, Candombe, was set amid the ruins of the Ansina district of the city. This barrio was the traditional home of the city's black community, many of whom had been forced by both social and economic pressures to abandon their neighbourhood for the countryside. In a similar vein, the Tvis community hall is both a functional location, since it is the only place in the village where large gatherings of the local community can take place, while at the same time, it is an environment invested with the community's collective identity. It is here that the community gathers for significant social events: the local clubs meet here, wedding receptions are held in the hall, local politicians conduct their meetings in the building. Almost all events that have communal significance to the local community, short of religious church located rituals such as Sunday service, burials, and christenings, are held in the hall.

The barter site is also a temporary liminal territory. To borrow the double negative that Richard Schechner applies to actors (1985: 110), the car park in Bahía Blanca was not-not a car park during the barter, but it was equally not-not a virtual environment that moved from stage to dance floor to parade ground. It was somewhere between the two; it was betwixt and between its functional self and the fantastical locations each of the performers demanded of it. Equally, the multi-purpose hall in Tvis was temporarily liminalized during the barter as it was not-not the place where the community gathered while at the same time it was not-not the various locations suggested by the performances it hosted. It was both home and familiar while at the same time it was collective and foreign.

In addition to being both a geographic and liminal space, a barter's location is a site of socio-political relevance. This relevance is often as much about the local as it is to do with the meeting between foreign cultures. The car park in the Bahía Blanca barter, for example, was at the edge of the middle-class building complex it served. It marked the border of the city proper and the slums that butted up against it. The tin shanties with illegal electrical wiring, no running water, and unpaved dirt tracks stood in stark contrast to the tarred roads and serviced multi-store apartment buildings that were their neighbours. But organizers arranged for one of the theatre groups to begin their performance in the slum and to encourage those who lived there to come and meet their neighbours in the car park. There was to be a double meeting, one between the foreigners and the locals, the other between the two estranged groups of local people. The choice of the barter's location in the Ansina district in Montevideo had a similar rationale behind it. The local organizers, the heads of the participating Candombe clubs, insisted that the barter be held in Ansina in order to draw attention to the barrio's deplorable state and to use the event as a forum to call for its rejuvenation. They arranged for television coverage of the entire event and included speeches by relevant dignitaries calling for action by the city and national governments to return Ansina to its former glory and inhabitants.

The most obvious socio-political relevance of barter is its role as catalyst to the meeting of cultures. Barters are borders which, to paraphrase Homi Bhabha, mark the boundaries of cultural difference and provide the means for a dialogue between those differences.[5] Barters are sites of cultural contact and negotiation predicated upon performance.

---

5   I am thinking here of Bhabha's concern with what he terms the 'post colonial space' which he characterizes as an 'in-between space' (1994: 1), an 'interstices ... [in which] the intersubjective experiences of nationness, community interest, or cultural values are negotiated' (1994: 2). This post-colonial space is, as in barter, one in which cultures meet and speak at/to each other.

The dynamics of cultural exchange in barter

At a casual glance, barter seems to be primarily concerned with a dialogue between cultures, but a closer examination reveals that things are somewhat more complex. Barter is a site of cultural meeting not necessarily of cultural engagement. It is less about the dialogue between cultures than it is about using its exchange of performance materials as a means of instigating contact. Just as at a personal level, in which the nature of contact between people may vary from the briefest of glances across a crowded room through to a formal greeting such as a handshake on to spending considerable time in conversation, the negotiations between cultures that meet varies. If one were to suggest a continuum to illustrate these degrees of negotiation, at one end of which is a mere passing contact and at the other a meaningful intercultural exchange, most barters would be decidedly toward the former. In barters, cultures touch. This touching maybe the catalyst to a significant intercultural exchange at some later date but there is little or no cultural imbrication or interpenetration during the barter itself.

This intercultural superficiality is endemic to the very nature of barter. Barter is but one tiny part of a complex gargantuan web, culturally speaking. Cultures are a complex of community, civil, social, economic, and political organization embedded in a world view and a plethora of symbolic values that give meaning to the real and mythical dimensions of each citizen's being. Culture encompasses at the very least the socio-familial, the civil-political, the economic, the scientific and technological, the intellectual, religious, psycho-behavioural, the ludic, and the artistic. Barter engages but a fragment of this cultural panorama, both in its action and in its consequences.

In order for a meaningful exchange to take place between cultures, a broader band of the cultural spectrum than is generated by barter would have to be involved. Barter is a form of what I would call shallow cultural exchange. Deep cultural exchange might well be performance based, but if it is, it entails a commitment of time and willingness to engage oneself in the other culture that is beyond the scope of Barba's notion of barter. This might be something in the nature of Heinrich Harrer's seven years in Tibet where he absorbed much of the rich ancient Tibetan culture by immersing himself in it while the youthful Dalai Lama incorporated what he learned from Harrer into a broader understanding of the world beyond the boundaries of his own country. Or, closer to home, Barba's own work in Latin America which is rooted in performance and, as I argue elsewhere in this book (in 'Barba's other culture'), has involved an ongoing relationship of mutual influence since the mid-1970s.

No matter how shallow the exchange in a particular barter, it raises questions of socio-cultural identity which are inextricably linked to location, history and origins. This is particularly true for the host culture in barter since Barba has consistently placed a great value on the deep-rooted significance of performance material to a particular culture's signature. Even in the earliest barters in southern Italy, when the young people did not know the traditional songs and dances of their community, Barba suggested that they ask the old people to perform in the barters and to teach them their 'history' (1986: 171). This implies that barter incorporates a performance of memory. The host culture's contributions to the barter are, at least in part, embedded in a reliving of a culture's performative heritage, and the deep significances it taps into, by the re-presentation of that heritage.

Despite the concern with authenticity, the signatures involved in most barters are far from simple. Host cultures are invariably relatively homogeneous social communities with a shared history, geographic roots, language, education and familial ties, what Baz Kershaw terms 'communities of location' (1992: 31). There is, nevertheless, no guarantee that the host culture will present material that is an expression of its cultural heritage. In the Tvis barter, for instance, there were certainly performances like the folk dances and traditional trumpet music which have their roots in the village's Danish identity, but, by the same token, the demonstrations of training by the local girl's handball team and the game played by the village scouts, both of which were done to the accompaniment of *English* language pop tunes, say much more about the internationalization of world culture than they do about the 'authentic' Tvis.

The cultural signature of the professional theatre performers in a barter are equally problematic, but for somewhat different reasons. The socio-communal culture of the Odin Teatret, much like other Third Theatre groups, is predicated upon performance. The Odin is what Kershaw, as a counter to his notion of a community of location, refers to as a 'community of interest' (1992: 31). It lacks the deep webs of significance rooted in shared ties of blood, language, geography, and experience that mark the host culture. Its culture is vocationally based. Its members have grown up, studied, and worked in a number of different countries prior to joining the group and the company's productions have never concerned themselves with the Danish reality; it is telling in this regard that, even though the Odin's headquarters had been in Denmark for more than twenty-five years and the company had been receiving financial support from the Danish government for most of that quarter century, when I interviewed the officer in charge of cultural affairs at the Danish

Embassy in Washington in 1990, I discovered that the group was, in his words, 'not thought of as being really Danish!'

The authenticity that interests Barba in barter is not so much concerned with the 'revelation' of one's cultural soul as it is with a genuine display of a culture's preoccupations. For the Odin this cannot be other than performative. For the home communities, as the barters in Tvis and Bahía Blanca attest, this is most often a mixture of materials drawn from their socio-cultural heritage, popular culture and current passions.

Barba's acceptance of a culture's preoccupations rather than its deep signatures in barter has its origins in the latter's dynamics. Barter is far more concerned with process than it is with product. As discussed earlier, barters are about meeting. They are about cultures touching; they are not about the quality of the presentations or deep intercultural communication, even though some, such as the Montevideo barter, have provided performances of a high standard, and other, long-term contacts, like Barba's ongoing relationship with Latin America, have lead to a meaningful intercultural dialogue. As Ferdinando Taviani points out in discussing Barba's barters, there is no question of an unequal exchange in a barter since all items are performatively and culturally equal (1979: 106). Barter is defined by the act of exchange itself!

As the word exchange implies, reciprocity is at the heart of barter. It is the give and take of barter that characterizes it, not the appropriation of cultural products. This is what marks it off from much of the recent neo-colonial criticisms made of the likes of Brook and Richard Schechner by Rustom Bharucha, Una Chauduri, Gautam Dasgupta and others. As Bharucha argues, Brook, Schechner, and Barba also, in his work at ISTA, are involved in an intercultural 'practice [that] cannot be separated from what could be described as a neo-colonial obsession with materials and techniques from the "third world"' (Bharucha, 1996: 207). Here is not the place to argue the merits of Bharucha's statement with regard to questions outside of barter. The latter is, however, unconcerned with the host culture's 'materials' or 'techniques' since they are but display items which are catalysts to contact. The intention of barter is to generate a barter community, not the theft of exotica.[6]

---

6   Members of the Odin deny ever having used anything from a barter in either their productions or training. Still, some critics have suggested that the Peruvian Scissor Dance, which was filmed during a 1978 barter in Lima and subsequently became part of the Odin film *On the Two Banks of the River* (Wethal, 1978), was used in the Odin production *Brecht's Ashes 2*. In this production, Iben Nagel Rassmussen plays the deaf-mute Kattrin from Brecht's *Mother Courage*. In a scene reminiscent of the one in Brecht's play in which Kattrin warns the townsfolk of the approaching troops, Rasmussen stood on a tower and clanged the two parts of a pair of disassembled scissors together to wake the village. In keeping with the Odin's habit

Of course, things are hardly so clear cut. It is virtually impossible in the present day to ignore the interpretive climate of post-colonial angst, despite the fact that there is a danger in viewing everything to do with cultural relations in this light. But, without becoming an apologist for Barba, who, as Bharucha rightly points out, has much to answer for in his ISTA practice on this point, barter seems to avoid many of the pitfalls of neo-imperialism. Uninterested in appropriation, it is equally unconcerned with confirming a dominant western professionalism and ethos over a submissive third world other. Barters are not engaged in the anthropological notion of identifying and cataloguing otherness, they are about performing difference in order for a meeting of cultural equals to take place. In fact, it is worth noting with regard to the 'inferior other' that the Odin's actors have mounted barters as frequently in so called first world countries including Denmark, Italy, Japan, the United Kingdom and the United States, as they have in poorer nations. Barter is an example of what Bharucha calls the 'ecology of cultures' (1997: 32), that is, an equilibrium in which the interaction of cultural difference sustains a balance between the cultures involved rather than one appropriating from the other.[7]

Barter is a strategy which incorporates both action and discourse. Even though barter's emphasis is on social process rather than on the imposition or usurpation of cultural models, it encompasses tropes on authorial positioning. Barba was the first contemporary theatre artist and theorist to formulate a conceptual and functional framework for barter. He published material about barters, he mounted many of them with his Odin colleagues, and he taught other groups with similar philosophies how to produce them. Many of these latter groups, such as Italy's Teatro Potlach and Tascabile di Bergamo, and Peru's Yuyachkani and Cuatrotablas, have developed their own forms of barter, but always with Barba as their frame of reference. Barba may not 'own' barter, but he formulated it and his discourse continues to inform it. Clearly, if, as Edward Said claims, knowledge is a form of power in cultural relations (1979: 5), Barba is a force to be reckoned with.

---

of collecting props that appeal to company members during their travels without regard for particular future productions, the scissors were bought in Peru (along with many other items). These scissors were similar to the one's in the Peruvian Scissor Dance, but the way in which they were used in *Brecht's Ashes* is very different from the way they are used in the dance. As Rasmussen puts it, 'I have been inspired and I have stolen the prop [but] I used the sound of the scissors in connection with the deaf and mute language of the hands (Kattrin) … it has nothing to do with the dance of the Peruvian magician' (1997).

7 It is worth noting in this regard that despite Bharucha's criticism of ISTA, he is very enthusiastic about Barba's barters which he describes as 'a very significant part of Barba's life that is of great 'use' to me' (1993: 61).

But, Barba's barter discourse is concerned with theorizing process. Unlike the notion of Orientalism put forward by Said, in which the West's constructs of the East are far more telling than the East's reality, Barba is uninterested in the 'Orient'. He is not attempting to formulate a conceptual framework for understanding the foreign in barter, he is solely preoccupied with the dynamics of meeting and exchange.[8]

In many ways, barter is the flip-side of Barba's more celebrated (and condemned) activity, ISTA. The latter's focus is on discovering universals, on negating cultural difference in order to find what underlies performance in all cultures. Barter, on the other hand, is about the skin. It is a celebration of difference that engenders epidermal contact between cultures.

In generating and theorizing this contact, Barba challenges those of us in the theatre. His praxis and the constructs that support it suggest questions: in our ever shrinking multicultural world dominated by technology and mass communication does live performance have a constructive role to play in the necessary dialogue between cultures? Has performance something to offer cultural pluralism beyond that of the museum, beyond that of merely exhibiting cultural artefacts through touring and at international festivals? Can performance be a part of a genuine exchange between cultures based on mutual respect rather than hegemonic instincts?

Difficult questions for difficult and exciting times!

References

Aristotle (1961), *Aristotle's Poetics*, with an introductory essay by Francis Fergusson. New York: Hill & Wang.

Barba, Eugenio (1986), *Beyond the Floating Islands*. New York: Performing Arts Journal Publications.

Bhabha, Homi (1994), *The Location of Culture*. London and New York: Routledge.

Bharucha, Rustom (1993), *Theatre and the World*. London and New York: Routledge.

Bharucha, Rustom (1996), 'Somebody's other', in *The Intercultural Performance Reader* ed. Patrice Pavis. London and New York: Routledge.

Bharucha, Rustom (1997), 'Negotiating the "River": intercultural interactions and interventions', *The Drama Review*, Vol. 41, No. 3 (T155), Autumn, pp. 31–38.

Carlson, Marvin (1989), *Places of Performance: The Semiotics of Theatre Architecture*. Ithaca, New York: Cornell University Press.

---

8 This is not to deny that some barters have had intentions beyond that of cultural exchange. At least one of the early barters in southern Italy, in Monteiasi, was used to help establish a library for the local community, for instance (Barba, 1986: 176), and, as discussed above, the Montevideo event was mounted in the Ansina district in order to draw attention to the deterioration of the neighbourhood and to encourage the authorities to revitalize it. Nevertheless, these intentions were secondary to the barters themselves and were prompted by lengthy discussions with local leaders about the needs of their particular community.

Carlson, Marvin (1996), 'Brook and Mnouchkine: passages to India', in *The Intercultural Performance Reader*, ed. Patrice Pavis. London and New York: Routledge.

Goffman, Erving (1967), *Interaction Ritual*. New York: Pantheon.

Kershaw, Baz (1992), *The Problems of Performance: Radical Theatre as Cultural Intervention*. New York and London: Routledge.

Roach, Joseph (1992), 'Slave spectacles and tragic octoroons: a cultural geneology of antebellum performance', *Theatre Survey*, Vol. 33, No. 2 (Nov.): 167–87.

Said, Edward (1979), *Orientalism*. New York: Vintage Books.

Schechner, Richard (1985), *Between Theatre and Anthropology*. Philadelphia: University of Pennsylvania Press.

Taviani, Ferdinando (1979), 'Ways of saying', in *The Floating Islands* by Eugenio Barba, Holstebro, Denmark: Odin Forlag.

Rasmussen, Iben Nagel (1997), Fax to the author, 29 April.

Turner, Victor (1969), *The Ritual Process*. Chicago: Aladine.

Turner, Victor (1982), *From Ritual to Theatre: The Human Seriousness of Play*. New York: Performing Arts Journal Publications.

Watson, Ian (1995), *Towards a Third Theatre: Eugenio Barba and the Odin Teatret*. London and New York: Routledge.

Wethal, Torgeir (director, 1978), *On The Two Banks of the River*, 16 mm. film and 1/2 in. video produced by Odin Film.

8

Borders, barters and beads: in search of intercultural Arcadia

Maria Shevtsova

Historiographers of the work of Eugenio Barba and the Odin Teatret have amply documented the origins of bartering as Barba and his actors understand it, that is, as a transaction between them and whichever group of people they target for cultural exchange. Ian Watson, for example, explains how this occurred in 1974 during the Odin's residency in Carpignano in the south of Italy (1993: 23). One day, Barba and the actors went to visit friends who were also staying in the village. They were dressed in their colourful work clothes, carrying their musical instruments with them. They were soon followed to the square by villagers who asked them to play and sing. To the Odin's surprise, they then reciprocated by singing their own songs, which had to do with harvesting, love and death. The point to be gleaned from accounts of the event is that these songs were folk songs handed down from generation to generation and, as such, were integral to the community's cultural identity. From this spontaneous encounter between a peasant society and one that surely must have appeared that day as a modern version of the *giullari* – Italian medieval minstrels and strolling players who performed in streets, fairs and market squares – came the idea of the barter, which Barba subsequently incorporated into his general theories of the Third Theatre and interculturalism. The idea, then, was neither premeditated nor part of an aesthetic, ideological or even purely utilitarian design. It simply happened by accident, in those happy circumstances when, in retrospect, chance looks like destiny, and necessity turns out to be a find.

Barba, when he recalls the improvised situation in Carpignano, refers to a similar one some five months earlier in Sardinia. This was in Ollolai in the central, mountainous region of the island where the Odin had brought *My Father's House*, its most recent production. After the performance, members of the audience composed of peasants and shepherds sang and danced, seemingly 'animated by a desire to present themselves to us, to do something that corresponded to what they had seen' (1979: 122). The Sardinian event was a precursor, a nascent barter preceding theoretical construction.

Watson's summary of the birth of barter in Carpignano draws attention, as does Barba's, to how the fateful outing in the village brought about the group's first appearance in public together. Before then, the actors had simply worked away in their secluded villa, going out individually rather than as a collective body. What is to be deduced from this is the importance of the group's *being together*, of being seen and identified by others as a connected, composite group – by others, moreover, who were alien, foreign, and neither theatre-making nor theatre-going people. In addition – a point Barba considers significant – the group was seen *out* in the street, in contact with people going about their daily lives. It was no longer training in its studio in Holstebro where a few, initiated spectators were allowed to observe. The training and experimenting, now both transformed by the unexpected interaction, took place in the public gaze. In other words, what emerges from all this is the importance of being *out* of the closet of self-absorption and *in* an interchange between two very different social groups that permitted unmediated, transparent communication. It is as if here, in this oddly anthropological situation, occurred that 'enabling conversation across societal lines' which is the task Clifford Geertz suggests anthropological writings might set themselves in the future (1988: 147). And, indeed, Geertz comes to mind yet again if only because the moment of epiphany for the Odin being out in the streets of Carpignano or, for that matter, out in the mountains of Sardinia, responds to Geertz's phrase of 'being there' for the complex bunch of difficulties involved in the face-to-face of fieldwork.

One of the principal difficulties evoked by Geertz is the question of *who* the ethnographer is, which question the ethnographer is bound, sooner or later, to turn back on herself, even if the 'savages' engaged with – here echoing Geertz's sly irony – do not ask it of the outsider in their midst. This deep question of being, which also, by the way, is a screen for a question about doing ('and what are you doing there?') was put to Barba by one of the southern Italian peasant women. Dissatisfied with the answer that they were actors, she retorted with an insistent, 'But, *who* are you?' Typically, Barba interprets the question as focusing primarily on the actor's ontological state or identity, the actor always being at the centre of his reflections. However, it is just as likely that the question was asking about *societal* identity, wanting to know where you are from and where you belong. Belonging is a way of specifying something bigger than yourself; call it a community in some sense of the term, or a *paese*, the word the woman might well have used to denote the village, countryside or region with which she identified and to which she belonged. When 'who are you?' is thought through in this context, it not only highlights the issue of what being an actor means, but also brings clearly into view the fact that the barter, although not described in this way by Barba or the scholars linked to him, is a form of ethnography: it is an attempt to present, represent and 'record' physically through the immediacy of performance actions – dance, song, ditty, gesture, mime – what is vital, or presumed to be vital, to the cultural cohesiveness of a community. The ethnographic character of the enterprise breaks through Barba's own, antiquated, Conradian comparison of the barter to an occasional meeting between 'two very different tribes, each on their own side of the river' when one or the other rows across 'to exchange something ... a handful of salt for a scrap of cloth, a bow for a fistful of beads' (Barba, 1979: 116).

Once they had been discovered, barters became a feature of the Odin's work. They have remained so ever since, and, as described in the previous chapter, have been mounted in a variety of rural and urban settings.[1] A particularly poignant barter is the one organized in Bologna, Italy as part of the 1990 ISTA. This barter took place among the Moroccan immigrant workers living near the station in a rather rough area away from the centre of town. Several barters were mounted during the Bologna session, but this one is particularly telling because it repeats, in a sophisticated European city with a strong intellectual culture, the quest for the folk motifs that bind all the barters across all the borders crossed by Barba and the actors. And the motifs arguably recall images of the 'simple folk', who are close to nature and cherished by the Romantics. What this search for authentic 'primary' sources suggests is that the barters, whatever else they may be, are opportunities for recovering, reviving and revalorizing traditional culture. The term 'traditional' is

---

1   For a detailed listing of ISTA sessions and their organization and objectives see Watson (1993), *Towards a Third Theatre*, pp. 149–73. Regarding barters in Venezuela and Peru see the videos *Theatre Meets Ritual*, for the first and *On the Two Banks of the River*, for the second. The earlier, Carpignano experience is on the video *Theatre as Barter*. All videos are Odin Teatret productions.

perhaps misleading because of its associations with notions of archaic, pre-industrial societies (and suggestions of the ubiquitous 'traditional music'). Some of this culture, like the music of the immigrant, industrial, workers in Bologna or the rhythms of the Candombe drummers in Montevideo, described earlier, would be best described as folk culture. The gatherings with food, talk and song during the barter in a Peruvian jail, featured in the Odin film *Theatre Meets Ritual,* could be termed local celebrations and festivities. The shaman's performance in the Amazon could fit into an anthropological conception of ritual. However, whatever the precise terms may be for the wide range of activities put under the umbrella of 'traditional culture', the activities of the different ethnic groupings chosen by the Odin for barters are all, in some way, instances of a people's culture or popular culture.

The issues raised by the notion of popular culture are no less intricate. If anything, they are more so because of linguistic nuances. The English word 'popular' is all too easily confused with 'mass'. Nor does it allude as clearly to politics as its homologue in such languages as Italian, French and Spanish. Since this is also true of 'the people', the most appropriate route to the argument unfolding here is via Italian and via Gramsci, who is still the major figure to be consulted in debates concerning the significance, let alone meaning, of popular culture. Gramsci, a Sardinian of peasant origin, was quite clear in his mind as to how the *popolo* – the people – were not anybody and everybody, but a distinct social class, a 'subaltern' class, as he put it, in respect of the establishment.[2] There can be little doubt as to the subaltern status – due to race, ethnicity, caste, class, gender, sheer poverty and/or political oppression – of the various peoples the Odin 'nosed' out for bartering. Their culture, then, is popular in so far as it is also determined and defined by how they are positioned by themselves and others, firstly, within their own societies, and, secondly, in relation to other societies. 'Other' refers not only to the contrast between, say, Denmark and Argentina, but also to the 'otherness' created when minority enclaves exist as a society within a society, neither in it nor beyond it and excluded from it more than included in it.

The Odin's performances cannot be said to be 'of the people' in the Gramscian sense of the phrase, which is essentially how Dario Fo con-

---

2 For what, in Gramsci, is a comprehensive argument concerning these issues see *Quaderni del carcere* (ed.) Valentino Gerratana, 4 vols. Giulio Einaudi Editore: Turin, 1975 and *Letteratura e vita nazionale*. Editori Riuniti: Rome, 1979. For an overview in English see *Selections from Prison Notebooks*, ed. and trans. Quintin Hoare and Geoffrey Nowell Smith. International Publishers: New York, 1971 and *Selections from Cultural Writings*, ed. David Forgacs and Geoffrey Nowell Smith, trans. William Boelhower. Harvard University Press: Cambridge, Mass., 1985.

ceived of it when he performed in factories and political demonstrations in the 1960s and 1970s. Fo, it must be remembered, openly acknowledges his debt to Gramsci. He was already a charismatic presence, and nothing short of a legend, especially in left-wing circles, at the time the barters swung into motion. Performances in Scandinavia had been arranged for him by Barba in 1968 and, although not a model, it would be hard to imagine that he did not inspire the Odin in some way, notably in the played-big comic effects used in the barters; and Fo contributed to the Volterra ISTA in 1981. Furthermore, the Odin's performances, unlike their counterparts in the barters, are made by professional performers for whom the barters are a professional act. These same performers initiate the exchange instead of being at the solicited end of it. This too is part of the performance-driven goal of a group whose common culture has very little to do with the socio-economic factors that still distinguish manual workers from intellectuals, the 'people' from the 'elite', and so on, and everything to do with the theatre that the members of the Odin create. The Odin group, quite unlike the groups who perform for it, is defined by aesthetics. Its culture, in consequence, is principally and fundamentally a theatre culture rather than a culture defined by ethno-social grouping.

Given its somewhat anomalous relation to its partners, what forms does the Odin's participation take? The answer must lie in how it adopts popular genres for its purposes, building a repertoire from them so that they eventually become the Odin's hallmark, its very own version of popular theatre. The entity has no particular national or regional identity. It is composed of bits and pieces of European popular theatre from the Middle Ages to the remnants left of it today, or whatever can be reconstructed from the living memories of those who knew it, or simply from the documents and other information still available. The parades, processions, flag-waving exhibitions, brass bands and other musical displays, walking on stilts, juggling, farcical sketches and clown shows – besides the usual songs and dances, and jokes and jibes to spectators – are all components of the street theatre that Mikhail Bakhtin includes in his landmark account of popular culture in Europe in the Middle Ages and the Renaissance and as well as in his analysis of how and why popular culture provided a combative alternative to the official, learned culture of the time (1984). Fo's own commentary on the multiple genres that make up popular culture and assessment of how, apart from being entertaining, they are able to challenge and undermine the status quo is remarkably close to Bakhtin's (1987). Yet his special favourite is the Italian *giullare* whose imputed style and skills were developed brilliantly by Fo as political tools for a theatre in which he ultimately equates 'popular' with 'political'. A glimmer of this kind of merger surfaced during the Odin's stay in

Peru when, to circumvent the authorities who had banned all mass gatherings, including street theatre, the actors appeared in their colourful costumes, on stilts or on foot in ones and twos, and gave a blow of a horn or a yell to attract greater attention to events that pretended to be mere happenings. This pretence at non-performance is, of course, a trick practised by all kinds of street theatre from the 1960s onwards.

Still, the Odin's popular ways of performing are not rooted in the ways of feeling, seeing and doing of the people from whom popular theatre is derived. Once again, Fo is the most useful comparison, since his performance processes are totally steeped in, and his sympathies completely allied with, the *popolo*, whom he did not hesitate to name the proletariat when he meant it. The Odin's 'free-floating' disengagement (by contrast with Fo's *engagement* or commitment) puts the barters in a peculiarly maverick situation and helps explain the prominent role – facilitating rather than activist – that Barba gave them in Third Theatre or group theatre meetings. (Perhaps even 'group-devised and group-controlled theatre' would be an adequate definition.) Barba specifies, while commentators like Erik Exe Christoffersen confirm his point, that Third Theatre is neither the established, what could be called 'mainstream', theatre, nor the experimental theatre of the avant-garde (1993: 62).[3] Glossing Barba would give something like the following: The Third Theatre is an alternative to existing varieties in so far as it is utterly motivated by the desire to do theatre, to think, live and breathe it so exclusively that the distinction between work and life and between art and preparatory process disappears. The person and the actor are one. If Barba's description of barter as tribal exchange resembles Marx's idea of 'primitive communism', my paraphrase here suggests a similarity between the Third Theatre and Kropotkin's ideal of a beautiful commune, where humans, labour and life are united in joy.[4]

Kropotkin's utopia could well be transferred across to Barba's vision of the Third Theatre as an autonomous organism which recognizes no external authorities, be they state, prince or the theatre, and which generates the absolute freedom for individuals from which their full potential may grow. If this interpretation is correct, the Third Theatre may be seen as a space where communal harmony and individual liberty do not contradict each other, but coexist for the greater benefit of all. The space appears to be an idyllic one, recalling the pacific peasant communes

3 See also Eugenio Barba 'Third Theatre' in *The Floating Islands*, pp. 145–7 on this point.
4 See especially, *Anarchism: its Philosophy and Ideology*. Freedom pamphlet: London, 1909 and *Anarchist Communism: its Basis and Principles*, ed. Colin Ward. Allen & Unwin: London, 1974.

Kropotkin had known in Russia, and which served as a blueprint for the self-contained, self-reliant small worlds envisaged by his anarchist project as an antidote to exploitative industrial society. Barba had glimpses of comparable idylls on his return, with the Odin actors, to his native Italy. Barters enter the privileged space of Third Theatre to circulate experience, knowledge, techniques and, perhaps above all, good will, which, like the surplus value of capital, is the extra, necessary touch to ensure the flow of the whole.

Just as significant is the way goodwill, as I have called it, can easily be assimilated in the idea of 'spiritual matter' which Marcel Mauss argues is exchanged along with concrete goods – things, animals and persons – in archaic societies. In his celebrated *Essai sur le don*, Mauss maintains that the exchange of gifts involves generosity as well as self-interest, and must do so to keep the exchanging tribes on an equal footing, that is, as peers in the transaction (1950: 145–279). According to Mauss, the principles of giving, receiving and reciprocating underlie the gift which, besides having economic, juridical, religious and ethical functions, is the condition for solidarity between social groups. The applicability of Mauss's argument to the barters is quite evident, not least because Barba's own thoughts on the subject have an anthropological ring. More specifically, the argument throws into relief the fact that the Odin's existence depends on its internal solidarity, which the exercise of the barters reinforces. At the same time, its internal solidarity legitimates its maverick status by giving it a 'tribal' identity, on which basis it meets other Third Theatre groups. Indeed, all the groups must function as 'tribes' in these meetings, whose success relies all the more heavily on the solidarity between them as they are disparate, heterogeneous groups. The inter-group solidarity is dependent, by the same token, on the solidarity within each group.

Barters in the Third Theatre might be described as a fusion of Mauss with Kropotkin, the former's depiction of the system of tribal exchange blending into the latter's aspirations to reach Arcadia. Flower power could not have imagined it better and, in this, as in other aspects, Barba and the whole enterprise for which the name Odin stands – odin means 'one' – are very much children of the 1960s; all the more so, because the Arcadia sought during these years was tribal-collective, and without the sanctions of anything other than its self-devised momentum.

The Third Theatre started out as an international workshop in Belgrade under the auspices of UNESCO (1976). Subsequent meetings were held over a twelve-year period in Italy, Peru (three times), Spain, Mexico, and Argentina. Wherever they were held, they drew on a wide, international spectrum of attitudes, approaches and techniques which, by the sheer density of their being together, brought out their idiosyncratic qualities, allowing participants to learn on the spot from the comparisons and contrasts available instantly. Irrespective of their theatre focus, the groups involved spoke a variety of different languages and, for all Barba's talk of theatre not having a country or culture, the members of these groups brought with them expectations, assumptions, values, objectives and agendas that differed precisely because of those differences. It is because they had something unique to offer that the exchanges were, and could be nothing but, intercultural in character. Thus, the 'cultural goods' given and received were caught up not in purely theatrical transactions, but in intercultural ones. Moreover, 'the tribes' driving the system were obliged to cede some of their beliefs and habits as well as concede to having other of their practices adapted by strangers. The operation is intercultural in this sense as well, loss and adaptation entailing a process of metamorphosis in which one cultural component willingly submits to another.

As is well known, Barba was to elaborate increasingly his research on the art of the actor through the prisms offered by interculturalism in any of the senses that I have given to the term above. Such concepts in the Barba canon as pre-expressivity and *bios*, which are supposed either to pre-exist or transcend culture, are, paradoxically, grounded in the very exercise of interculturalism, by which I mean simply in the fact that it is done. They are rooted in there, however, for reasons opposite to those implied in my adjective 'unique'. In other words, the intercultural prisms are used by Barba to reflect the same or closely similar images (steps, movements, gestures) rather than refract and break them up so as to let what is dissimilar break through. Michel Foucault's notion of 'archaeology' would be very useful here in that Barba's investigation into recurrences lead him, as does Foucault's, to a map of elements that have no choice but to be seen to be being repeated again and again, give or take some minor variations on the pattern drawn (1969). Foucault was intent on demonstrating the elemental units or minimal structures of linguistic/thought patterns in which knowledge was enunciated and which, because they were ahistorical and thus immanent ('always already' there), merely repeated themselves as permutations and combinations of the same. Barba's assumption is similar in that, instead of linguistic/thought patterns, bodily patterns are at issue, and their imputed permutations and combinations across cultures is not only what 'proves' the immanent state of pre-expressivity, which is there 'always already', irrespective of cultures and cultural differences, but is also the condition on which all intercultural transaction is necessarily dependent.

In Barba's theory, this repetition is predicated upon the energy of the *bios*, which is an eternal-like force that is ever present across time, space

and history. This is why the global '*the* actor', who incarnates the principles of '*the* theatre', is conceptually possible in his schema in the first
place. I have argued elsewhere against Barba's erroneous universalist
assumptions, which presuppose that historical and cultural particularities can be transcended, and, similarly, against what I take to be the biol-
ogism and naturalism of his thought (Shevtsova, 1993: 21–52). What is of
central interest here is how intercultural meetings in whatever shape or
form they may take, as Third Theatre, ISTA, studio workshops, public
demonstrations or productions, are presumed to facilitate the dissolution
of all cultural boundaries and yet leave Barba musing on the panorama
which 'when seen close up … resembles an intricate tapestry of minute
and diverse cultures' (1995: 144). Even so, to his way of looking, the intercultural work does not throw into relief the individual contours of these
diverse cultures, nor does it single out what makes one quite dissimilar
from the next. Although diverse, when seen close up, their diversity serves
the tapestry above all else, where they simply disappear into each other
for the sake of an impersonal whole – as occurs in a crowd, in effect. As is
usual for him, Barba dislocates them, virtually abstracts them from their
territories. Twenty plus years on from the birth of the barters, Barba,
instead of employing the tropes of the banks of rivers (which, incidentally, are like a no man's land, belonging to none) uses the metaphor of a
canoe. Thus, like the canoe: 'Everything travels, everything drifts away
from its original context, and is transplanted. There are no traditions
which are inseparably connected to a particular geographical location,
language or profession' (1995: 146). The elegiac tone of this – in fact, of
the whole text from which the fragment is taken – has none of the spring
of Christoffersen's ode (no other word will do) to the metaphors of
islands, nomads, immigrants, outsiders, outcasts, and more, that Barba
has used, resiliently over the years, to describe the Odin, its actors, and the
theatre profession (Christoffersen, 1993: 187–95).

So, if everything is flux and change and drift, why do it? Why do theatre, why do barters, and what is their purpose anyway? Ferdinando
Taviani claims a political purpose for the barters at their beginnings, even
though their politics were neither explicit nor ideologized and certainly
not a politics of content and dogma (in Barba, 1979: 103). They were
political in so far as they subverted establishment-imposed norms, presumably – although Taviani is discrete on this point – whether it was a
matter of an establishment left or an establishment right. This would
include the major political parties, thus also the PCI, the Italian Communist Party, whose role and influence in the early 1970s cannot be under-
estimated. When this line of thought is pursued, the barters would appear
also to be political in so far as they by-passed and thereby implicitly

opposed any form of authority. In doing so, they could be said to have weakened the grip of domination, political, social and theatrical (that is, as exercised by the established theatre) and, in the same instant, empowered those who were disempowered and/or marginalized by the official structures in place. The impulse behind all this is decidedly anarchist, without authority, without masters – *ni dieu ni maître*, as the slogan goes. But it comes from a non-violent, non-terrorist version of anarchism behind which Kropotkin, pacific anarchist par excellence, hovers like a ghost. To call the motivation anarchist is to get more clearly into focus the small-scale, alternative, radical, interventionist, grass-roots, even 'green' or environmentalist and ecological (the last eco-grouping being a quasi-institutional alternative to party politics) nature of the barters. Their fundamental character comes into focus even more when the barters are set in Third Theatre performances. What appears extremely clearly then, when they rub against each other, is how all the adjectives cited just now for the barter are just as applicable to the Third Theatre.

Taviani gives an illuminating example of an Odin barter in Paris which, in my view, confirms my argument about the nature of the barters and the Third Theatre and how, in political terms, they may best be seen. The barter was organized in 1977 by the Théâtre de l'Unité, which had been doing political theatre since 1968, the date being apocryphal, of course. By 'political theatre' it is to be understood that the Unité was a didactic theatre, *militant,* as such theatres in France were known at the time, and which mounted pretty standard sorts of scenes about working life and working conditions. Like other groups operating in a similar fashion, it aimed to help sustain the sense of working class solidarity that had been achieved before and during May 1968. The group had the cooperation of the unions, which would have been necessary for access to the factories where the Unité performed. Taviani makes a point of stressing how the Théâtre de l'Unité had failed to interest the workers and, worse still, to explore the cultural wealth at its disposal in the neighbourhoods where they lived. The Odin, on the other hand, managed to succeed where the other had failed precisely because it brought to bear on this situation its outreach approach: going into the communities to elicit from them what they themselves had to say and do. Underpinning Taviani's criticism of the one and his praise of the other is the assumption that the Théâtre de l'Unité had taken the wrong turn because, when all was said and done, it was part of official political culture, albeit of the left. As a result, it was unable to get to the heart of the real problems in the factories or the community at large. Among these problems was the isolation of North Africans who were present at the barter. They eventually dropped the inhibitions imposed upon them by cultural incomprehension and racial discrimination when they realized that no one was boss.[5]

The Odin's apparent transgression of any kind of politics that might confer power and, consequently, the status of being a 'boss' is part and parcel of both the flower power and the militancy of the 1960s – the one passive, the other on the attack, as if each were the reverse side of the same phenomenon of contestation against social control, whatever form control may assume. It could, indeed, be argued that the Odin's 1977 barter ran counter to the idea absorbed by the Théâtre de l'Unité, to whatever degree consciously, that a certain amount of expertise, or what Foucault generically called 'knowledge', automatically authorized doing, and invested power in the knower/doer. In other words, the Odin took up a perspective that is nothing if not Foucauldian in how it sidelines authority or authoritative distinction, barter here attempting to be an encounter with non-'expert', one might say, 'ordinary' people. Foucault's adamantly anti-institutional position is integral to the period (and the temper of the 1960s spilled well and truly over into the 1970s). Apart from finding its expression in small-scale group theatre and other small-art forms, this anti-institutionalism – an updated *ni dieu ni maître* – is evident in the writings of the prominent intellectuals, who, like Foucault, were activists, in one way or another, in May 1968. It may suffice to cite among them Jean Baudrillard, Gilles Deleuze, Félix Guattari, Jacques Derrida, Jean-François Lyotard – the pantheon, in short, of the leaders who had an immediate and great impact on French and Italian intellectuals, and,

---

5   For Taviani's commenatry on the Théâtre del'Unité see *The Floating Islands*, pp. 104–5. For extremely interesting and pertinent insights into the politics of the non-party, independent and small-is-beautiful left-wing groups of the 1960s in France to which I refer here see my interview with Jean Baudrillard 'Intellectuals, commitment and political power' in *Baudrillard Live: Selected Interviews*, ed. Mike Gane. Routledge: London, 1993, pp. 72–80. Reprinted from *Thesis Eleven*, 10/11, 1984–5, trans. by Maria Shevtsova. In this interview, Baudrillard emphasizes what can only be called the transgressive role of intellectuals, here sharing a point of view that was widespread among intellectuals of the 1968 generation. Thus Foucault, another notable figure of this generation, also ascribes to the idea that the role of intellectuals is, above all, to contest power, authority and institutions. Foucault's argument in the *Archaeology of Knowledge*, whose main drift regarding the permutations and combinations of linguistic/thought-patterns-knowledge I summarize in my text, assumes that knowledge, by dint of establishing its authority through repetition over time, is instrumental in social control. This becomes quite explicit in Foucault's notes and interviews where knowledge is understood to be the instrument by which institutions hold sway and dominate society. See *Power/Knowledge: Selected Interviews and Other Writings, 1972–1977*, ed. Colin Gordon. Harvester Wheatsheaf: Brighton, 1980. Watson and Christoffersen above both document Barba's and the Odin's positive evaluation of the autodidacticism to which I refer in my following paragraph in relation to the issues of power and authority – and the role of institutions in maintaining them – raised here.

soon afterwards, on North European and South American ones. They hit the Anglo-American intellectuals with considerable force only some time later, arguably in the late 1970s, and held sway in the decades closing the century. These details of cultural history are embedded in the story of the Odin, and help throw its trajectory into relief, including the place of barters in the latter. The Third Theatre's anti-institutionalism, for instance, and the emphasis placed by both Barba and the Odin actors on the value of autodidacticism may certainly be seen as mistrust of the knowledge-power nexus, as Foucault understands it.

It has to be said that the Odin's intervention in Paris resembles *animation culturelle*, the practice of facilitating creativity among ordinary people in a community which marked a number of small-scale groups in Europe generally, and in France and Italy, in particular, during the 1970s. On other occasions, as in the example of Peru above, its actions have a guerrilla quality. Nor is this surprising, given the importance of guerrilla warfare in the Latin American countries in the 1960s and 1970s, which, together with the charismatic power of Che Guevara, fuelled the 'third worldism' of European intellectuals. 'Third worldism' was especially widespread and potent in Italy, even though the most visible, because most media-publicized, of third-worldists was a Frenchman, Régis Debray. (Debray had briefly been a companion-in-arms of Che Guevara, for which he was imprisoned in Bolivia.) Barba, although not in the thick of things, could hardly have been immune to the enormous political vitality of the time which, in Central and South America, was a matter of life and death. Nor could he and the Odin actors, who were constantly in search of a theatre unlike anything in existence, be immune to the theatrical possibilities suggested by the variety of non-institutionalized and/or guerrilla-type theatre groups working, to whichever degree politically, in Central and South America. Considering that these groups were endogenous and locally meaningful, it would have been decidedly odd if the Odin's barter/Third Theatre had *not* had a receptive, if not captive, audience, among theatre practitioners in the *Latino* world. They and the Odin were bound to have a great deal in common.

A sociological overview of this kind helps to place the barter/Third Theatre and, incidentally, suggests that Barba is less of a 'floating island' than he imagines (or than others have imagined for him). The implication of this is that he owes more culturally to Italy than he might wish to acknowledge (or than others have thought to acknowledge for him). Moreover, Italy's presence is there, in the language spoken, and manner of thinking and being, of the Italian scholars who have collaborated with him for so long. Be all this as it may, the process of sociological placing, and hearing in it not an indistinct, but a culturally distinct voice, does not

amount to defining what type of political theatre the barter/Third Theatre is. Or, indeed, whether it is political theatre at all. Barba has likened
himself and the Odin to Brecht, but, on closer inspection, the Brecht most
referred to is Brecht the exile or 'immigrant'. The latter is Barba's word for
Brecht, and indicates just where he may well most identify with him. Yet
the Odin's theatre is neither Brechtian political,[6] nor, despite possible
superficial traits in common, is it like the theatre of Augusto Boal. It is
even less like the community-centred, politically-focused and goal-
directed Teatro Campesino. Nor, again, is it *popolare* political in the
manner of Dario Fo. Nor, despite a certain teasing flavour about it, does
it have the panache (and the sheer gall) of that urban guerrilla which Fo
and Franca Rame describe as 'the politics of the hoax' and which I would
describe as the politics of provocation.[7] Decidedly, it is easier to say what
the Odin barters and Third Theatre forays are *not*, than what they actually are.

The imprecision, it could be argued, is the beauty of the thing. It
cannot be categorized or pigeonholed. It is intercultural for it crosses all
cultures. It sits on all borders, but settles for none. It is ambiguous,
although was probably less so in the 1970s when barters were seen to have
social and political uses and implications. This is all well and good, for the
issue of definition is not, after all, of primary importance. What counts is
what is achieved, what remains, and what the consequences of the doing
are. Christoffersen notes that, apart from the desired exchange between
cultural differences, 'one of the consequences of the barter is that it
demonstrates the spectator's principal and necessary role in the theatre'
(1993: 191). Yet, what emerges principally from Christoffersen (and also
from related accounts by Odin actors in Christoffersen's chronicle) is that
the spectator is necessary in order that actors may become spectators of
other spectators who perform. It is this which, all things considered, takes
the upper hand: play for the sake of playing, for the sake of theatre *sui
generis*. And this, in the accounts of the main players, appears to be a
vision of paradise. The paradise, though, is ascetic and terribly self-
centred since the Odin's world of play appears to be peopled only by indi-

6 For references to Barba the immigrant see Watson, *Towards a Third Theatre*, p. 137.
   See also Barba, *Beyond the Floating Islands*, trans. Judy Barba *et al.* PAJ Publications:
   New York, 1986, pp. 220–1, where Barba claims that what led Brecht to write 'was
   not faith in ideals, but in his own actions'. For opposing views regarding Brecht's
   ideals see the essays in *The Cambridge Companion to Brecht*, ed. Peter Thompson
   and Glendyr Sacks. Cambridge University Press: Cambridge, 1994. For my own
   view on the subject see my 'The Caucasian Chalk Circle: the view from Europe' in
   The Cambridge Companion to Brecht, pp. 153–64.
7 See Franca Rame's account of the phenomenon in Fo, *The Tricks of the Trade*, 1987:
   pp. 191–6.

viduals, each one seeking his/her own personal improvement. Christof-fersen explains: 'The point of departure is each individual's need to change himself or herself through the theatre' (1993: 190). This may be a secular form of spiritual enlightenment and/or salvation, and is essentially of a personal, private nature. The larger, public arena entailed in the barters, where the personal and the public could only be disentangled with difficulty, goes into retreat.

Enter Antigone. Enter Barba, speaking about his production *Oxyrhincus Evangeliet.* Barba is thinking about the 'ingenuous girl who is trying to change things with her useless gesture' (in Christoffersen, 1993: 185). He is trying to understand why Antigone defies Creon's law by burying her brother. Why 'this symbolic gesture of burial which accomplishes nothing?' Barba:

> I finally understood it when I asked myself what the intellectual's weapon is, what the intellectual could use to fight against the law of the city. I think that the weapon is a handful of dust, a useless and symbolic gesture, which goes against the majority, against pragmatism, against fashion. A useless, inefficient, symbolic gesture, but a gesture which must be made. This is the intellectual's role: *to know that the gesture is useless, symbolic, and to have to make it* (Barba's italics). (Christoffersen, 1993: 185)

'Intellectual' can just as easily be replaced by 'actor', since Antigone is played by one. Can we speak of politics when gestures are useless, even if they have to be made? Such gestures are gratuitous, and gratuitousness is nothing else but itself. As for politics, there surely can be no politics without the *intention* to bring about change – in legislature (say, gay rights), in structures (say, democracy contra-totalitarianism), in mentalities (say, women's independence), in destitution, and so on.

As for the symbolic side of the gesture. One might well return to the notion of '(inter)cultural goods' exchanged in barters and look again at the symbolic value they hold. Mauss, although using the term 'spiritual' rather than 'symbolic', did not underestimate the symbolic value of the gift in that the latter's giving, receiving and reciprocity involved respect, dignity, self-esteem and honour for all concerned, collectives no less than individuals. The bonds of solidarity were likewise implicated in the presentation. Thus we could say that, in Mauss, solidarity also constitutes the symbolic value of the gift. Theorists of post-industrial societies at the end of the twentieth century are as aware as Mauss of the non-material meanings passed through objects and actions. They claim that symbolic value, or 'symbolic power', as Pierre Bourdieu calls it, is attached to 'cultural goods' (1979). Furthermore, it may have as much force as economic power or political power, depending upon how much 'capital' all told (economic, political, social, cultural – knowledge and the arts – all combined) has been accumulated. The symbolic power of cultural goods, as Bourdieu conceives of both, is far from gratuitous. It can confer actual, real power on those who have symbolic power. Irrespective of Bourdieu's emphasis on how cultural goods are tied up with concrete, material factors, the point to be inferred from Bourdieu is that the former's symbolic power is semiotic. That is to say that what cultural goods might mean semantically and, therefore, also socially and politically may be superseded by what they signify semiotically.[8]

Now, this is very relevant to the idea of the useless, symbolic gesture evoked by Barba, except for one crucial difference that makes all the difference. Semiotic power, as it might be understood through Bourdieu's argument concerning symbolic power, is anything but useless. It is useful for those who have it, and exceedingly damaging for those who do not, because, among other advantages, it confers distinction. By doing so, it enters the real, socio-economic, cultural and political world of exchange, interchange, communication and information. Semiotic signification, in other words, is an active force to be reckoned with, not least in political transactions or negotiations. The symbolic gesture, as Barba conceives of it via Antigone, is a sign pure and simple. In other words, it has *no consequence*. And the implications of this for Barba's 'gesture which must be made' are rather startling. For, all questions of politics aside, when performances, as theatre or barter, are nothing but useless gestures, they are

---

8 'Cultural goods' when they are performances of whatever kind (spectacular, that is, pertaining to the theatre arts) or musical, or intellectual (that is, the knowledge acquired from, say, a book rather than the actual object 'book') are non-material, which does not prevent them from having what I have called semantic meaning. In other words, they mean something in socio-political and economic terms. They are purely semiotic when these 'other terms' are no longer applicable, and the signs merely turn in on themselves. They become signs of signs. It is here that Bourdieu's notion of 'symbolic' is potent, for it indicates how signs that function as signs of signs signify such non-material ideas as prestige, social status, desire and so on. The theoretician par excellence of how material objects signify these kinds of ideas is Jean Baudrillard. See especially his *Le Système des objets*. Denoel: Paris, 1968 (not available in English). However, see also Scott Lash and John Urry, *Economies of Signs and Space*, Sage Publications: London, 1994, whose theses regarding the semioticization of the post-industrial world are very useful for understanding how things represent signs. According to Lash and Urry, both signs and things in contemporary post-industrialism are catapulted (my term) out of the socio-economic world with its social relations, the result of which is that they have virtually nothing but symbolic value now treated purely as sign value. It is worth suggesting that Barba's notion of the useless, symbolic gesture is in accord with this line of thought; also, perhaps, worth suggesting that my observations regarding play for its own sake refer to the semioticized universe, which, Lash and Urry argue, is the present state of affairs across the globe. This would make Barba and the Odin very much a phenomenon of these so-called postmodern times.

also semiotically useless. At which point they lose all their power, including the power to exchange, dialogue, communicate and play. The deep pessimism emerging from Barba casts dark, dark shadows on the Odin which undertook its long journey so as to exchange beads for idylls where play was the sign-thing, and bright play the desired thing.

References

Bakhtin, Mikhail (1984), *Rabelais and His World*, trans. Helen Iswolsky. Indiana University Press: Bloomington.

Barba, Eugenio (1979), *The Floating Islands*. Odin Teatret Forlag: Holstebro, Denmark.

Barba, Eugenio (1993), *Towards a Third Theatre: Eugenio Barba and the Odin Teatret*. Routledge: London and New York.

Barba, Eugenio (1995), *The Paper Canoe: A Guide to Theatre Anthropology*, Routledge: London and Paris.

Bourdieu, Pierre (1979), *La Distinction: Critique sociale du jugement*. Editions de Minuit: Paris. In English as *Distinction: A Social Critique of the Judgement of Taste*, trans. Richard Nice. Harvard University Press: Cambridge, Mass., 1984.

Christoffersen, Erik Exe (1993), *The Actor's Way*, trans. Richard Fowler. Routledge: London and New York. See also Eugenio Barba 'Third Theatre' in *The Floating Islands*, pp. 145–7.

Fo, Dario (1987), *Manuale minimo dell' attore*. Einaudi: Turin. In English as *The Tricks Of the Trade*, ed. Stuart Hood, trans. Joe Farrell. Methuen: London, 1991.

Foucault, Michel (1969), *L'Archéologie du savoir*. Gallimard: Paris. In English as *The Archaeology of Knowledge*, trans. A. M. Sheridan Smith. Tavistock Publications: London, 1972.

Geertz, Clifford (1988), *Works and Lives: the Anthropologist as Author*. Polity Press: Oxford.

Mauss, Marcel (1950), *Sociologie et anthropologie*. Presses universitaires de France: Paris, pp. 145–279. In English as *The Gift: the Form and Reason for Exchange in Archaic Societies*, trans. W. D. Halls. Routledge: London, 1990.

Shevtsova, Maria (1993), 'Universal culture/universal theatre' in my *Theatre and Cultural Interaction*. Sydney Studies, University of Sydney.

Watson, Ian (1993), *Towards a Third Theatre: Eugenio Barba and the Odin Teatret*. Routledge: London.

9

Theatre presence: sea lanes, Sardinia, 1975

Eugenio Barba, Iben Nagel Rasmussen, Tony D'Urso
and Ferdinando Taviani

During the summer and early autumn of 1975 the Odin was in residence in southern Italy for a second time. During the company's first residency the previous year, Barba and his colleagues had begun their experiments with street theatre and barter. They continued these experiments during their second residency in Sardinia. This article chronicles an unusual barter that took place during the second residency, one between a solitary performer and an entire village. Barba played little role in the barter. He was not present during it and, as is made clear in the article, only gave advice to the actress prior to her beginning the barter. His advice highlights the dual aspect of what takes place in the meeting. The first being the meeting of two, quite separate, hermeneutic worlds, what he terms 'planet Theatre' and the everyday life of a remote, tiny Sardinian village. The second is the way in which this meeting will provide the actress with an understanding of her professional identity by, as Barba puts it, allowing the actor to 'measure himself [herself, in this instance] up against others'.

The director referred to in the piece is Eugenio Barba, the actress, Iben Nagel Rasmussen, and the photographer is Tony D'Urso. The chronicler is Ferdinando Taviani. (Ian Watson).

The lane between the old and the new

THE PHOTOGRAPHER (6 August 1975, morning) We arrive by lorry near Sarule and stop just on the outskirts of the village. I have my two cameras with me. Iben is wearing the white costume with the red stripe which she wears in *The Book of Dances* [an Odin street theatre production premiered in 1974] and the white mask with red tears, three on one cheek and two on the other. The big drum with ribbons is attached to her waist and a little flute hangs from her neck. She is walking barefoot. We decide I will go into the village before her. She follows me closely. She is stopped at once by people coming out of the bar, very near the place where we parked the lorry. They ask who she is, what she's doing, and they touch her costume ... I watch the scene from a distance. They are a small group of five or six people, the proprietor of the bar, his son perhaps, his daughter-in-law and a few customers. Then Iben approaches the village. People in cars stop to speak to her, but I don't know what she replies. Even a shepherd on a donkey turns around, curiously.

THE CHRONICLER We [the Odin theatre group] try lots of things: how to make theatre throughout the whole village by using the colours of its walls, the regular localities which an outsider can revive, its ascents and descents, its arches, roofs and terraces; how to make the first contacts; how to present ourselves; how to inspire confidence without using promises or fine words; how to go about creating a situation which allows the villagers themselves to improvise, at first rather timidly, then with more and more assurance, their own entertainment. We try to see by which lanes we can set up a series of actions and reactions; how we can effectively confront the representatives of a society whose most entrenched conventions escape us.

We try all these things: but now our attention is fixed elsewhere. We look at the skeleton of theatre. We see what it consists of. Now the actress (or the figure she presents, which is almost sexless) goes into the village of Sarule, with her sounds and colours alone.

THE DIRECTOR On arrival in Sarule you will meet a reality which is not expecting you and which does not make you feel wanted. Here it is not theatrical action, but human action which is necessary.

That will be a moment of loneliness.

You cannot conquer other people; throw them into confusion. You are an outsider and you will feel an outsider. It is as if you have to find the justification for your presence in the eyes, gestures, and reactions of others.

How do you make your need meet that of theirs, when theirs has nothing to do with the planet Theatre? Deep down you know the answer: you must destroy it, burn it with a violence each man here will recognize.

You will go to Sarule all alone, with your costume, mask and drum, not with the idea of conquering, but of becoming an image in its memory, of someone who became an actor to find herself by measuring herself up against others.

THE ACTRESS (6 August, Sarule, morning.) I put on the mask, get down from the lorry and the drum falls to the ground. Some people from the bar come up, having heard the noise; three men approach while I attach the drum to my belt. They appear to be curious and amused. They are not laughing in a nasty way.

'Why are you wearing that mask?'

'Because I am a character and the mask is part of the character. I am an actress.'

'Where do you come from? Are you Italian?'

'We are a theatre group of Danes and Italians. We are living in the school at Ollolai.'

Then I ask: 'Where can I find some skins for my drum?' And I show them the broken drum, which has no skin on the bottom. The men tell me that there are no tanners in Sarule. I reply that maybe I'll be able to find one and move on.

Tony has gone on in front. I realize that this is the first time I have found myself alone, completely alone as an actress. But to say 'as an actress' is not fair, since just before joining Odin Theatre group ten years ago, I travelled and had to obtain the necessities for survival alone. Once I had made the choice to live as an actress, there followed a long developmental period. And now I ask myself if that long period can give me the strength to survive here with what I have with me, my drum and my flute. Now I am here as a person-actress.

I stepped down from the lorry and immediately I felt very alone and defenceless, but free too, as if what had given me security and protection, the shell of the Odin, had been taken from me.

The village I have to go into is now visible for the first time. It is in front of me, slightly elevated. I start walking along the road leading to Sarule. A car stops. Someone opens the window to look at me and asks me what I'm doing. I ask them if they know where Antonio Sini lives. They are not from the village and they say they don't. Then they ask if Antonio is a communist.

THE PHOTOGRAPHER Contact in the village of Sarule is made in one of the first houses, a workshop where carpets are woven. Iben goes in, attracted by the materials and the colours. In a small room are three looms and behind each loom two women. I take the first photographs here. Iben is still wearing her mask, she stands in front of the looms; I photograph the hands of the women working, their faces and Iben. When we went in, the women's faces suddenly appeared from behind the looms, their hands separating the curtains of threads so that they could see.

THE ACTRESS White threads, black women. They ask us many questions: why I am wearing the mask, where we live and what we are doing. They show us how to work the loom. I play the flute. I don't look around me or try to see their reactions, whether they are openly responsive or whether they are frightened. I concentrate on what I am doing and on the way in which I establish contact. I feel that if I am confident and open, they too will be confident and open. I am an outsider in this room. I feel that every gesture I make is charged with a slightly magical significance for the women. I, too, see the looms, the woman and the whole room as a super-reality.

On the other side of the street there is a very old woman sitting on one of the steps in front of her door. She is like a mummy, her skin forming enormous wrinkles on her face. I play the flute to her, but I am not certain she can hear me. I ask the girl with the baby in her arms who is standing next to the old woman, if she can hear or not. We talk a bit, Tony takes photographs:

'What a big house this is.'

'No, not so big.'

I ask her, as well, if she knows anything about skins for the drum and where I can find Antonio Sini. The old woman is still motionless. Perhaps she can't see me either. Further down the street there is another group of women. I approach and play the flute. They watch me and seem pleased. A very fat woman with an enormous smile comes out of her house to see what we are doing. Immediately another woman comes out, extremely angry and brandishing a broom to make me go away. She makes the fat woman return, as if she is sweeping her back into the house.

The lane of Sarule

THE CHRONICLER Normally one doesn't admit to it, but the first sensation here is that of fear. It is a vague fear that cannot, however, be reduced to the simple dread which precedes every first performance.

I remember the first evening we put on *Min Fars Hus* [the Odin production first performed in 1972] in the school at Orgosolo. We had gone out of our way but only found sixty spectators; no one in the village would vouch for this outsider's theatre. The unexpected reactions, the loud commentaries and the yells during the moments of blackout seemed like threats. Which part of this fear comes from the fact that we find ourselves in front of people who seem to us to be 'different', and which part comes from the fact that we know that they are not simply 'different', but also 'excluded?' What does this distinction mean? The 'fear' we are talking about is very similar to the fear we feel towards an unknown class. It is a fear through which one has to pass. It is very easy to come to a little village and bring it theatre. That is, to make a cultural gesture, protected in advance by the party, or one's renown, or by the evident superiority of one's 'own culture'. One can do that without fear, the only concern being the degree of success. It is a completely different matter when an actor or actors arrive without having anyone to present or defend them and, when they jump and dance like the travelling player, to whom you could say anything. It is completely different when they don't bring with them their aura, coming from a 'well-brought up' or ideologically correct world: born, grown up, formed, known and recognized in the upper strata of that superior world where Theatre lives. Here it is in the hands of others. Here only the skeleton of the actor's brilliant theatre remains.

THE ACTRESS (6 August, Sarule, morning.) We leave the main street to follow one of the side alleys. An old woman is sitting on one of the steps in front of her house. I ask her if she knows where Antonio Sini lives. At that moment a young girl, her grand-daughter perhaps, comes out and tells the old woman that she is being photographed. The old woman promptly adopts a pose, closing her legs and arranging her hands.

THE PHOTOGRAPHER The old woman is very beautiful in her black costume. She is startled when Iben begins to beat her drum. The heat echoes in the tiny street. She jumps, but her grand-daughter calms her. I now photograph the details: the rosary in the hands of the old woman; her peaceful face. The camera disturbs nothing. Sometimes Iben's presence erases mine; sometimes she makes it more natural and something which people have no need to avoid. The camera, like the actress, is carrying out its work. What binds them is the fact that they are both strangers in the village and they are both in harmony with each other. This reciprocal harmony removes any element of violence from their impact on the village and therefore they don't seem like invaders.

We go up towards the church. A string of children start to follow us at a distance. The church is high up, at the top of the alley. Several old people are sitting by the wall in the church square. Iben does not go straight towards them, but turns to the left towards some rough ground, full of brambles and glass. The old people look amazed at her bare feet. Iben tries to climb onto the wall to get back to the road. One of the stones gives way and falls on her foot, making it bleed. The men chorus: 'Why don't you go the normal way? Careful you don't hurt yourself! Ouch!' Iben runs along the edge of the wall and down to the road … A man is coming up by the same road towards the square. He joins in the comments with the others sitting higher up and pretends, with a sudden movement, to try and touch the masked girl. They laugh at her again in a friendly way. In the square there are also two or three very small children being carried by their grandfathers and there is one in a stroller. We are bombarded with questions. I say that we are a theatre group, that we live at Ollolai, that we have come to Sarule to find people we know, that Iben, in fact, is working since she is an actress, that she speaks Italian, and they can, therefore speak to her. As soon as they hear the words 'theatre group' they find Iben's costume, her mask and drum and our presence natural. Iben begins to play the flute. One of the little girls being carried by her grandfather starts crying, saying she is frightened and wants to go home. The old man tries to calm her: she doesn't have to be frightened, Iben is someone just like us but she has put on a mask. Iben takes off her mask and tries to play with the child. The little girl calls her grandmother. The old woman comes and takes her in her arms. The child stops crying and Iben asks the old woman if she can go into the church. She says, yes, provided that she does not wear her mask. Iben goes into the church, still followed by the children. When we come out we wave to everyone and everyone gives us a friendly goodbye. We go towards the village. It is midday and we want to find Sini's house. A woman leaning over a garden wall takes us by surprise: she is very beautiful, in peasant costume, with very, very long grey hair hanging loosely down her back. She smiles and asks Iben who she is.

'An actress.'

'Oh, an actress. Then you've got a lot of money. How lucky, you're rich.'

'I am an actress and I make theatre. No, I haven't that much money.'

'But still you travel.'

THE ACTRESS She seems different from the other women we have met up to now, because she isn't the least bit frightened. Perhaps I get that impression because I associate long, loose hair with something freer and more open than hair done up in a bun, which most women have at that age. I am rather embarrassed by the blood on my foot and I ask one of the children following us where I might find a fountain. They show me the way, but a woman invites me into her house. She comes back with a bucket of water, washes my foot and puts a plaster on it. She wants to wash the other foot too.

THE PHOTOGRAPHER We carry on towards Sini's house. Some old people sitting on the edge of the road question Iben but she passes them without hearing. So they stop me.

'Who is she? What's she doing?'

'She's an actress from a theatre group.'

'What, in Sardinia? Are you tourists?'

'The group is working at Ollolai for a month.'

'Yes, yes. I see. OK, OK … But tell me, the mask, why the mask? The mask is too strange. Don't you see, it could frighten the children.'

'But the children are following us, they're not frightened.'

'Yes, but often … Oh, well, O.K., but the mask is a little too strange. O.K., good work. Cheerio!'

Iben asks a group of people outside the front door of a house where Antonio is. Someone calls him. Antonio comes out of the house with his three sisters. We introduce ourselves. He gives us a friendly welcome. He tells us that he saw us in the village, as he was driving down the main road, when the old woman was threatening us with a broom. He had suspected something then: I knew that all of you from the Odin were in Sardinia. Pleased to see you. Antonio has published two books and written some poetry. He is 'the poet of Sarule' and works at Nuoro as a 'teacher' of maladjusted children. There are two of them living in a community with five or six young people. To see him, he looks exactly like the Barbagia shepherds. When young, he was arrested and spent six years in prison. He says that prison was his 'university'. Antonio lives with his three sisters, who work on the loom, weaving carpets, covers, belts and handbags. Recently, nearly all their works have been on show at the craft museum at Nuoro. They show us the loom and the wool they dye with plants, which they collect themselves. They invite us to eat with them. We tell them why we have come to Sarule: we want to establish the foundations of our theatre group's presence in other villages around Ollolai. And we are also looking for something more concrete: flutes and skins for the drum. Antonio and his sisters tell us that there is a tanner at Ghilarza. A drum can be found at Giuseppe Lavra's in Gavoi.

THE ACTRESS Antonio screws up his eyes and speaks in a low voice. I take off the mask and drum to sit at the table. No, I am not afraid to be alone – as an actress, in a country I don't know. I have no physical fear that the people will laugh at me or hit me … It is a different type of fear, like the one I have during an improvisation. In that situation I never feel at ease, and I am frightened I won't succeed in making things seem real and alive. Today I was frightened I wouldn't be able to do that. To begin with, I thought it was the first time I had done something like this, alone, but afterwards I decided that it was similar to an improvisation. It involved the same way of facing a situation, with no idea of a beginning, but remaining open only to what happens. It is not that one thinks of being open, it is simply a matter of being so. In both instances it is like a journey which has only a certain point of departure and whose destination you don't know. It is a matter of being ready.

THE CHRONICLER In Salento and other areas of Sardinia, but not in Barbagia, there were evenings which could be considered real 'victories'. They happened when communication seemed to have failed, or when the organizing group was too weak, or when people were particularly reticent in coming forward to find out what was going on. Once, at the end of *The Book of Dances*, after the grotesque, masked character of Torgeir had thrown himself to the ground for the last time, the people who should have joined in with their contribution to the action from the outside, hadn't arrived. The strangers from Odin waited. The thing had been arranged: something had to be done. So a young man came to the microphone with a harmonica … then a choir of boys, who were embarrassed but determined to save the situation by doing something all the same … Amid the confusion they sang songs they didn't know too well. And, as at the most banal country parties everywhere, the children broke into the circle, running, jumping, mimicking the adults who were dancing. Two or three young people decided to have some fun and became infantile as they broke into the circle, too. The middle-aged and the old people around the little square and in the courtyard wore a smile of commiseration for the youth of the village. The miserable parody of a popular fête left us feeling embarrassed and even ashamed. But the moment we had given up trying to organize and no one had the evening in hand, the old people started to filter through the crowd towards the front. One started to dance, another took up his accordion or his guitar or his harmonica; fat mothers who had, until then, remained seated with the air of those who amuse themselves by watching the young make fools of themselves, suddenly got to their feet with the bearing of queens of the dance. In very little time the 'old' were dominating the scene. Something compact and adult replaced the original uproar: dignity, precision and strength, without wasting energy. One had the impression that, from the depth of stone, the fire of a volcano was making its way to the surface. Evenings like those were the victories.

THE ACTRESS (6 August, Sarule, afternoon.) We go out with Antonio. It is very hot outside; it is three in the afternoon and everyone is indoors. We go towards the oldest quarter of the village. I get the impression that Antonio knows every house and every person who lives there. Each time we stop, we meet someone. Antonio stands a little apart, as if he is not sure of what we are able to do; he is ready to intervene and give explanations should we need them. I think he sees us as rather crazy children who don't know what they are doing, or perhaps don't know what they should be doing.

THE PHOTOGRAPHER 'An old friend of the party,' Antonio tells me. The old man is sitting on a bench near the door of his house. He greets us. Antonio responds and carries on. But Iben goes towards the old man. The old man turns and stares at her. Iben gives a roll on the drum and then starts playing the flute. His face quite still, the old man makes signs of approbation with his head and says softly: good, good. Well done. I stop to take photographs. Antonio comes back and introduces us. The old man gets up and goes to fetch wine, liqueurs and water. Inside the house his sister is ill, which is why he doesn't invite us in. He doesn't ask what we are doing and says we can go back to his place for a drink whenever we like. Evidently it is enough for the old man to have seen us with Antonio. He speaks to him, in Sardinian, about local problems and about a meeting to take place the next day. From time to time Antonio translates and explains to me: he is a good friend. We have been places together …

THE ACTRESS A very old woman with a stick is sitting on a step. From her chin hang long white hairs, a real beard. On the fingers of her left hand she is wearing two huge rings. I go up to her, but when she sees Tony and his camera she hides her head behind her shawl. She shakes her stick in the air in my direction. Behind the closed door I can hear dogs barking. I ask her why and of what is she frightened. I tell her that I wish her no harm and squat down in front of her and play the flute. The woman hides behind her shawl, swearing. With little, sudden movements she tries to frighten me with her stick. I can't understand what she is saying, but clearly she is threatening to hit me on the head or backside if I don't go.

THE PHOTOGRAPHER Antonio says: Don't worry. Zi' Gavina is always like that. The children following us continue to tease her, making it necessary for us to leave. At the bakery, a small room in semi-darkness, Antonio shows us how Sardinian bread is made. The women cannot stay for long in front of the ovens, the heat is unbearable. They ask Iben why she is wearing the mask and what we are doing there. One of them says to Antonio: 'You're taking those photos for the newspaper, aren't you?'

An old woman comes in and starts giving explanations for us. She says we want to see the Sardinian bread because it's special. No photographs of her though … she doesn't want to be in our newspaper. She hides to avoid the camera, laughing and gesticulating expressively.

THE ACTRESS We arrive back at our lorry. There are people sitting in front of the bar. We speak to the proprietress, who had already seen us in the morning, and she asks us what it all means. She submits us to a real interrogation session: where do we come from? Where are we living? What are we doing? What does the mask mean? Antonio stands us several beers. I take my mask off. The people are surprised by my face, but they seem to get used to it quickly.

THE DIRECTOR People seeing *The Book of Dances* sometimes say: 'If that meant anything I didn't understand it. But one thing is obvious: there was violence.' They often use the word violence in connection with the production.

It is difficult for people who have lived in a world where the rules are more or less known to confront another truth. There is (or there was) in Sardinia the *attitu*, the funeral lament or 'ritual wail', and there is also the *contre-attitu*. While the mother, wife or daughter cries and sings the dead man's praises inside the house, outside, in front of it, there is another who denigrates him, explaining that, on the contrary the man was not a huge tree, but a tiny shoot that trembled at the slightest breath of wind.

Violence. Situations which do not correspond to our ideas, our prejudices, or our theories. Like that woman of eighty who told us an amusing story, the most amusing she had ever heard. She told us about woman who was expecting a child: a set of baby's clothes had been prepared, the godparents had brought presents and everyone was waiting and waiting for this child who was finally born, only to die straightaway. The old woman shouted with laughter describing the mother who cried: my son, my son, I wanted you to become a doctor … And we looked at her embarrassed. That is violence, one that you breathe in the 'reality without theatre'. It is the violence of people who, on the one hand are exuberant, welcoming you warmly and, on the other, hold you at a distance, as though to neutralize your presence, because too often 'outsiders' have stabbed them in the back.

The lane of yesterday

THE ACTRESS (7 August, Sarule, afternoon.) We park the lorry, as we did yesterday, in front of the bar. I go on. Tony follows me at a distance.

Today I will use my voice and the drum. I think people are beginning to become accustomed to my strange way of being and will, therefore, not be afraid. I start playing the drum and dancing at the outskirts of the village. The house with the looms is open: I can see the women working. For a moment I think of going in, but I carry on, in order to preserve my 'theatricality', which would disappear the moment I opened my mouth to exchange greetings or reply to questions or ask questions myself. Further on there is a balcony with a box full of flowers. Some young women and two children come out. They take a red flower and throw it to me. I do a short dance. They throw me another flower. I pick it up and attach both to the drum. I start dancing again. I say goodbye to them and continue along the main road.

Today is different from yesterday. Yesterday it was as if I was someone else. I was a figure who surprised everyone; they asked me questions and I, in my turn, asked them questions about their world, their carpets and materials, their houses and bread. Yesterday I played only gentle little tunes on the flute, so as not to frighten. Today another world is radiating from me. It is different from theirs, not just because of the costume and mask, but also because of what is behind and inside. The sounds and movements awaken apprehension because they are unknown.

Once again, I feel defenceless, infinitely vulnerable and at the mercy of their shouts and reactions. It is very different from our usual performances, which open out into spectacles in which there is nearly always a victory … that of the clown who provokes laughter, laughter which is on our side; or that of a dance which reveals a subjugating force. Here there is no spectacle for me to lean on and I am only what I am at this moment: a thing which dances and sings and which is totally alone. And this fact of being alone is frightening and it is difficult to understand such an extreme madness. Tony, coming up slowly behind me with his camera, helps me to find confidence. Only a few women take refuge, hide behind doors or turn their faces away, saying they don't want to be photographed. Yesterday I made the old people and the children afraid with my mask: the women from the weaving house tell me that. They come out and surround Tony, just after I pass them. They want to know what we are intending to do and why we have come back. Tony is a bit surprised, because before they were offering me flowers. We decide to go and ask Antonio Sini's advice. He says everything went well yesterday and that he has spoken to a lot of people who seemed to have accepted our presence in the village.

Yesterday he spoke to us about a very old woman of ninety-five he would have liked us to have met. She lives a stone's throw away from his house and he takes us there. He reckons that it is better if I appear initially with my mask off. Antonio introduces us first to Zi' Lucia, who is a mere sixty years old and then to Zi' Angelica who is ninety-five. We are in their patio-garden. Zi' Lucia brings some chairs and we sit down.

The yard is small, full of green plants, huge containers and small pots of water. We sit in a circle; one of Antonio's neighbours and his child have come with us as well. Several children's heads appear at the door which opens out onto what one could hardly call a street, it is more like a narrow alley between two houses. Zi' Angelica speaks in Sardinian and everything she says has to be translated for us either by Antonio, his sister, or one of the grandchildren who are with us.

We talk. I am at the same time very near and also far away …

I ask Zi' Angelica if she would like to see my mask. I put it on. She looks at me for a moment and then recoils in her chair in disgust: Why do you put that on? Ugh! Ugh! Ugh! she says several times.

After five minutes she accepts the mask.

We talk of her brothers who emigrated to America and died there; of the little field on the hill, where they cultivate potatoes and where they go every day at four in the morning; of Zi' Angelica who carries huge bundles on her head, erect as a soldier. Zi' Lucia brings out an old newspaper cutting with a photograph of Zi' Angelica standing in the street, barefoot, with a huge bundle on her head. The newspaper dates from the previous year. The cutting is passed from hand to hand and finishes up in Zi' Angelica's, who asks what it is. Zi' Lucia says: but can't you see it's you? Me? What do you mean? It's as if there was no connection or recognition possible between the shadow on the paper and the woman on the chair.

Wouldn't we like something to drink? Then we must at least take some potatoes with us. I accept, saying that potatoes will certainly be used.

Zi' Lucia brings a large plastic bagful which they themselves have gathered from their field. It is a significant gift.

Time passes and I take off my mask to say goodbye. Zi' Angelica cries out: 'Oh, it's beautiful.' But she is suddenly annoyed that I have been wearing it, and says noisily: 'Why? Why?' Tony suggests that to thank them I do a dance using my stick with ribbons. I look around: the space we are in is tiny. I move back a chair and I try to find some space between the plants and pots, so that I won't kick someone in the face. I start dancing and Tony shouts: 'Carefully,' so as not to frighten them. I continue carefully, almost in slow motion, the yellow stick with its multicoloured ribbons – red, white, purple – making pictures in the air. I sing and speak as quietly as possible, bending my body in all directions, flattening myself nearly to the ground to avoid colliding with the trellis. I hear exclamations, shouts and bursts of laughter from the children at the door.

Tony tells me that the few minutes of the dance were ones of intense concentration. He says that it was the first deep rapport we had succeeded in establishing with Sarule, that we had been accepted and that what I did pleased and charmed. He also says that Zi' Angelica now seems to better understand who I am. We could even do a show from courtyard to courtyard. Antonio's sister says I must repeat my little ballet (as she calls it) at her place too and that we must have coffee with her. Tony must also take some photographs of their carpets on the terrace. It is almost sunset. We take the drum, mask and potatoes and say our goodbyes over and over again, promising to return.

We are back at Antonio's again, where the sisters have prepared coffee and Sardinian cakes. No one sits down and we go out onto the terrace where there's a huge loom. Antonio's other two sisters and a young girl we have never met, are working on it. They say hello to us through the threads. They carry on working while Tony takes photographs. I start dancing, as I had promised, and suddenly other heads appear through the threads … As we are leaving the village, a man stops and asks: 'Why aren't you wearing the mask? Masks are made to be worn over the face.'

I find the question funny, because people have kept asking me why I am wearing it. I had taken it off and thrown it round my neck, behind me. I am tired and we walk quickly towards the lorry to return to Ollolai. Tony is tagging behind, he has stopped and calls me. He is speaking to a little group of people, a family: the wife is asking if I wouldn't like to do a short dance. She must have seen me before when I went into the village or at Zi'Angelica's.

'Just a little dance in front of the house.'

They clean a corner of the street, I set down my drum and dance with my ribboned stick. I improvise, but suddenly I feel tired and stop.

Tony said their faces seemed to echo the rise and fall of my voice, smiling and full of expression.

'Great, great. But when she arrived she was dancing better. And she was also beating her drum. I saw her, you know. Will you take a photograph of us both? And afterwards you must send it to me.' Tony takes the photograph. Another says that the dance was too short. The woman who begged me to dance asks me if I would like some bread. I accept and she comes back with a large bag full of bread. We thank her and carry on. In the lorry I realize that it is late and that perhaps we won't need the bread. But I accepted it even if it does turn out to be superfluous and stays in our kitchen at the school till it becomes dry. I want the lorry to drive on and on, travelling far into the night. I too can survive with what I have learnt with my yellow stick like a loaf of bread that I have made myself.

A month after the barter in Sarule, Barba and his colleagues conducted a seminar at the Venice Biennale. During the seminar, Barba, in his typical philosophical poetic style, reflected upon theatre and what had happened in Sarule. The point of departure for his reflections was a metaphor drawn from ocean travel, the sea lane, a line that joins and divides distant shores but that only really exists on the navigator's chart.

The question is not: how is the theatre defined? Nor: what statements does it make? Nor even: what use is it? But rather: between which adjoining points does it create a barrier? And: between which does it break a bond? Or: what does this theatre draw our attention to, if not to a gap? And: what does this gap break and what does it join together? 'Lane' according to the origins of the word, means a semi-path, something which is not a real road, a real way, a genuine route. The 'lane' also skirts a field, that is, it separates a person from his neighbour. It is a frontier.

What is the actor's new role to be? What position is he or she to take in the town or village and amongst which people? The 'sea lane' is an intangible frontier whose future is lost in the past, between the theatre to come and the theatre as it has always been.

One can understand then that the trail is broken into several discontinued, diverging lines, that it will be difficult to follow and that it mingles with the trails of other ways and other times. Words are exchanged, not as dialogue, but as reflections, the voices alternating, typical of things which are fluid and still undefined. Typical, too, of things that attract us.

A longer version of this chapter first appeared in the journal *Theatre Papers* (no. 7, The Third Series, 1979–80: 2–26) ed. Peter Hulton.

10

Provocation anthropology: bartering performance in Africa
Mette Bovin

Most anthropologists recognize Sherlock Holmes in themselves. Like Conan Doyle's detective, we surreptitiously creep about in our eagerness to collect information untainted by our intrusion. What happens if we come out from behind the bush and meet face-to-face with the people we wish to learn about? What happens if we provoke interaction? An adverse shock effect needn't be a concern – the 'natives' may find the stranger just as foreign and no more odd were she to abandon her hiding place and well-known disguise.

In 1982 I made a journey to Upper Volta in West Africa (renamed Burkina Faso after the 1984 revolution) accompanied by Roberta Carreri of Denmark's Odin Teatret and a two-person camera crew. What follows is my account of the dynamics of our interaction with the people of Burkina Faso with whom we bartered performances. I believe that an ethnographer's 'presentation of self' in field work can be an *active* presentation of her/his own culture to the foreign population.[1]

This way of working – I call it 'provocation anthropology' – is partially the product of upheavals generated by the 1970s and 1980s shift from demands for objectivity to an acceptance of subjective, reflexive

---

1 The ethnographer's presentation of self, of his own culture to the foreign population, should be presented at specifically chosen times and after consultation with the local authorities, either at the initiation of the project (as was the case in our experiment) or during the course of the fieldwork.

approaches; from quantitative anthropological studies and towards more qualitative work. This shift towards being a 'participating anthropologist', an approach which represents my personal transition from a traditional perspective, is also part of a growing tendency over the past fifteen years in women's research to enter into exchange situations and to give expression to personal experience (see Golde, 1970; Ardener, 1975). A large part of women's research takes place as small-scale, interpersonal exchanges of experience, based on giving of oneself in direct relation to what one takes from others, rather than through formal interviews and the traditional one-way transfer of information. Such exchange has proven valuable not only in women's groups, but in research situations in the fields of sociology, psychology, history, anthropology, etc.

That 'the natives' also ask questions can no longer make us wonder. One-of-your-stories for one-of-our-stories has been tested in the field. The classic example is Laura Bohannan, who told the elders of Nigeria's Tiv tribe about *Hamlet* (Bohannan, 1966). The Tiv found it morally and politically correct that Hamlet's uncle should marry Hamlet's mother; that's surely what one does – the taking of a dead brother's wife is the norm. The Tiv sensibly declared Hamlet a mad fool, and in doing so supplied Bohannan with information concerning Tiv concepts of madness, witchcraft and kinship. The fact that Bohannan told the Hamlet story *provoked* reactions and information which she otherwise might not have obtained.

This method of provocation elicits a reciprocal rather than a one-way stream of information. The stranger and the native exchange roles as actor/storyteller, spectator/listener. Thus, there arises a possibility for role equality by means of reciprocal input and output, especially if the provocation originates sometimes with the native, sometimes with the stranger.

Eugenio Barba and the principle of barter

The principle of barter in the context of performance was introduced by Eugenio Barba, who first used the Norwegian term *byttehandel* to describe the particular performative approach of Odin during the group's extended stay in the town of Carpignano, southern Italy, in 1974. Byttehandel in Norwegian, *tuskhandel* in Danish, *le troc* in French, barter in English. He compares theatre to the exchange of objects that takes place when people from one tribe cross the river to meet another tribe.

> Each tribe can live for itself, talk about the other tribe, praise or slander it. But every time one of them rows over to the other shore it is to exchange something. One does not row over to carry on ethnographic research, to

observe the other's way of life, but rather to give and take: a handful of salt for a scrap of cloth, a bow for a fistful of beads. (Barba, 1986: 159)

The wares that Odin Teatret exchanged were cultural. The performers began with simple situations: singing Scandinavian songs for southern Italian peasants and receiving local songs as responses. Later, they expanded the barter to include fragments of their actor training, which looked like dance, and the people responded with examples of their own cultural material (Barba, 1986: 159).

As touched on in 'The dynamics of barter', by 1982, Odin Teatret had exchanged cultural performances and tested the method of barter among people of such diverse societies as the Japanese of Tokyo, Amazonas Yanomami Indians in Venezuela, Gypsies in Yugoslavia, Indians in the Peruvian highlands, the poor of Paris slums and those in such institutions as hospitals and prisons. But they had never been to Africa.

In 1979 in Holstebro I took part in a course for actors given by Odin Teatret. I also attended two sessions of ISTA, first in 1980 in Germany, then again in 1981 in Italy. At the German ISTA, I was present as an anthropologist, at the second session as an actor/dancer along with participants from twenty-two countries. At ISTA we analysed, among other things, what it is that makes an actor expressive – 'extra-daily presence' – and studied its manifestation across cultures with the help of professional performers from Japan, India, Bali, Europe and America. This research work in such an intercultural laboratory generated many of my ideas about the possibility of barter in West Africa.

The experiment

Since my first fieldwork experience in Africa in 1964, I have been interested in the problem of entering the field. How could my entrance be made stronger, more sure, more honest and amusing – in short, less sly? This introductory phase is often neglected in descriptions of fieldwork, though it is during this initial period that the boundaries are marked and limitations laid down. At the beginning of the fieldwork, strategies concerning the collection of data are worked out. These strategies consist of more than fieldwork permission papers and authorization by the chief administrative officer of the region, the chief of the tribe, and the inhabitants. What happens when our status as guests who enjoy privileges without giving anything in return grows stale? The old Danish saying, 'fish and guests start to smell on the third day' is valid the world over. Friendship and local 'sponsors' are not enough.

It was obvious that my presence in Burkina Faso would necessarily affect the subject of my study. A European in Africa can never be invisible. As Erving Freilich has observed: 'to participate is to influence the environment. Once the anthropologist is observed by others, he necessarily influences the environment, even if he speaks to no one and just stands in a corner doing nothing' (1969: 563). Of course, if I wished to get close to the people I studied, my presence was unavoidable. I wondered, then how could I best present myself in such a way as to benefit my research and bring me closest to the subjects of my study while giving something to the people in return?

My aim in 1982 was to examine the degree of Islamization of the Fulbe, Taureg/Bella, and Hausa peoples, among others, in an ethnically heterogeneous area of the Sahel zone in Africa.[2] Before leaving on my journey, I set up two hypotheses which I wanted to test. First, that through African performances, which included dance, song, music and mime, I could come into closer contact with the non-Islamic[3] elements of the culture. And second, that by actively presenting myself through the sharing of a 'little bit of culture' from Europe, I would provoke an expression of corresponding bits of culture from the local society. Rather than 'to disturb', which is the ordinary meaning of the word provoke, I was inspired by the Latin root *pro-vocare*, which means 'to bring about; to awaken; to give rise to'.

I thus chose to come with something from my own culture which corresponded with what I hoped to see in the foreign culture. To this end, I would use theatre – an experienced and very good theatre – as a catalyst by which I would come into closer contact with the people. I recalled that many years ago in a town in Niger, I had drawn and painted the Sahel landscape after a day's 'real work' was done. No one present found the flat art on flat paper in the least bit interesting, but when I showed them dances from Europe, or played the guitar, the response was very different. Dance and music are sacred as well as social messages, and are thus very provocative.

I wanted to show that Europeans are just as 'exotic' as people from other continents. I wanted to provoke revisions of African stereotypes about Europeans and European stereotypes about Africans. The villagers in Burkina Faso had become accustomed to the white French travellers who passed through during the colonial and neocolonial periods, as well as to visits by a few Americans and other Westerners. But they were not as used to white women as white men. And not so familiar with people who

2 'Sahel' means coast. The coast of the 'sea' of the Sahara desert and the southern coast of the caravan routes where many religions meet, transform and conflict in a process which definitely did not end with Mohammed in the year 632, nor with the first Muslim trans-Sahara caravans which followed in the 700s.

3 I intentionally write 'non-Islamic' rather than 'pre-Islamic' since the Sahel is Islamic.

were neither rich, nor colonialists, merchants, missionaries, or tourists. I wanted to 'come in another way'.

I proposed the project to the Odin Teatret in 1979, but it wasn't until 1981 that something began to happen. We agreed that I should take Roberta Carreri, an Italian who had been living in Denmark for ten years. One of Odin's professional actresses and a woman with a varied repertory, Carreri had been on the journey to Venezuela where Odin had collaborated with the French anthropologist Jacques Lizot (D'Urso and Taviani, 1977). In 1977 she had been in Brazil, in 1978 in Peru, where the theatre collaborated with the Peruvian anthropologist Palonino Flores among the Indians of the Andes, and in 1979 she travelled with the Odin Teatret to Japan. We also agreed that a film crew, as discreet as possible, would accompany us.

For two months Carreri trained and rehearsed in Holstebro, directed by Barba and his assistant Walter Ybema. Her actions were composed of six parts in various styles which could be used as the situation demanded, from spontaneous contact to planned performances. In addition to these actions, Carreri wanted to bring her street performance figure – a clown whom she called 'The Little Man'. 'I had learned from earlier experiences with the Odin Teatret in the Amazon jungle that a clown performance can be perceived as very aggressive,' Carreri told me, 'while a dramatic performance can be perceived as being full of humour.' This was something I was interested in testing in Africa, and it more or less proved to be true in Burkina Faso.

All of our activities were to be completely legal by means of pre-arranged, agreed-upon performative exchanges, open to everyone who wished to take part, and taking place mostly in public squares, alleys, streets and markets rather than in private homes. I wished to alternate between participating observer and observing participant, the actor-spectator roles being exchanged by 'us' and 'them' in turn. Indeed, the fact that the people of Burkina Faso could reciprocally study their European guests was perhaps the most innovative aspect of our project.

We decided that the anthropologist would 'turn up from nowhere', bringing with her a 'catalyst' who would create a confrontation. Our triad looked like this: the actress was to come in between the anthropologist and the 'informants' in the town. Sometimes we would appear together, other times and in other places we would be on our own. We would attempt to let the actress enter the arena first, alone, going ahead toward the Africans. I would follow and observe what happened. The actress would in effect, function as a catalyst for the researcher-informant meetings. That was in fact what happened, and it worked. Glimpses of this can be seen in the film *Dansen i sandet – et møde mellem Europa og Africa*

(Dances in the Sand – A Meeting Between Europe and Africa 1984)[4] which was made along with the anthropological research.

Upon leaving Denmark, Carreri and I first travelled to the Republic of Niger where I had worked years before and where the film crew was assembled. Jean-Pierre Kaba, the cameraperson, and Moussa Hamidou (Jean Rouch's soundperson for twenty years) were both Africans from Niger. They recorded the situation in which the other three parts of the equation were at work, providing an important link for us by preserving interaction that would otherwise be lost. In Niger I had wished to confront the Odin Teatret with the nomadic Fulbe and Kanuri farmers I knew, but we were unfortunately refused permission to perform. It was Ramadan and the government of Niger wanted no theatre or dance during that month of religious fasting. After sixteen days without being able to work, the four of us travelled to Burkina Faso where permission was granted at once. An interpreter joined the group and we became five.

We began to film (16 mm) after Carreri and I had been in Africa for twenty-three days and had thoroughly discussed the project with the Prefect, and the assistant Prefect (in Dori), and with the local cultural mediators. I had chosen a Fulbe district in Burkina Faso: the Liptako Emirate. We filmed there for two intensive weeks, from 10 to 21 July 1982. Seven months later, in February 1983, I returned to Liptako alone and did more filming, covering various ethnic groups that were in the area daily and interviewing people who had experienced the meetings and the barter in 1982.

The performances

Carreri describes as follows:

> The first time I stepped into the marketplace and began to perform, I immediately felt that the women were afraid of me: a white woman, dressed as a man, who moved in a strange way and made bizarre noises … 'She must be crazy – only crazy people walk about on the street and make themselves ridiculous'. Children, on the other hand laughed as we looked each other straight in the eye. 'She's entertaining the children,' said some of the women, and they calmed down a little. The next day, they also laughed.

On 13 July 1982 I wrote in my journal:

> Roberta danced as 'The Little Man' for the first time today with a top hat, white shirt, black trousers, red suspenders, a big red flower in her button-

4   *Dances in the Sand – A Meeting Between Europe and Africa*, 1984 (16 mm, colour, 45 mins) may be rented by writing: Mette Bovin, Film Producer, Piskemaldet 8, DK-3000 Helsingor, Denmark.

hole, and a flute sometimes in her pocket, sometimes in her mouth. There was a tremendous reaction: people in the Dori market were with her right from the beginning, yes, even in the street before the marketplace there were five, seven, ten, then fifteen children, especially boys between six and twelve, who followed her, laughing, wanting to communicate with her, touch her – and inside the market itself, Roberta swept around with her hat and flute, making faces, stretching her suspenders, moving her arms and legs. I stayed in the background, I was just the ethnographer today, watching both her and the others. She ran, stopped in the small market alleys, lifting her hat and raising her eyebrows to the market people in their sheds – men, women, children – and in one place she was given a caramel. At another spot at the entrance to a tailor's hall, she came out with a flock of children following her in a veritable procession. Three young Fulbe women in a stall asked me: 'What's she doing here? Is she crazy?' ('*O kanado?*' in Fulfulde, the language of the Fulbe).

Jean-Pierre and Moussa had trouble shooting today because Roberta whirled quickly through the small alleys of the market, and there were about 150 people following her as things got going. The children tripped over the cables and the shooting had to be started all over again. The film crew couldn't get close enough to Roberta and there were shadows in the market stalls where she stopped and where they otherwise would have been able to shoot. Sometimes she jumped through empty stalls and made her own route, zigzagging through the market at flying speed with her 'gwak-gwak' in her mouth. Some women asked me: '*Yallah debbo na gorko?*' (Is it a man or a woman?) Some boys asked: '*Yallah Carlot-na?* (Is it Charlie Chaplin?) A used-radio salesman said: '*Tobago kanado!*' (a crazy white person!) A cola nut seller asked if she was there to make children laugh. When Dicko [the interpreter] and I answered 'Yes,' he replied that she really could do it!

Carreri's very first performance, a mask dance in Dori, was exchanged for the performance of three orchestras. After Carreri's performance, some of the spectators cried '*Wallah!*' (Tremendous!) and '*Wellien, wellien!*' (We're satisfied, satisfied!). Others said '*Huunde-fo buraniye welde!*' (Nothing could more interesting than this!), and urged the Bella orchestra to play again and show what they could do – which they did. The barter was underway.

The next time Carreri performed, she appeared in the same white mask. Some adults remarked: '*O nginaro*' (It's an imaginary creature, a phantom) – and they meant that she could not be human. Several children ran away because the mask was white and therefore dangerous.

We never told the people of Burkina Faso where Carreri's props were from. It was irrelevant that her mask was originally from Bali – it was now incorporated into the completely different context of a Scandinavian/Italian costume assembled by Carreri during improvisations in

Denmark. Some of the text was from Shakespeare and some from popular Italian street songs, but that was irrelevant as well. To the average African it was all 'something that whites did' – something from far away – in the same way that the average Dane could not tell the difference between a mask from West Africa and one from East Africa, not to mention Melanesia.

The barter

People in West Africa give money and/or cola nuts to performers. We did the same. Some transactions were exchanged without the use of money because the exchange was a performance for a performance. At other times we exchanged our performance plus a gift (most often money) for an African performance. A third type of transaction occurred when we exchanged our performance and a series of gifts for a sequence of several performances from different ethnic groups. The first type of transactions occurred in situations where we did not film, as when, for example, Carreri danced alone for a group of women in return for an African hair styling. The second type of transactions took place when I gave money above and beyond Carreri's performance because: (a) the group was being filmed by us and therefore the barter was unequal; (b) the African performance entailed many performers and musicians while Carreri was a single performer and therefore the barter was unequal; or (c) it was we who took the initiative and they were asked to give something in exchange, making the barter somewhat unequal.

The gift of money was always an effort to 'equalize' because, in my opinion, there was an inherent inequality in the latent, though unspoken, colonizer/colonized relationship – 'they' were African and 'we' were European and implicitly wealthier. That we were from countries that had never colonized Burkina Faso was irrelevant. France had done so, followed by multinational companies, and the townspeople rarely differentiated between 'white/Westerners' and 'colonizers'. The fact that we usually filmed during the barter and that I, moreover, was researching the entire process, made it especially fitting that we should pay more. In Odin Teatret's books and descriptions of their journeys to Latin America, southern Europe, and Asia there is no mention of extra payment. Since the entire group was usually present and the number of their performers was far more substantial, they bartered directly – a performance for a performance.

Provocation: the European and African *griot*

A *griot* is a troubadour, a professional artist, musician, praise-singer – a very dangerous person, inferior and low-caste – a teller of epic tales, an intermediary familiar with devils, a court bard, a wandering minstrel who knows the genealogies of thirty generations by heart, a living newspaper who sings, dances, does acrobatics, flatters and derides the stingy rich, begs, crosses barriers, breaks taboos, entertains, scorns. In short, a *griot* is the opposite of what the norm dictates. The word *griot* has been used throughout most of West Africa since 1690. It comes from the Portuguese *criador* and *griado*, 'one who has been brought up, educated, and lives in his master's house'; in other words, the client of a patron. The *griot*'s aggression is a 'condition generated by deviance' (Camara, 1976: 180).

One can still read in popular travel books that 'when the moon rises, all Africa dances'. This is a favourite European stereotype of the 'dark continent'. In point of fact, among the West Africans only a few dance or play musical instruments. Particularly after the introduction of Islam to the African states in the Sahel and the Savannah (from approximately AD 900–1300), there were only a limited number of specialists who danced. Other dances were separated by sex or danced only on ceremonial occasions. Only the *griot* has the freedom to dance. Most people just watch.

In Burkina Faso Carreri would occasionally meet with professional musicians and singers – such as Boureima Arba, a flute player known to all the Fulbe. But most of the time we bartered with semi-professional musicians and amateur dancers; or more accurately, with anyone who danced, sang, or performed and belonged to a particular ethnic group of the town we visited. The women and men always performed separately, in keeping with the prescribed tradition of any given dance, but the audience was composed of anyone in town who wished to observe.

We tried to determine how Carreri and I were perceived by the local people. Carreri's energetic body movements made the people wonder, and a female film director was very odd, too. We were two strange white women who wore trousers instead of dresses and presented dances and music which deviated from both the African norm and the African image of the European norm. In a Muslim society we were very atypical figures.

It is certain that our experiment provoked performances and social situations which opposed the norm. The Africans pulled out their anti-structural behaviour and anti-social individuals such as Hassan, a handicapped Bella man who whirled about in front of the drummers. 'The marginal Europeans' met 'marginal natives' – we attracted each other, reciprocally provoking one another to come forward. The situation made it very easy for me to research those who were marginal or outsiders – musicians, dancers, singers, mountebanks, mimes, magicians – which was precisely the goal of my research project: to examine possible non-Islamic elements in the culture of an otherwise Islamic area in West Africa's Sahel. Performance became our transcultural meeting point.

The experiment in Africa caused Roberta Carreri to reflect on the differences between West African dances and her own.

> Until Mette Bovin suggested I make this journey to Africa, I had never before been obliged to confront my tradition with that of another group *alone*. I experienced very strongly that my dances were *mine* because I had created them myself. I had seen each one of them being born, and I will see them die. *Their* dances are *theirs* because they belong to the community, the dances have an origin and every performing dancer has a fragment of them – like a part of an endless line that is lost in time.

In our film *Dances in the Sand*, this continuity can be seen in the way a piece of cloth is passed from one dancing Bella woman to the next. The African performances are an integral part of their daily social/religious life, while our performances are 'extra-daily' – 'theatre' as manifested in a highly industrialized society, separate from daily social/religious life. If all eleven Odin Teatret actors had been in the square in Burkina Faso, the public would have seen eleven individual dances combined into a single and unique performance form.

Of course I could have taken a Danish folk dance troupe to Africa instead of the Odin Teatret, as Anders Bodelsen suggested in his review of my film (1984: 13), but would doing so have represented our culture today? I don't think so. And would the people of Burkina Faso have responded by presenting their more marginal performers, as best benefited the subject of my research? I doubt it.

The presence of a catalyst in the fieldwork provoked the presentation of cultural products I would otherwise not have discovered, seen, or heard about. People in the towns of Dori, Wendou and Oullo came out because Carreri had a performance to present and because their performances responded in kind. A hyena-tamer appeared with his hyena; an 'invulnerable magician' danced a knife dance accompanied by talking drums. To have seen these without Carreri would have taken many years. Only the ritual Dodo dance of the Mossi men would have been performed had we been there or not. Every other performance was brought out in response to our initiatives.

Another advantage to our approach was that it became easier for me to obtain translations of songs and information about music or dance traditions specifically because I could provide a similar service regarding our English, Italian and French performance texts in return. Interviews about instruments, symbolic meanings, or religious significance were informative in an organic way – I didn't have to 'drag it out' of the people. When I returned to Burkina Faso seven months later I could still profit from the exchange and promised to give the town a copy of *Dances in the Sand*, which I did on my third trip in 1986.

My interviews in 1983 showed that by far the majority of the people of the Fulbe district of Liptako Emirate had been impressed by Carreri as 'a radiation of energy' and power. Many were confused by the fact that she was a woman and yet wore men's clothing in some of the performances. In the street I would hear *'Debbo tobago! Debbo tobago!* (White woman! White woman!) Where is Chaplin? Isn't he with you this time? We want to see him dance again!' Some believed that she was *kando* (mentally ill). Many people gained a new perception of white women and were surprised to think that they could be 'so strong'.

Not all impressions, however, were reversionary. The belief that Europeans are ungodly was confirmed for many people. Some of the more aristocratic Fulbe in Dori confided in me that they would have liked to have seen the performances, but that it wouldn't do for them to be seen in the crowd of spectators – since it was, after all, rather ungodly – and it was the month of Ramadan. They didn't want to jeopardize their social standing. It was a collection of minority ethnic groups, rather than Fulbe, who had been active in the barter both as performers and audience. Those Fulbe who did participate were low status, professional or semi-professional musicians.

Interestingly, I experienced in the Fulbe the same contradictory mix of contempt and fascination held by Danes. As Geert Egger has written:

> In all, the double behavior is … just a convenient coupling of civilization's built-in arrogance and the distorted conditions of development for the needs. That which is not found inside civilization's own walls, since it is constantly tamed and deported, must be compensated for with a trip out into the 'wilderness: ' context, sensuality, sexuality, freedom etc. (1983: 111)

The Fulbe culture is extremely strict: *pulaaku* (the way, morals) and *semteende* (shame) guide their lives and prohibit dancing or wild play. The *griot* functions for the Fulbe as provocateur of that which they themselves dare not provoke and as mediator of the 'trip out in the wilderness'. *Griots* are an essential part of the society precisely because they are somewhat outside its boundaries. As I played my European flute for some Fulbe in Dori I was told a story: 'The son of a Fulbe chief wanted very badly to be a flute player. He could not resist the temptation – he had to be an artist. But when his father died, he was not allowed to become the new chief. One could not, after all, have a flute player as a chief!'

To the Africans, Carreri and I became 'the wild whites', or 'the whites gone wild', who performed side by side with their own 'wild' professionals – the *griots*. And yet the African dances seemed tame, controlled and at times self-conscious in comparison to Carreri's large, wild movements and daring vocalization. In fact, Carreri's presence in the African towns where I was conducting research presented a tremendous challenge – not only to the public she excited, but to myself as an anthropologist as I constantly confronted the training which had so strongly encouraged me to 'go native' and practise 'participant observation'. The actors of Odin Teatret do exactly the opposite of such training by remaining 100 per cent themselves and refusing to assimilate. They call assimilation 'fraternization' and entirely reject it. The Odin holds firmly to: 'We are us, you are you. We respect you as you are. We would also like you to respect us.' There is no cultural rapprochement; nor do either of the two confronting partners imitate the other. They meet, coming together precisely because of their 'differences which fascinate'.

After we had bartered performance in the village of Oullo and returned to Dori, people came to us and confided that the villagers of Oullo were 'not real Muslims' and that the chief of Oullo was in reality a kind of heathen priest. They told us that the Oullo people practised ancient rituals and had altars where they slaughtered sacrificial animals instead of having a mosque. It was through an Oullo song about how it was not possible to 'conquor Oullo with violence' that I learned the history of the Bellabe people. It was clearly no accident that people of Dori had suggested Oullo as the prime place for us to meet performers, for though Islam has incorporated dances and rituals from earlier periods in a flexible and syncretic way, the practice of dancing (among adults) is in inverse proportion to the degree of Islamization.

All Fulbe in northern Burkina Faso are 'Muslims by definition' (Riesman, 1977: 96). Islam is part of their ethnic heritage. But the difference in Fulbe society between *rimbe* (aristocracy) and *rimaibe* (slaves, captives of war) was obvious. There were more former captives than aristocrats taking part in our exchanges. The *rimbe* in Dori said to me, 'Of course, among real Fulbe, only children dance.'

Spaces selected for dancing were distinctly separate from normal living areas. Our exchanges characteristically occurred as they did the first day in Dori: in an open square before the abattoir, the slaughterhouse. For Muslims, the slaughtering of animals is an unclean occupation, usually done by people of other ethnic groups. In pre-Islamic times, animal sacrifice was part of a religious tradition offered to ancestors, spirits and gods. Blacksmiths and leather workers often took care of drum playing in connection with such offerings. Interestingly, when the society converted to Islam, it was the blacksmiths who played the drums for offering feasts (see Tubiana, 1964: 69). Something similar turned up in our experiment – the dances around the drum belonged to the blacksmiths' wives and the *gargasabe* (women leather workers) were the only female drummers.

The few Hausa magicians in Dori covered themselves with leather amulets and left their torsos naked, as their pre-Islamic ancestors would have done. Both the Hausa magical hyena dance and the dance of the 'Knife-That-Doesn't-Wound' were clearly non-Islamic phenomena. The Dodo dance, or 'The Myth of the Hunter and the King', is performed ritually during Ramadan. The story goes like this:

> A long, long time ago, there lived a great hunter in the Hausa empire in Nige-ria. The king forbade the hunter to hunt on Fridays, but the hunter defied the order and, one Friday, went hunting. When he didn't return to the castle, the king became very angry and sent his men to find the hunter. They had little difficulty finding him though he had changed into a mysterious being, half man and half animal, with a long tail. One day during Ramadan they followed him home. Children began to clap for him and started to dance. The king then locked him away and allowed him out only once a year during Ramadan, to entertain the people as they fasted. He was called *Dodo*, which means 'a strange phenomenon'.

According to the old people, the Dodo tradition was introduced to Burk-ina Faso by Hausa merchants around 1832. Since that time the Dodo dance has been performed by young Mossi men who dance around the chief's house and around the houses of the rich to 'greet' them and receive gifts in return for their performance. In preparation for the dance, the young men secretly construct masks of calabash, cloth, or tin, which they then paint. The masks are always destroyed after Ramadan and new masks, each representing one of Dodo's personalities, must be made the following year. An adult Mossi will perform as a hunter while the young men portray large or powerful animals such as elephants, lions, giraffes, monkeys, gorillas, zebras, antelopes, or snakes. The dancer/singers and the drummers gather at night and perform from about 9: 00 p.m., to 2: 00 a.m.

I came across the Dodo phenomenon in the 1960s in the real Hausa country of northern Nigeria. The performance was clearly non-Islamic; the design of the masks dated from pre-Islamic times. There, Dodo is the town's guardian spirit, and in the 'heathen' ethnic or social groups the ritual is performed for funerals and manhood initiation rites as well as at Ramadan. I found it fascinating that the very same young Mossi men in

Burkina Faso who dance in non-Islamic Dodo masks at night would go to the mosque and pray to Allah during the day, all the while considering themselves 'good Muslims'.

My goal in pinpointing the non-Islamic traits in Burkino Faso was not to note their 'survival' from an earlier period, but rather to suggest that they represent tensions and contradictions in the Islamic society of today. Examining the performative manifestations of non-Islamic elements can illuminate processes underlying the struggle between the structure of a centralized state and stateless, segmented society. The contradiction between 'civilization' and 'primitivism', a struggle in which many West Africans are deeply involved, is played out in some performances and tackled in different ways in the various ethnic groups and social classes that make up modern Africa.

Criticism of the method

Scholarly puritans among anthropologists will most likely find my suggestion for an active, provocative field research too dependent upon 'artificial stimuli'. And yet we field ethnographers have not been criticized for distributing medicine to 'our natives', nor for helping with transportation in emergencies – activities which have actively interfered with local cultures. The dilemma is not if we will disturb, but how we will disturb. Of course, one can ask whether our provocative approach was more disturbing to the local culture than a 'Man with the notebook and the thousand questions' might have been. Carreri and I gave pleasure to perhaps 1000 people in Burkina Faso, and we frightened about twenty. But whether the reactions we provoked were more or less 'disturbing' than reactions induced by a more traditional approach is difficult to measure.

Uncommon field experiments had taken place in Africa before 1982, but most involved field anthropologists handing out otherwise inaccessible material things. One experiment allotted new bicycles to a limited number of families in a small and otherwise bicycle-free society. Allan Holmberg gave steel nooses and machetes to the Siriono Indians and brought about a measurable increase in in-group hostility (see Holmberg, 1954: 108). Holmberg advises against such experiments, as does Pertti Pelto (1970: 310–11). Such handing out of material things is nevertheless distinct from our experiment with theatre. Our performances were public – no one was prevented by us from taking part; we left nothing behind when we departed; and we created no social inequality among individuals, materially speaking, with our intervention. We quite probably exchanged with some and not with others, but all had the invitation to barter with us.

If one considers the exchanges from a profit-oriented point of view, as Freilich and others have done, the results of our project can be seen as an advantage for the African informants as well as for the anthropologists. Carreri's performances in the town meant that input from or cost to the Africans was low, but that their output was high. Similarly for us, the 'price' of our barter was little compared with the return. If one has a craft, an art or skill, a lot of time has been invested to acquire this 'bottomless capital'. Such a skill cannot be run out of – as often happens with money in the field – the advantage being that such an approach as ours almost erases the fieldwork depression that ordinarily occurs during the course of research.

Another advantage was that the barter radically decreased the need to explain the purpose of my presence in the field. It was easy to say 'I will see and learn something about your dances, songs, music and masks in the same way that you can observe our dances, songs, masks, etc.' There was an equality in the exchange that made for an increased understanding between the partners. We, as they, had become informants. They, as we, had become observers. This was our common ground. And though the equality was not entirely complete since we were the more active 'merchants', the provocation inspired both parties to become self-observers. Inspired by the reciprocity of exchange, no one was restricted to the position of 'object' of study.

Yet I do have certain reservations and advice about the approach. Provocation anthropology is exhausting and has the potential to frighten the local people away. The provocation must be disciplined and controlled. The methods and the materials brought to the field must be closely adjusted to the particular culture being researched. I couldn't have come with theatre had I wished to study African kings. Once in the field, care must be taken to avoid blasphemy and violation of the people's important taboos. If Carreri had performed near the mosque in Dori, for example, we would have only provoked a disaster.

As demanding as the method was, however, there were things I discovered through barter that I would never have discovered otherwise. I was astonished at the African children's immediate recognition of Chaplin in Carreri's movements, her clothes, her hat. Because of their cries for *Carlot-na*, I learned that a couple of people in Dori had seen *Charlie and the Kid* on video somewhere. Carreri was also amazed and said, 'If we come back to Dori years from now, these children will be old and will sit and tell their grandchildren, 'When I was young, Charlie Chaplin came to Dori – he was right here in the marketplace!'

If our method is called 'obtrusive', I will agree. Some of the Africans obviously saw our presence as a diversion from the town's monotonous life. Children would stand and shout through the fence around our house: 'Chaplin, Chaplin, come out and dance again!' Theatre is always something which causes a change, a variation – it is obtrusive. If theatre is not distinct from the everyday, then it is not theatre. The question is: can we westerners enter the so-called Third World and behave like Dario Fo, or is it only the industrialized West that we dare disturb? In encountering the Third World are we obliged to limit ourselves to a one-way transfer of information that assumes a hierarchy of privilege? If so, what might we miss? And what might we provoke?

When combined with experience and respect, barter and provocation anthropology are very effective. After Burkina Faso in 1982, I will never again go into the field empty-handed. I will always bring along 'cultural baggage' and prepare its presentation, whatever form it may take. Perhaps another group of artists, perhaps a book learned by heart, or another flute recital. Perhaps something even more unexpected.

A version of this chapter first appeared in *The Drama Review*, Vol. 32, No. 1 (T117) Spring 1998.

References

Ardener, Shirley (ed.) (1975), *Perceiving Women*. London: Malaby Press.

Barba, Eugenio (1986), *Beyond the Floating Islands*. New York: Performing Arts Journal Publications.

Bodelson, Anders (1984), Review of the film *Dansen i sandet: Et møde mellem Europa og Afrika*, produced and directed by Mette Bovin. *Politiken*, 8 April: 13.

Bohannan, Laura (1966), 'Shakespeare in the bush', *Natural History*, 72: 28–33.

Bovin, Mette (1969), 'Rapport fra en nigersk landsby', *Jordens Folk Ethnografisk Revy* 5 (no. 1): 24–9.

Bovin, Mette (1984), *Dansen i sandet: et møde mellem Europa og Afrika*. Film: 16 mm, 45 mins. Distributed by Mette Bovin, Helsingor, Denmark.

Camara, Sory (1976), *Gens de la parole: Essai sur la condition et role des griots dans la société Malinke*. Paris: La Haye.

D'Urso, Tony and Ferdinando Taviani (1977), *L'Etranger qui danse: Album de L'Odin Teatret 1972-77*. Holstebro, Denmark: Maison de la Culture de Rennes and Odin Teatret.

Egger, Geert (1983), 'Dem om vendte verden – om antropologisk formidling, paedagogisk utopi og moderne ungdomskulterer', in *Havd kan vi leare af andre kulterer?: Proceedings of the 10th Scandinavian Meeting of Ethnographs*, ed. Niels Fock, pp. 106–24. Copenhagen: Copenhagen University Press.

Freilich, Erving (1969), *Marginal Natives: Anthropologists at Work*. New York: Harper & Row.

Golde, Peggy (ed.) (1970), *Women in the Field: Anthropological Experiences*. Chicago: Aldine Publishing Company.

Holmberg, Allan R. (1954), 'Adventures in culture change', in *Methods and Perspectives in Anthropology*, ed. R. F. Spencer, pp. 103–16. Minneapolis: University of Minnesota Press.

Pelto, Pertti (1970), *Anthropological Research: Structure of Enquiry*. New York: Harper & Row.

Riesman, Paul (1977), *Freedom in Fulani Social Life: an Introspective Ethnography*. Chicago: University of Chicago Press.

Royal Anthropological Institute (1951), *Notes and Queries on Anthropology*, 6th edn. London: Routledge.

Tubiana, Marie-José (1964), *Survivances préslamiques en pays Zaghawa*. Paris: Institut d'Ethnologie.

11

Invisible cities: an interview with Pino di Buduo

Ian Watson

Pino di Buduo is the founder and director of the Italian theatre group Potlach, which is based in Fara Sabina outside Rome. This interview was carried out in the Louisiana Museum, Copenhagen, Denmark on 11 May 1996.

IAN WATSON Early in your career you studied with Eugenio at the Odin?

PINO DI BUDUO Yes. In 1975 I studied for six months in Holstebro after seeing the Odin's work for the first time. I saw *Min Fars Hus* (My Father's House) in Rome where I was teaching anthropology at the university. In addition to my teaching, I was working in the theatre part time. The theatre was a personal rather than professional interest in those days. After the performance of *Min Fars Hus*, Eugenio taught a short seminar where he introduced some of his ideas about the theatre. Afterwards, he invited me to have dinner with him during which I told him about the thesis I had just completed on magicians, story telling, and superstition in the south of Italy. I explained that the magician's rituals and the performative nature of story telling was one of the sources of material for my work with actors at the time. Eugenio was interested because of his recent residencies in the south and because he had just begun his barter work with the people in the region. Eugenio told me that he was about to mount an eight-month seminar in Holstebro and that if I was interested in taking part I should write to him. I did and he accepted me and my professional partner Daniela. We went to Holstebro where we worked with the company. We studied their physical training techniques and worked on Jean Genet's *The Maids*. Towards the end of the seminar, Eugenio asked me what I wanted to do. I told him that I would like to have a group in a small village in Italy. He told me about Fara Sabina.

ɪᴡ   He knew about Fara Sabina?

ᴘʙ   Yes, he first mentioned Fara Sabina to me. He told me, there is a village near Rome, a little village of three hundred people, which has space that could be suitable for a theatre group.

ɪᴡ   How did he know about it?

ᴘʙ   Through Nando Taviani [the Italian scholar mentioned earlier in the introduction to 'Lecture/demonstrations at ISTA: examples of a transcultural dialogue' by Nicola Savarese]. Nando had been looking for a house for the Odin in Fara Sabina, but there were no suitable houses. What he did find, however, was a large laboratory-type space that could be used for theatre training and performances. When I returned to Italy, Nando and I went to the mayor of Fara Sabina with a proposition and he accepted. I continued teaching for another year, then I resigned from the university to work full time in theatre.

ɪᴡ   Did what you had learned in Holstebro become a model for your work in Fara Sabina?

ᴘʙ   The physical training, yes. I taught our actors acrobatics and the other physical techniques that Daniella and I had learned in Denmark. We also began to develop a performance through improvisation. Our beginnings were this; and building a relationship with the villagers in Fara Sabina. The latter took many years because people from the village do not accept outsiders easily. There was a man living in Fara Sabina for forty-five years, for example, and still the people did not regard him as a local. We had to decide what kind of relationship to have with the village.

ɪᴡ   How did you do that? You had two very different cultures in contact, the new immigrant theatre culture and the indigenous village culture. You were outsiders and your interests were far removed from the local people.

ᴘʙ   I first thought of what we should not do, what we should avoid in order not to antagonize the village. Our first point of contact was with the young people. I began to work with the young people, especially in the schools. In addition we made a point of being respectful, we did not discuss politics, we did not speak about religion, and we avoided any kind of scandal. The people from the village did not accept us because they were sympathetic to what we were doing, they did not understand what we were doing. But they did accept our work ethic. We were very disciplined; we began work at 7:00 a.m., every day and worked through till at least 5:00 p.m., in the afternoon. We were friendly but never became involved in local problems. We would say hello to everyone but work came first.

IW All the people in the group were Italian at this point?

PB No, they were from Switzerland, Italy and Germany. We have been international from the beginning. But despite the international nature of the group, the villagers could see that we worked hard, that we were disciplined, that we avoided discussing contentious issues, and that we were friendly. Then after the first year they began to ask, 'What are you doing inside a space for so many hours?' So we presented our training for three hours to show them.

IW Did the people come?

PB Some did, but they really had no idea about what we were doing. They told the others that the only thing we could do was acrobatics.

IW You had not created any productions at this point?

PB Yes, we had begun to do some street work, small-scale projects.

IW Did you develop the street theatre yourselves or was it something you had studied in Holstebro?

PB I had only seen a few images from Eugenio's street theatre in Denmark, but, of course, I did speak with him about it. However, street theatre was very new for the Odin at the time also, and Eugenio used it mostly as a means of establishing relationships with the villages in the south of Italy. We used it in much the same way, to make contact with the people of Fara Sabina. It gave us an opportunity to present something to the people and to be accepted. Performance, especially street performance with its colourful props, its costumes, and use of music, generates immediate contact. Our street theatre also avoided questions about meaning since we were able to say that it was done just to make the village visible, to catch attention, to bring life to a street. They accepted this.

IW Is there a tradition of street performance in Fara Sabina?

PB No. It was completely new for them. But it was one of the means of building bridges between us and them. I am an anthropologist by training so I had an understanding of what a culture means, and of how to build relations between different cultures.

IW What you say is interesting because my understanding of anthropology is one in which anthropologists avoid building links with the 'other' culture for fear of distorting their study of it. Most anthropologists use their training to objectify and analyse cultures while

you used yours to personalize and create relations between yourselves and the villagers.

PB The street work, our behaviour in the village, and the work we did
with the young people was only the first phase of our bridge building. Later we looked for institutional support to mount larger events
such as conferences. People came and studied with us, and we invited
performers from Japan, India, Bali, South and North America. The
people from the village could see that something was happening.

IW The strategy you were using is essentially one of barter. You displayed
your cultural interests to the village who in turn presented their traditional village culture. Through this mutual display contact and
relations were established.

PB I did not think of it in barter terms at the time, but now I have a
better understanding of what I was doing.

IW But you were aware of Eugenio's barter ideas at the time?

PB Yes. But barter was something he had done in the south of Italy.
When I thought of barter in those days, I though of the south of Italy,
of villages where there were traditional forms of dance and singing
that the older villagers, especially, brought to the barters. Southern
Italy has a rich heritage of performance but the Fara Sabina region
has no such tradition. I understood how Eugenio's barters worked,
but I didn't think that Fara Sabina was suitable for such an exchange.

IW Did you see any of Eugenio's barters at the time?

PB No. I saw the film made for Italian television about the Odin's residency in the south of Italy, which includes footage of barters, and I
talked with Eugenio about them, but I did not see any in person. In
1990, however, I began something of my own that is, I think, barter.
It is ironic, that the name of my group is Potlach. Potlach [or pot-
latch] is a barter. But I was not thinking of barter at the time, I was
thinking of another aspect of potlach. In a potlach goods are
destroyed, a great effort is made to accumulate items and then they
are destroyed in a ceremony. Theatre is like that, you work and work
to prepare a production which is 'destroyed' in a kind of way as you
present it to your audience then eventually abandon it altogether.
Theatre is a potlach of sorts. But now I think a little differently about
the potlach, I am more aware of the exchange involved in our name.
Prior to 1988 I focused exclusively on theatre, on the work of the
actor especially, the training, the physical work, the voice, improvisation. But from 1988 on I began to develop an interest in other disciplines. I have friends who are architects and musicians, I have one
friend who teaches scenography; through these friendships I
attempted to build a new relationship among the different disci-

plines in the theatre. I began from my experience, the work of the actor. I am used to being in the training and rehearsal room watching the actor working with the body for hour after hour every day. By 1990, when I began to plan my first interdisciplinary project, I had been doing this for fourteen years. The project was created around the historical centre of my theatre life, Fara Sabina. I wanted to include Fara Sabina in what I did. Since I knew the people of the village, I asked if I could use the cellars beneath their houses, the gardens, and inner courtyards which cannot be seen from the street. Everyone gave me the keys to his house without question. The villagers also arranged to accommodate the guests who came to take part in the project. There are no hotels in Fara Sabina so the local people hosted more than thirty artists, one guest per family. These guests included architects, musicians, visual artists, writers, dramaturgs, dancers … I invited people I know from each of these professions. I invited them to work together in this way to build new relations.

I W   To build new relations between you, your group, and these various friends of yours?

P B   Yes. Between myself, Potlach, and the others I invited, such as the architect Luca Ruzza and his architecture students, Fabrizio Crisafulli and his students of visual arts, the musician Danilo Tarenzi along with a group of his fellow musicians. I also invited local amateur artists from Fara Sabina, as well as local musicians and actors. The theme of the piece was the village. Together we began to work on the memories of the village, the memories of Fara Sabina.

I W   But how do you know the memories of Fara Sabina? You have only been in the village for fifteen years and your friends, the colleagues you worked with, they do not even live there.

P B   There are two aspects to this kind of memory, one is the local memory. Those from the village have internal memory. Those who worked with me from outside the village observed with the eyes of strangers, they tried to make the invisible traces of the local people's internal memories visible. Secondly, I invited a historian and an archaeologist who have studied Fara Sabina to work with us. They told us the history and gave us archaeological information about the village. They knew about streets that no longer exist, the origins of the village's name, even why Fara Sabina came into being. I also asked every family from the village for photos from the beginning of the century. I even selected some of these for the piece. I made slides of some photos and projected them on to the wall of the church in the village courtyard, huge eight-metres square projections. Fara Sabina was founded in the Middle Ages. The cellars in the older houses are really grottoes, they are hewn out of solid rock. There are often two or three grotto-like caves underneath one house, many of which are decorated with medieval arches which form the foundations of the houses. These grottoes gave me a thematic idea for what we were doing. They made me think of Italo Calvino's novella *Invisible Cities*. In the book, Calvino describes the fantastical cities that Marco Polo told Kubla Khan about on his visit to China. The Kubla Khan knew nothing of these cities so Marco Polo could exaggerate or invent and make the invisible cities visible through his tales, which were often told through pantomime, singing and physical gestures because Marco Polo did not speak Chinese. The hidden dimension of Fara Sabina is like these cities, there are invisible spaces, island cities. It was my job to build the connections between them.

I w Between the various grottoes, gardens and courtyards?

P B Yes, as in Marco Polo's Venice. Venice was originally many islands. The founding fathers of the city built bridges between these islands to create the city. I think it is possible to read any city like Venice, like an archipelago. A city consists of many connected 'islands'. My job in Fara Sabina was to create the connections between the separate invisible cities underlying the village. Streets form a natural connection between spaces so I decorated them. I placed a canopy of white transparent drapes over the streets that suggested paths to the spectators, paths that led to secret places. I didn't give directions, the spectators began to travel and discover the cities for themselves. They began to understand the relations between the spaces created by the various groups of actors, musicians, and visual artists. But that was later, while creating the piece we always began our work with the space. We went into each of the cellars and courtyards that had been closed to the public for thirty years with the information given us by the historian and archaeologist. There were more than sixty locations; each group had to choose a location and develop a proposition for the space. At first I asked the groups to spend time in each of the spaces that interested them. The groups remained in these spaces for three days without making a proposition to me, just listening to the space, living in it. At the end of those three days we decided the space and proposition for each group.

I w Did you merely accept each group's proposition and choice of space or was there a process of selection and discussion between you and the groups?

P B Each group indicated a preference and suggested a proposition for the space. Everything must come initially from the group. This is the way I always work. I work this way with my actors. the actor has to make a proposition for the performance in rehearsal. Why? Because it is *their* proposition. During the work in Fara Sabina, I gave the groups three days to make their decisions. Each group had to make its own proposition separate from the others. I suggested adaptations at times, I asked some groups to prepare propositions for two or three spaces when I knew that several groups had the same space in mind. There were conflicts but I had to resolve them.

IW Each of the groups developed a proposition based upon their discipline, musicians created a musical response to their space, actors a performative response, visual artists developed a design response and so on?

PB Yes. And as the propositions were developing I would give suggestions, especially about ways of making more connections with the local nature of the space. In addition, we had meetings every morning and afternoon in which we mapped out the development of each of the cities and tried to solve concrete problems, such as where we needed lighting, where we had to be careful because a group was using fire, the placement of lighting cables, etc. Through these meetings everyone came to know the work of the others and to understand their place in the evolving map.

IW Once everything was prepared how was the city presented to the public?

PB The entrance to the village is a wide street that passes under an arch, which is part of the outer wall surrounding the town. Once you pass under the archway, the street, which leads to the main square, has many smaller streets running off it. The cellars, gardens and courtyards of the invisible city were all in these small streets. When we were ready to show our city, we invited people to come to the archway at the entrance to Fara Sabina. They were met by the artists, those who had prepared the city. Once everyone was gathered, Daniela read out a proclamation inviting people to visit the invisible city. Then, as the people entered the village, the artists went to the spaces they had created and prepared to greet the public. Once inside the village, the spectators found many pathways and streets they could follow. There was not one single pathway but many and it was left to the individual spectator to decide his or her own journey. It was much like visiting a strange city in your travels. When you visit a city you have never been to before, you are attracted to certain things, other things are less interesting and you ignore them. Each presentation went on for around one and a half hours. It varied from night to night, but at a prearranged cue, the artists invited everyone who was in their space or on the street nearby to move to the main square for the ending.

IW So it was a journey of sorts, with the spectators meeting at the entrance to the village then travelling through the pathways and secrets of the invisible city until they gathered once again in the heart of the village to say goodbye.

PB Yes.

IW Was it possible for a spectator to see all of the invisible city?

PB Not in a single visit. But many came for several nights until they had seen everything.

IW You described the invisible cities project as a barter earlier, but exchange is central to my understanding of barter. Where is the exchange in what you have described?

PB There are different levels of exchange. One level involves the various nationalities of participants. The next invisible city project is to take place towards the end of the summer in Liverpool, England [it was presented in the first week of September 1996]. I have invited a number of groups from different countries to take part: one from Liege in Belgium, another from Giessen, Germany, one each from the Austrian cities of Vienna, Klagenfurt, Lienz and Graz, a number of Italian groups from Cosenza, Fara Sabina, Trento, Rome, Catania and Bologna, as well as one from Dublin. There are about sixty people in all, two or three from each town, who, in addition to working together, will also work with visual artists, actors and musicians from Liverpool. These local artists will have to exchange their experience of the town in which they were born, their culture, their way of looking at space with everyone else. Another level of exchange lies in the space itself. Each location is unique, the medieval village of Fara Sabina suggests a different exchange from the lake at Klagenfurt [where an invisible city project was mounted in 1992], or the abandoned dock where the Liverpool event is to take place. In each of these settings, the artists have to exchange their knowledge, their different sensibilities about the management of space. Visual artists view space in a certain way, actors in another; but there is common ground. For example, one visual artist in Fara Sabina, Fabrizio Crisafulli wanted to create the illusion of a chair floating in the air. He used very thin, near-invisible threads, but he discovered that in order for the illusion to be more convincing, he had to tilt the chair rather than keep its seat parallel with the ground. It is the same for an actor, if he wants to bring life to an action he must distort his equilibrium [he is referring to Barba's notion of the energy generated by manipulating equilibrium, see Barba and Savarese, 1991:34–50]. Fabrizio knows this law in some way, I don't know if he is aware of it, but he knows it in his sensibility. There is also another level of exchange, that between the strangers and the memory of the city, between the people from the city who have lived its history with those who come to the city for the first time.

IW Why do you feel the need to create these forms of exchange? Why not just go to towns, perform, possibly conduct some workshops and leave, as you have done many times before during your theatre tours in Europe, Latin America and elsewhere.

PB It is not enough to present your work to those who come to the theatre. I feel the need to have a relationship with those who do not normally come to the theatre also. How can you have an insight into a people without understanding something of their cultural expression? How can one build a relation or, to use your terms, have an exchange, with those who do not normally come to the theatre? One way is to give them the space to create with us, to present their music or their design sensibilities. When I build a true relationship through work in this way I see in the other an energy, a desire to meet and exchange with me. It is the same when I work with an actor, I watch the actor in rehearsal discover something, he works and works then suddenly something new appears, something is born. Out of this birth of energy a new relationship takes shape. This gives sense to my work.

References

Barba, Eugenio and Nicola Savarese (1991), *A Dictionary of Theatre Anthropology: the Secret Art of the Performer*. London and New York: Routledge.

Latin America and the Third Theatre

12

Barba's other culture
Ian Watson

Eugenio Barba's concern with cultural pluralism is hardly limited to his research at the International School of Theatre Anthropology (ISTA). It permeates most every aspect of his work, from his unusual dramaturgical structures, to his productions, performer training methods and his use of barter performances as a means of instigating cultural exchange. Cultural pluralism is equally important in Barba's relationship with Latin America.

In a paper presented at the UNESCO-sponsored meeting on Latin American theatre in Lima, Peru in April 1987, Luis Peirano cited Bertolt Brecht, Jerzy Grotowski and Eugenio Barba as the three major European influences on modern Latin American theatre (1987: 10-13). However, unlike Brecht and Grotowski, Barba has made a major commitment to the continent.[1] Since 1976, when the Odin performed in Latin America for the first time at the Caracas Festival in Venezuela, Barba and the members of his Nordisk Teaterlaboratorium have returned many times

---

1 Brecht never travelled to Latin America, and his company, the Berliner Ensemble did not tour the continent during his lifetime. Grotowski, on the other hand, did have limited direct contact with Latin America prior to his departure from the theatre: several Latin American actors and directors worked with him at Barba's Third Theatre gatherings in Belgrade and Bergamo; his Theatre Laboratory performed once in Latin America as part of the 1968 Mexico Cultural Olympics; and he lectured and led seminars in the continent on several occasions (for full details on these lectures and seminars see Osinski, 1986: 36–125).

to perform, conduct workshops, lecture, run seminars, rehearse Odin performances, and Barba even directed the only production he has ever mounted outside of the Odin, *Otelo*, in Brazil, with the Candomblé dancer Augusto Omolú.

Venezuela and Brazil aside, Barba has also spent extensive amounts of time in Mexico, Columbia, Peru, Chile, Argentina, Uruguay, Costa Rica, and Cuba. In turn, he has invited leading theatre artists from various parts of Latin America to Europe to conduct workshops and/or to work with him and his Odin colleagues at their headquarters in Holstebro, Denmark, at ISTA, and at the international meetings of group theatre that Barba refers to as Third Theatre gatherings. In addition, all of Barba's major theatre writings have been published in Spanish and are readily available throughout the continent.

Barba's commitment to Latin America is in essence a relationship, and, like all good relationships, it involves exchange. It is an exchange between cultures in which questions of otherness are tempered by a shared preoccupation with theatre. Barba has influenced theatre in Latin America. Equally, the various national cultures of the continent have had an impact on Barba and the fundamental premises that underlie his work in the theatre.

Barba's influence on Latin America

Group theatre

Barba's major impact in Latin America has been on those who, like himself, regard actors as the creative focal point of theatre and the group as the theatre's basic social unit. This influence has its origins in Barba's own history. One of his primary concerns has always been what in Europe are referred to as free groups, that is, groups which are independent of the state or city financed theatre complexes which constitute the 'official theatre'. This preoccupation has not only found expression in the way Barba makes theatre but in his theoretical writings, through his concept of what he terms Third Theatre.

Despite the variety of rehearsal/training methods and forms of expression among the groups who comprise the Third Theatre, its distinguishing feature for Barba is the socio-creative need of its members to make theatre without regard to monetary rewards, stardom, or even the accolades of aficionados. Its very existence questions how and why theatre is made, and in so doing reorients theatre's focus from being concerned with either expressing present cultural values – which is the domain of institutionalized theatre, or aesthetic experimentation, as in the avant-garde. This concept of Third Theatre, first published in 1976, found an echo in contemporary Latin American theatre mainly due to developments inside the continent during the same period.

The 1960s and 1970s saw a proliferation of group theatre in Latin America[2] and a number of these groups found a kindred spirit in Barba that led to his ideas being widely published throughout the continent. This dissemination of his ideas was augmented by continued personal contact between him and several important Latin American groups, such as Teatro Núcleo and Libre Teatro Libre from Argentina and Peru's Cuatrotablas, which culminated in Barba and his Odin Teatret being invited to the first Third Theatre gathering mounted in Latin America, organized by Cuatrotablas in Ayacucho, Peru (1978). This gathering, which was modelled on Barba's Third Theatre meetings in Europe to which he had invited Cuatrotablas, marked the first significant exchange between Barba and his Latin American colleagues on their own soil.[3]

Barba has provided both models and an intellectual infrastructure for many Latin American groups which, rather than merely copying, they have adapted to their specific needs. Strategies he discovered that helped the Odin survive economically during its difficult early years, for example – publishing a journal containing material that had influenced him and in so doing generating interest in his work without waiting for favourable critiques to build an audience, and realizing that both mounting workshops and screening films for a fee can supplement income earned from performances – have been employed by groups like Argentina's Comuna Baires, Teatro Núcleo and others.

His theoretical writings on Third Theatre have also had an important influence since they provide an intellectual justification for a theatre that is forced to exist on the cultural periphery with little money, and whose members frequently find themselves forced to earn a living outside of what is the major focus of their professional lives.

In addition, Barba's international reputation as a champion of those on the fringes of the mainstream has provided a source of psychological support for many groups; and the Odin's longevity and continued success has suggested it both as a social and aesthetic model to many.

Similarly, Barba's Third Theatre gatherings in Europe have inspired their Latin American counterparts. The original premise of the Third

2   Internationally famous groups such as ICTUS, Galpón, Teatro Experimental de Cali, La Candelaria, Cuatrotablas, Rajatablas, Libre Teatro Libre and Teatro Núcleo were all founded or came to prominence during this period. But, these are only a small part of a much larger picture. Enrique Buenaventura, for example, claims that there were some 2000 groups in Colombia alone in 1979 (in Luzuriaga, 1986: 85).

3   See 'The Third Theatre: a legacy of independence' elsewhere in this volume for a more detailed discussion of the Third Theatre gatherings.

Theatre meetings was that they would serve as a point of contact between groups outside of the theatre mainstream who share similar philosophies but which are often separated by huge geographic distances. This is precisely the function they have served in Latin America. Groups from all over the continent, and even a few from as far afield as Europe and North America, have taken part in the region's Third Theatre meetings.[4]

The major components of Barba's European Third Theatre meetings have been workshop/training sessions and the sharing of techniques as well as ideas, all of which have also played an important part in the Latin American gatherings. As discussed in greater detail in 'The Third Theatre: a legacy of independence' in this volume, at these latter meetings, participants have performed and demonstrated their training and/or approaches to dramaturgy for each other. The gatherings have also provided training sessions. And, as a balance to the focus on practical concerns, several meetings have invited respected scholars and/or critics, like Italy's Ferdinando Taviani, Jean-Marie Pradier from France, and Peru's Juan Larco,[5] to conduct seminars with participants.

Taking theatre to those who rarely see it

Another important influence Barba has had on Latin America stems from his research into the social value of theatre. Most of this research has focused on using performance as a means of meeting those who would not normally attend the theatre by presenting work outdoors in city streets and village squares and by engaging local communities in barter performances.

---

4 The majority of groups taking part in each of the Third Theatre gatherings have been from the host country. However, there have always been groups from other countries at each of the meetings. The Odin Teatret has been to all three of the gatherings in Ayacucho (1978, 1988, 1998), for instance; at the 1981 Zacatecas, Mexico meeting there were a number of groups from Latin America, Europe and the United States including: Teatro Taller and Acto Latino from Colombia, Grupo Quebranto from Brazil, the Argentinean group El Centro de Cula Experimental, Contradanza from Venezuela, Peru's Teatro del Sol, La Rana Sabia from Ecuador, as well as the Spanish group El Teatro Vivo, Ciotola and Teatro Núcleo of Italy, the Theatre of the 8th Day (Teatr Osmego Dnia) from Poland, and New York's Talking Band. And the Odin Teatret took part in the 1987 Bahía Blanca meeting, as did Denmark's Farfa and The Canada Project, the Italian groups Potlach and Tascabile di Bergamo, as well as Grupo Emanuel from Chile, Mexico's Teatro Campesino de Milpa Alta, and Teatro de la Comuna from Uruguay. For more details on these meetings see 'The Third Theatre: A Legacy of Independence', elsewhere in this volume.

5 Ferdinando Taviani took part in the Zacatecas gathering, along with two other European intellectuals familiar with Barba's work: Peter Elsass and Jean-Marie Pradier. Fernando de Toro was at the Third Theatre meeting in Bahía Blanca, while Taviani and Larco were at the meeting in Chaclacayo.

Despite Barba's innovative work in the field, he can hardly be credited with initiating the concept of taking performances to those not used to attending the theatre in Latin America. Most of the continent has a tradition of open air performance-oriented spectacles like parades and street festivals, while in countries like Cuba and Peru there is a history of presenting theatre in small towns and villages.[6]

Barba's contribution to taking theatre to the masses in Latin America can best be characterized as complementary and supportive. His theoretical writings on barter and Third Theatre have provided a conceptual matrix for the work, and a number of groups including Cuatrotablas, Peru's Yuyachkani, and Libre Teatro Libre, before it disbanded, incorporated many of Barba's street theatre techniques into their work – including his methods of gathering and controlling crowds, his use of spectacular props and stilt figures, as well as using barter-type performances as a point of meaningful exchange with various communities.[7]

Performer training

As might be expected of someone who began his theatrical apprenticeship as Grotowski's assistant, Barba has devoted a large part of his time to a study of the acting process. And a number of Latin American groups have been influenced by his findings.

Through the work of groups such as Comuna Baires, Cuba's Tercer Mundo, and Cuatrotablas, Latin America has a history of theatre workers who, under the initial influence of Grotowski especially, focused at least part of their activity on exploring the actor's art. And, even though some of these groups have been disbanded, those that remain and others that have sprung up to take their place (such as Yuyachkani and Mexico's La Rueca) have continued this line of research and have had contact with Barba, through his writings or as participants at festivals and/or Third Theatre gatherings he has attended. All of these groups have experimented with some or all of Barba's ideas on training and have adapted them to their particular needs. Yuyachkani, for example, was initially opposed to Grotowski-influenced concerns with the actor, but, in experimenting with Barba's concept of daily, individualized training, they have

---

6   In the early 1960s Cuban groups like Grupo Teatro del Tercer Mundo and Teatro
    Escambray toured small towns and villages in Cuba with the express purpose of
    taking performances to those who did not have the opportunity to attend the
    theatre (Tunberg, 1970: 50, 54). In 1973, Augusto Boal headed a Peruvian
    government-sponsored literacy programme that worked among the illiterate
    peasants throughout the country, using theatre as a means of developing reading
    and writing skills (Boal, 1979: 120–56).
7   For more details on Barba's street theatre techniques see Watson, 1993: 108–17.

found that they are better able to explore and convey themes they are working on through the expanded physical and emotional range it affords them.[8]

Dramaturgy

Barba has a somewhat unusual approach to creating a performance text. Rather than beginning rehearsals with a written script, the source of material for productions is improvisation. Each actor develops segments of improvised action based on given themes individually. These segments are then learned so that the actor can repeat his improvisations at will. Barba uses these various fragments, which are rarely causally connected, much as rough drafts of scenes to which he adds texts that he and the actors have collected during rehearsals from various sources such as books, poems and plays. He then gradually combines these vocal and physical montages into a cohesive whole, the production.[9]

In the late 1960s through into the 1970s, collective creation, that is, groups developing their work collectively rather than basing rehearsals on an already existing script, became popular in Latin America. Most of this work, like that developed by Teatro Escambray from Cuba and the Colombian groups Teatro Experimental de Cali and La Candelaria, centred on addressing particular social or political issues;[10] and there is little evidence to suggest that these types of endeavours were influenced by Barba's unusual approach to dramaturgy, other than possibly indirectly through his theoretical writings.

There are a number of groups in Latin America, however, which have incorporated and adapted Barba's dramaturgical methods directly into their work. These groups are generally those who share his concern for individually developed daily training, and his view that the actor is the central figure in the theatre. These include groups such as Cuatrotablas, Yuyachkani and La Rueca.

---

8   Despite this history, the value Barba has always placed on training and individual research has not been shared by all Latin American groups. Primarily under the influence of Brecht, many groups regard ideology and a committed body of work as the most important components in the theatrical formula. To be concerned with technique or training is felt to be mere bourgeois formalism by these groups. And, regardless of the fact that Brecht's influence has waned somewhat during recent years, this theme persists in much of the continent.

9   For a more detailed description of Barba's dramaturgical methods see Watson, 1993: 73–103.

10   For details on the type of work developed collectively by these companies see Tunberg, 1970: 54–5 (Teatro Escambray); Buenaventura, 1978 (Teatro Experimental de Cali); and Luzuriaga, 1986 (La Candelaria).

Criticism of Barba in Latin America

There is little doubt that Barba has an important place in the history of group theatre in Latin America, but that is not to say that he is without his critics. Despite his ardent supporters, he has been attacked for a number of different reasons. He is frequently accused of being a formalist, for instance, because his productions rarely have a demonstrative political point of view, and because of his concern with training and dramaturgical structures. He has also been accused of being an elitist because his studio-type productions limit the size of the audience and because they are often difficult to understand. As a counter to this, even though his street performances and barters take theatre to the masses, others have attacked them as a misuse of theatre. These critics argue that to take theatre to those who are unprepared for it has a negative rather than a positive effect because it may only frighten and alienate them.

Barba's response to his critics has been much the same all his life, he generally ignores them. His actions, however, have gone a long way to answering many of their attacks. With regard to his political commitment, for example, it is true that excluding Odin Teatret's *Ornitofilene* (premiered in October 1965), which used the conflict between local villagers and an ecologically conscious group of developers to explore the horrors of a Nazi occupation of the village some twenty years earlier, and *Come! And the Day Will be Ours* (premiered in May 1976), that dealt with the encounter between European immigrants and the North American Indians, none of his productions has been based on an overtly political theme.[11]

But Barba's entire approach to his work is a political ideology. He is devoted to theatre as a way of life, to continually exploring the creative and social boundaries of theatre. Despite ample opportunity, he has never abandoned group theatre for the financial rewards of commercialism. And he has always openly supported those on the theatrical periphery, as well as colleagues opposed to repressive cultural cartels and authoritarian regimes. In a similar vein, his barter work has brought the very value of theatre into question by discarding money as the means of measuring its worth. For Barba, the currency of theatre is social exchange.

---

11 This is not to say that the Odin's work is apolitical. The group's work could hardly be described as overtly leftist or Marxist, but most of Barba's productions deal one way or another with the individual in relation to the polis, that is, to the state and/or his socio-historical context. Apart from those already mentioned: *Ferai* drew heavily on Greek and Nordic mythology but also dealt with the conflict between a democratic king and a people who yearn for dictatorship; and *Brecht's Ashes 2* was the biography of a committed communist.

It should also be remembered that even though Barba's studio-type productions limit audiences, they are the result of the extensive research he and his actors have conducted over the years. Since these productions are often at the cutting edge of technique and new developments in dramaturgy, they appeal to a limited audience. So, despite the fact that Barba has often consciously limited audiences for the sake of intimacy in his productions, he is also aware that what he is doing will not appeal to everyone; it calls for a special audience. And it should further be remembered that these productions, and the research they are based on, are the primary source of Barba's theoretical writing, much of which has had a major impact on Latin America.

Latin America's influence on Barba

Latin America's influence on Barba can be seen most clearly in his productions. As touched on in 'Contexting Barba', for instance, two of the original sources of *Oxyrhincus Evangeliet* were the Jorge Luis Borges' story, *The Dead Man* and the Brazilian outlaws in the novels of writers like Euclides da Cunha and the films of Ruy Guerra (Barba, 1985: 30); similarly, the inspiration for the tale of a false Messiah and his impact on those around him, which was the central plot of *Oxyrhincus*, was drawn in part from Mario Vargas Llosa's *The War of the End of the World*, while many of the costumes in the production were authentic Latin American pieces collected by Barba and other members of the cast during their travels in the continent. This Latin American influence was carried through into the company's following production, *Talabot*, the initial rehearsals for which were conducted in Chicxulub, Mexico during a three-month residency in early 1988, with the express aim of allowing the cultural and geographic environment to influence the work (Barba, 1987).[12]

The culmination of Barba's creative links to Latin America is his production of *Otelo* (premiered in August, 1994). As mentioned earlier, this work, which features the Candomblé dancer Augusto Omolú and his musicians, is the only fully mounted Barba piece done without his Odin actors. The *mise-en-scène*, rehearsed partly in Holstebro and partly in Brazil, is based on Shakespeare's tragedy and combines the *Orixà* dance vocabulary of Candomblé with recorded fragments of Guiseppe Verdi's opera *Otello*.

---

12 This residency was from February until April 1988 and follows in the tradition of the Odin's earlier residencies in southern Italy in the early 1970s which led to their street theatre work and barter performances.

These obvious examples of the continent's influence on Barba are only the tip of the iceberg, however, since Latin America has in fact become a major frame of reference for him. In the Odin's formative years, Europe was Barba's locus. He was, after all, a European making theatre in Europe; the ideas of his Polish mentor, Grotowski, were gradually becoming better known; many free groups were beginning to emerge; and through the work of people like Grotowski, Brook, Ronconi, Fo, and the Living Theatre there was a dynamic theatrical pulse in Europe. This dynamism was a reflection of the general artistic, political and social ferment throughout the continent, which culminated in the student and worker uprisings of 1968.

In the years following this social and cultural revolution, Europe gradually settled once again into its bourgeois complacency. Barba began looking elsewhere for inspiration, for a world in tune with his philosophies that everything tends to change rather than to stability, and that taking risks rather than repeating proven formulas is the only way to continue growing as an artist. He found this in Latin America.

Barba's affinity with Latin America is both personal and professional. His personal rapport stems from the Latin roots he shares with the majority of the continent, and with the question of identity, which is an issue for both him and Latin America in general. Many from the continent, especially those from countries dominated by European immigrants and the descendants of colonial rule, are unclear about what it means to be Latin American. Some are of mixed blood, others are of European stock, but even the latter are no longer Europeans. The majority of Latin Americans were born in countries that belong to others, the Indians and their descendants, but they also come from these countries. They are racially different from those of the land and their roots and heritage are from another world, but in many ways they are closer to them than to their former kin in Europe. Yet Europe's shadow hangs over them in their language, in their history and in their culture.

Barba may share the Latin origins of those he is closest to in South America yet, like them, he is separated from his roots: he was born in Italy but lives in Denmark. His actors come from many different countries, he speaks a number of languages fluently, and he is constantly travelling. He carries a Danish passport, however, his swarthy skin and accent betray him as a foreigner. Little wonder that when reflecting upon a professional life of over thirty years in the theatre in the mid-1990s, Barba wrote that he has 'experienced theatre as emigration' (1996).

Barba's professional point of contact with Latin America lies in the importance of group theatre throughout the continent. Many of these groups are similar to the free groups in Europe that have always been

Barba's theatrical territory, and the majority of them are quin
examples of his concept of the Third Theatre. Most are on the
of the theatrical mainstream, both politically and economicall;
them have taken great risks in their ideological commitment and are (or
have been from time to time) under threat from the authoritarian
regimes they oppose.

In addition to this threat, most group members are paid very little, if
anything, for their theatrical work and have to maintain full-time jobs
outside of the theatre in order to earn a living. But, regardless of this
necessity and the awareness that their theatrical efforts will receive little
recognition from others, theatre is the focus of their lives. In such an environment, questions like 'what is the value of theatre?' and 'why make
theatre?' are not merely part of a larger metaphysical investigation of performance, as they are in most of Europe and the United States. These are
ever present, fundamental questions for most Latin American theatre
workers. These are also the very questions that Barba has wrestled with all
his professional life. Thus Latin America confronts him with his *raison
d'être*. The combination of his own preoccupations with the ever-present
need to address these same preoccupations in this vast continent forces
Barba continually to measure his work and the work of others against the
socio-political reality of theatre in Latin America.

Barba and his 'colony'

It is understandable, given the nature of Latin America's history with
Europe, that Barba has been accused by some of being a colonialist, of
being the European 'master' intent on enlightening the 'natives'. As one
might expect, he rejects any suggestion of imperialist-type motives in his
contacts with Latin America. But, there is little doubt that even though
the continent consists of many regional and national differences, it is the
'other' culture for Barba. In fairness to him, Barba's meeting with the
Latin American other is best characterized by negotiation rather than by
the typically colonial bipolar relationship of the dominant versus the subaltern. Between Barba's theatre culture and that of his Latin colleagues lies
what Homi Bhabha terms an 'in-between' space (1994: 22). This space
denies delineated borders between cultures. As Bhabha sees it, cultural
contact is marked by a discursive, negotiated territory rather than a clear
line in the sand that cannot be crossed. The discursive space for Barba and
his Latin American colleagues is a combination of the multicultural on
the one hand (i.e., the inclusion of separate, clearly identifiable cultures
existing side by side) and the intercultural or creolized relationship (con-
noting penetration and merging) on the other.

The Latin American performance culture is separate and independent from that of Barba's Odin practice. But, once the two cultures interact, or, as Bhabha would have it, negotiate their borders, the result has most often been a synthesized creolization. The Latin Americans who have worked most closely with Barba, such as Miguel Rubrio from Yuyuchkani and Cuatrotablas' Mario Delgado, have made elements of Barba's theatre practice their own; similarly, Barba's work is no longer what it was prior to his involvement with Latin America.

Contact and negotiation aside, Barba has been criticized, most especially at ISTA, for exoticizing the 'other'. Both at ISTA and in his relationship with Latin America, this criticism is rooted in Barba's authorial positioning and the perception that otherness entails passivity and a lack of agency.

Barba's relationship with Latin America is in many ways predicated upon a master discourse, a body of knowledge developed by him as a means of understanding performance and framing his theatre practice. As described above, Barba and his Odin colleagues do not merely perform and leave when touring in Latin America, they rather teach, lecture, conduct workshops, as well as encourage ongoing contact between themselves and local groups. They perceive themselves as the bearers of a knowledge that is worthy of transmission. Barba is the locus of this knowledge. His research led to its formulation, his writings explicate it, his actors practise it. Barba, and those who work closest with him, are the 'owners of a truth'.

Barba's authorial stance implies a division between the dominant and the submissive, between those who have the knowledge and those who do not. Given Latin America's colonial history, this division has echoes of what post-colonialist commentators like Rey Chow might characterize as that between the 'ignorant natives' and 'wise Europeans' (1993: 33). This division is hardly Barba's intention, but history's long shadow all too often assigns the best intentions to darkened corners. It is ironic that, in their desire to share what they have learned from years of research and experience, Barba and his Odin colleagues revive the ghosts of imperialism and reaffirm a bipolar difference between self and other.

Implicit in this bipolar construction of power is a passivity and lack of agency on the part of the other. This is because the Eurocentric bias that lies at the root of otherness implies a colonial rhetoric: the local other is subject to the protagonist, imperial self. The reality is more complex. Cultural interaction is a dialectic of sorts in which original cultures subsume, adapt, and/or incorporate cultural fragments each from the other with the potential of becoming creolized versions of their original selves. Creolization is the ultimate conclusion of the relationship between self and other and even if the so-called other culture is not an equal partner to the creolization, it is as capable of absorbing and discarding elements of the dominant culture as the latter is of appropriating and ignoring the former.

As Edward Said so rightly points out, questions of equality, the configurations of power, and ownership of knowledge are central to an understanding of the relations between cultures in contact (1979: 5). But Barba's relationship with Latin America is limited. It is a meeting between artists with a common creative passion, the theatre. This meeting hardly entails the sustained contact and array of potential socio-cultural conflicts ranging from one's world-view and fundamental belief structures to eating habits and fashion statements that mark contemporary multi-cultural societies.

Barba and those he is in most contact with in Latin America exchange, influence and negotiate a creative discourse that they both share. Within this creative discourse each appropriates, subsumes, adapts, co-opts, and absorbs from the other. Questions of who brings more and who benefits most from these interactions are difficult, if not impossible, to quantify, especially when the currency of exchange is a combination of aesthetic techniques and the world of ideas, while the traditional notions of majority and minority are inverted. The reciprocity of these exchanges only serves to confirm that, even though Barba is cast by some as the atavistic heir to European colonialism, his place in Latin America is much closer to a fellow other than it is to an imperial archetype.

Despite having celebrated his 65th birthday (29 October 2001), Barba remains deeply involved with his fellow artists in Latin America. Likewise, he continues his research and creative work with his ISTA and Odin colleagues. Given these ongoing commitments, it would seem reasonable to assume that he will continue to influence Latin American theatre through his teaching, writings, and productions, at least in the near future. Equally, it would seem reasonable to assume that he will continue to be influenced by Latin America, since it persistently forces him to re-evaluate his personal and professional ethos. This interaction stems primarily from the fact that Barba's notion of the Third Theatre is the reality of most Latin American group theatre: that is, theatre based on a duality in which the actor is at the centre of the creative process while the group is the central focus of the social dynamic. In this conception, making theatre is a way of life rather than a mere profession: so it is in much of Latin America, so it is for Eugenio Barba.

An earlier, shorter version of this chapter, entitled 'Eugenio Barba: The Latin American Connection', appeared in *New Theatre Quarterly*, Vol. 5, No. 17 (1989).

References

Barba, Eugenio (1985), *The Dilated Body*, trans. Richard Fowler. Rome: Zeami Libri.

Barba, Eugenio (1987), Personal communication to the author.

Barba, Eugenio (1996), 'The paradoxical space of theatre in multicultural societies' in the programme for the ISTA symposium 'Theatre in Multicultural Society' in Copenhagen, Denmark 9–11 May (no page numbers).

Bhabha, Homi K (1994), *The Location of Culture*. London and New York: Routledge.

Boal, Augusto (1979), *Theatre of the Oppressed*. New York: Urizon Books.

Buenaventura, Enrique (1978), 'Esquema general del método de trabajo colectivo Del Teatro Experimental de Cali', in *Popular Theatre for Social Change*, ed. by Gerardo Luzuriaga. Los Angeles: University of California, Latin American Center Publications: 42–66.

Chow, Rey (1993), 'Against the lures of Diaspora: minority discourse, Chinese women, and intellectual hegemony', in *Gender and Sexuality in Twentieth Century Chinese Literature*, ed. Tonglin Lu. Albany: State University of New York Press, pp. 23–45.

Hastrup, Kirsten (ed.) (1996), *The Performers' Village: Times, Techniques and Theories at ISTA*. Graasten, Denmark: Drama.

Luzuriaga, Gerardo (1986), 'El proceso de creación teatral según el modelo de La Candelaria', in *Gestos*, No 2.

Osinski, Zbigniew (1986), *Grotowski and His Laboratory*. New York: Performing Arts Journal Publications.

Peirano, Luis (1987), 'Notas sobre la creación teatral en America Latina', paper presented at the Seminario Regional sobre Creación Teatral en América Latina y Caribe, a UNESCO-sponsored conference on Latin American theatre held in Lima, Peru, 13–16 April, published in *Conjunto*, No. 73 (1987).

Said, Edward W. (1979), *Orientalism*. New York: Vintage Books.

Tunberg, Karl A. (1970), 'The new Cuban theatre', in *The Drama Review*, Vol. 14, No.,2, (T46): 43–55.

Watson, Ian (1993), *Towards a Third Theatre: Eugenio Barba and the Odin Teatret*. London and New York: Routledge.

13

The house with two doors
Eugenio Barba

This article was written by Barba in the Yucatan village of Chicxulub, Mexico during rehearsals for the Odin Teatret production *Talabot* in the early part of 1988. Barba specifically chose to begin rehearsals for his new production in Latin America in response to the growing importance of the continent on his work and ideas about theatre. He wanted to see what, if any, influence the region would have on the new production that he and his actors were about to embark upon. Given Barba's reflective and analytical bent, it is understandable that the three-month residency in Chicxulub led to more than a production that premiered later the same year in Holstebro. 'The house with two doors' is Barba's attempt to explain his relationship with Latin America and to context that relationship through his ongoing history with the continent and the dual notions of professional and personal identity that he feels lies at the heart of a deeply felt connection for him.

This article was first published in Spanish as 'La casa con dos puertas' in *La Escena Latinoamericana* No. 2 (Buenos Aires: Editorial Galerna/Lemcke Verlag: Kiel, 1989). (Ian Watson)

I feel as if everything I have learned in the theatre was somehow a preparation for Latin America.

For a European, Latin American theatre is both recognizable and unknown since it stems from European roots but is marked by its own history.

The *ethos* (i.e., the ensemble of social, political, existential, community and ethical behaviour), that characterizes Latin American theatre should always be present for those who question the meaning of theatre, no matter where.

The *ethos* is a series of answers-in-action to this question. It constitutes the theatre's third dimension. However, many think about the theatre in two dimensions, as if what mattered was only aesthetics, ideological tendencies, artistic results, or different techniques. The *ethos* is the dimension of depth, the measure of the relationship between one's individual history and History.

The bi-dimensional view does not specifically acknowledge the value of Latin American theatre. It does not consider geographical or cultural distance; it is the product of the same lack of subtlety that in Europe leads to whole areas of European theatre being ignored.

On a plane to Caracas, more than ten years ago

What is the meaning of making theatre nowadays in Latin America, in such a dramatic socio-cultural reality, where tensions are so high and tragedies so striking?

We were talking this way more than ten years ago, during a long night flight to Caracas. The answer seemed obvious and it was typical of an all too speedy reasoning that places instant blame on something or somebody.

'What a waste to organize a big international theatre congress! Isn't this a way of closing one's eyes to serious problems?'

The Odin Teatret and I were part of a group of actors, directors and authors invited to the Festival of Caracas, directed by Carlos Giménez and the International Theatre Institute (ITI) about the future of theatre in Third World countries. It was the spring of 1976.

'The future of theatre in Third World countries? Isn't this a good example of a senseless problem?'

Behind these rhetorical questions was the assumption that theatre could only nourish well-fed nations.

We were discussing carnivals. For us, as Europeans, carnivals are completely lost: 'Why should theatre, this art for export, be more potent than the rituals, celebrations, or popular and collective performances that thrive in Latin America?'

When our group of European actors, directors and authors got off the plane, we dispersed into the frenzied atmosphere of the festival. My Odin colleagues and I met a few key people and ended up staying in Venezuela longer than expected. We met with La Candelaria, whom we had hosted in Holstebro, Denmark, in 1971. We saw their production *Guadalupe años sin cuenta* the title of which, as Santiago García and his actors explained to us, is based on a word play in Spanish: *Sin cuenta* (without importance) also connotes *cincuenta* (fifty) [hence the piece, which is entitled 'Guadalupe, Years Without Importance', also has connotations of 'Guadalupe, Fifty Years', translator's note]. The piece was based on a fragment of unwritten, officially censored Colombian history, which was recreated with rage and irony; and, despite its depressing content, was thoroughly fulfilling because of the professional skills of the cast. The production was successful in the international milieu of the festival, even though it referred to a specific social reality. It not only told a story, it also managed to evoke the context in which this story had its fullest meaning.

We met Mario Delgado and his group Cuatrotablas from Lima for the first time. One morning, while we were in the headquarters of the Contradanza group, they showed us their new piece *La noche larga* (The Long Night). They told us it was a first step in their search for a new road. They were looking for a theatre perhaps less 'spectacular' than what they had been doing up to that point, yet closer to their dreams and personal obsessions. We had expected a theatre of auto-confessions. Instead, we saw a series of images, which were a reflection on the meeting among the diverse cultures in their nation. We have retained a close relationship since then.

We met the Teatro Libre de Bahía. Two years later, they hosted a couple of actors from the Odin for months.

We met the Libre Teatro Libre, directed by María Escudero, actually, only three actors from the original, much larger, disbanded group. Libre Teatro Libre from Córdoba had been well known for the quality of its artistic work and its political message. The new group of three actors presented *El rostro* (The Face): they were using self-referential irony to explore their tragedy. They were already on their way to exile.

In inviting us to Caracas, Carlos Giménez provided the Odin Teatret with an experience that became a turning point for us when, in keeping with our desires at the time, he gave us the opportunity to move outside the parameters of the festival. We did a few barters in working-class neighbourhoods of Caracas and in Barlovento, an area of black culture. These were centres where small cultural or theatre groups, inspired by our presence, felt free to define themselves in front of foreigners.

A film cooperative and several anthropologists took us into the Venezuelan Amazonas, to a Yanomami *shabono* (a high-walled wooden complex in the jungle which is village to an entire tribe), where we were received according to their rituals. We showed them all our pieces, even those that we used to perform for a reduced number of spectators on special occasions.

'It is not a good idea,' we said to the anthropologists when they originally invited us to come. 'Our theatre does not mean anything to the Yanomami. We will not be able to communicate with them.'

They answered that they wanted to present the Yanomami with a face of the white man they had never seen before, 'They have only seen missionaries, anthropologists, and government officials.' Here, theatre met ritual. It was the most incisive of barters: the representatives of a culture that believes in progress in front of a community on the verge of extinction.

Before going to Caracas, I thought I was well informed about Latin American theatre. I subscribed to *Conjunto* (the Cuban journal that focuses on Latin American theatre), knew the groups and personalities that appeared in international publications, and I had seen many productions in European festivals. I was under the impression that Latin America was an example of a 'low density' (and 'low need') theatre reality. After the first meetings with Latin American colleagues in Caracas, I realized that the phenomenon that had sprung up in Europe existed in their countries as well: a myriad of scattered groups, ignored by critics, and each driven by personal and social needs to invent its own theatre. There was a theatrical density that was surprising and underground. Just as in Europe, the group theatre movement in Latin America was invisible to the eyes of the bi-dimensional theatre.

I realized that there was a third dimension to the theatre: a Third Theatre.

The Third Theatre

My theatrical formation took place during the 1960s, in almost complete isolation. The Odin Teatret had camped outside the walls of the theatre. We did not choose this position. We did not share the avant-garde debates against the so called 'traditional theatre'. We were victims of circumstance. Sometimes somebody would come to visit us. Other times, we were invited inside the walls and we were praised for our diversity.

We felt we belonged to the same biological mutation as that of the Living Theater, Grotowski's Teatr-Laboratorium, the Open Theatre, the Bread and Puppet Theater, and Teatro Campesino. We were travelling the same road they had travelled or were still travelling. Others were talking to us through their books: Craig, Stanislavsky, Vakhtangov, Copeau, Artaud, Meyerhold, Decroux, Brecht, Sulerzhitsky, Osterwa ... they had kept to themselves or were left outside. Some years later, a great Italian satirical actor participated in one of our seminars in Holstebro. He was very successful commercially in his own country. But Dario Fo was also starting to camp outside. He was leaving the theatre establishment and positioning himself among the most radical leftist political organizations.

During the 1970s, it started to become crowded outside the walls of the theatre. Those outside were mostly groups. Generally speaking, these groups consisted of people who were not particularly interested in the 'true' theatre that was made within the walls. They wanted to form their own groups and make their own theatre. What were they searching for? They did not have a sophisticated education in the theatre; they were not attempting to be part of the 'avant-garde'. Many had seen the Living Theatre's work or had read Grotowski's book, had seen our work or had heard about it.

In September 1976, a few months after our trip to Caracas, UNESCO and the Theatre of Nations Festival of Belgrade (BITEF) gave me the opportunity to organize a conference on theatre research.

A theatre researching what? New forms, new languages, or maybe a new meaning to the theatre?

I combined the recent memory of Caracas with what I knew about group theatre; it wasn't a question of Europe or Latin America. It was necessary to prove the existence of a theatre that had no recognition thus far, a dimension of theatre that did not respect geographical borders. I invited European and Latin American theatre groups to Belgrade. None of the professional organizers had heard of them. These groups were not doing 'traditional theatre' nor could they be labelled avant-garde. Within the framework of the larger festival, they seemed to be the representatives of a 'minor' or marginal theatre. They were not. In order to show this, we ended the conference with a collective performance, right in the heart of Belgrade, that lasted the whole day from dawn on into the night. For the first time I used the term 'Third Theatre' to introduce these groups.

The Third Theatre does not indicate an artistic tendency, a 'school', nor a style. *It indicates a way of giving meaning to the theatre.* From the beginning of the twentieth century, many have posed the question – and still do – whether theatre can convey meaning in our times. I believe the question is not well formulated. Is it perhaps the theatre that sometimes *has* and at other times *loses* meaning, as one has or loses money? The problem is ours alone, because we are those who make theatre. The answers must be individual, embodied in our actions. The question is, are we able to give meaning to what we do?

Theatre research includes a search for meaning. How, otherwise, can we understand the work done by groups who are often autodidacts lacking the respect given those who enter our art in a recognizable manner? I am talking about groups that live as immigrants, who manage to earn the right to exist with their own sweat and for whom there are no schools.

Since the 1976 festival in Caracas, Latin America has became an essential point of reference for me. It keeps the questions about the meaning of my work alive. I was in Peru with the Odin in 1978, in Colombia in 1983, in Peru, Colombia and Mexico in 1984, in Argentina in 1985, again in Argentina and Uruguay in 1986, in Argentina, Uruguay, Brazil and Mexico in 1987. In addition to these long tours, each of which was between two and three months long and included performances as well as barters, I went alone many more times to Latin America to meet with groups, give seminars, travel, to see, and to learn. In 1987, I was there for a total of five months.

I am writing this article in a house on the outskirts of Chicxulub, on the coast of the Yucatan, where the Odin has retired for a few months to prepare our new production.

A Cuban colleague told me once: 'You are a Latin American who was born in exile.'

Is there any truth in this compliment? I believe so.

I grew up in the South of Italy. I became an adult in Norway, as an immigrant. I obtained my theatre education in Poland. The theatre I founded is Danish. Yet, I feel at home in the theatres of Latin America.

In Europe and in North America the theatre shells prevail. They are stone theatres, buildings/institutions where people are recruited according to the demands of particular productions, where one director comes after the other, and where continuity is dictated by the organizational structure of statutes, rules and legal recognition. In Latin America, the human theatre prevails. This type of theatre, that is for minorities elsewhere, occupies the entire panorama here. With the exception of a few metropolises like Mexico City, Rio de Janeiro, São Paulo and Buenos Aires, Latin American theatre is characterized by groups.

The differences between Latin American groups and their European counterparts are as important as their similarities. In Europe, fashion is very important. Some people saw the Third Theatre as a fashionable artistic trend, a novelty transformed into a 'genre'.

Latin American theatre groups have never enjoyed the favourable waves of fashion and are less influenced by its ebb and flow.

Generalizing, one could say that the European Third Theatre is an existential choice, a reaction to excess, indifference, and an artistic overabundance which is unable to convey a sense of urgency and necessity.

The Latin American Third Theatre is also an existential choice, but it is one that reacts against a situation of penury.

In Europe, many run the risk of being seduced by an apparent security. We are citizens of welfare democracies. We must appeal to our historic and existential conscience, both as human beings and professionals, to retain perspective on the precarious nature of our existence.

In Latin America you would have to be blind and deaf to forget it.

Easter 1987

In the 1970s I received a letter from Bahía Blanca, Argentina. Coral and Dardo Aguirre, the leaders of the group Teatro Alianza, told me about their work, their precarious life, and the importance of knowing that we existed: 'Do not forget that you live in a privileged situation.' Their theatre was attacked. They were beaten, one of their actresses was sexually abused and killed. Dardo and Coral were both jailed. They managed to save themselves through the road others had chosen as well: exile. They found themselves jobs playing violin with the Turin Symphony Orchestra. They stayed for about a year. In Turin and in the rest of Italy 'the war against the state' led by armed groups was in progress. 'Violence for violence, we'd better go back to ours,' they reasoned. They returned to Argentina in 1981.

In Bahía Blanca, with an effort akin to a miracle, they managed to organize a group theatre encounter in the vein of those begun in 1976 in Belgrade and continued in Bergamo (Italy), Madrid-Lekeitio (Spain), Ayacucho (Peru) and Zacatecas (Mexico). This meeting in Bahía Blanca was called *Primer encuentro de teatro antropológico* (first encounter of anthropological theatre). They invited groups from Mexico, Chile, Uruguay, Brazil, Argentina and also a group of Mapuche origin. They also invited the Odin Teatret. At the end of the Encounter, we went to Buenos Aires to perform and organize barters.

There was a military revolt in the capital. For three days the country feared that the rest of the army would join them. The shadow of yet another military coup darkened the horizon.

On Easter Sunday we were all in the Plaza de Mayo, including the Odin Teatret. There are situations in which one does not feel like a foreigner and following the days of threats and angst, there was euphoria. We were almost drunk with the joy of living such a historic act of justice: democracy's victory over the military.

The next day, the local papers made us understand that we had lived an appearance, a joke; the victory had been 'won' on *their* conditions.

Everything was in flux. Everything *could change* from one day to the next. The military forces' conditions were being accepted at the very moment we were excited about our triumph. We felt that our actions had no value, that we had no weight as individuals. The precariousness of the political reality transformed into an existential experience that was nesting in the heart of our identity.

How much fatherland does a theatre need?

Hans Meyer thought he was German. His countrymen told him he was a Jew. He migrated. He was seized by soldiers and the police of *his* country. He was taken to Auschwitz. He survived. He became a writer. He translated his name and made an anagram with his last name. This is how he became Jean Améry. Now his name is just like any other from Provence in France, the land of poets and medieval heretics that were exterminated at the beginning of the thirteenth century by the Catholic army which transformed France into a nation, a new fatherland.

Jean Améry devoted his work as a writer to remembering: 'All of this has happened, *therefore*, it can happen again.' He continued repeating it until too many people became impatient with him *still* talking about Auschwitz and its tragedies, which were *definitely* buried. While some historians were beginning to use scientific methods to demonstrate that Nazism had not been so different from other regimes of our times after all and that it deserved 'fairer' historical recognition, Jean Améry published *The Intellectual in Auschwitz*. In 1978, he committed suicide.

A chapter from his book is entitled 'How much fatherland does one man need?' In German there are two words for 'fatherland': *Vaterland* and *Heimat*, 'mother country', and 'home, the particular place one comes from'. These are not simply two different expressions, they are two different realities.

In Latin America I often hear 'What does it mean to be an Argentine …, a Peruvian …, a Colombian …, a Venezuelan? What does it mean to be Latin American?'

How much fatherland do we need? Let's try being more precise: how much *Vaterland* and how much *Heimat* do we need?

Let's now think in terms of theatre.

An awareness of how precarious and uncertain one's cultural identity is, historically speaking, threatens the soul. In many cultures they say that the soul always wants to escape. Men feel constantly threatened by 'a crisis of presence'. Something similar happens to us: the source of our creativity seems to exhaust itself when it does not reflect a history and a set of values with which we can identify. We want to discover our identity as members of a community rather than as individuals; to discover, that is, to reconstruct and restore, a past that we may call *ours* and to travel its many roads. But to go where?

This question confronts us with two problems. Above all, it puts us on guard because the path which turns back is but one side of the coin. Roots alone cannot guarantee anything, even if they are not the product of an illusion. The second problem is that of illusion itself.

It is true that there are some 'vital illusions'. But *when* are they vital and *how* vital are they? Furthermore, illusions are mortal. Many of those that we call 'old traditions' are mere illusions. They are nothing but roads surrounded by archaeological ruins. These 'old traditions' can help us a great deal because they retain traces of knowledge from many generations. However, we must decide upon the sense and direction to take. It is not the traditions that choose us, but it is us who choose them. A Frenchman may convert to Islam and an Indian may become a fabulous orchestra conductor of European classical music. The fact that one is born in a particular land to specific parents does not mean that one's identity is reduced to that land and to those parents.

How much fatherland (*Vaterland, Heimat*) do we need? How much capability of being or becoming foreigners do we need?

What does it mean to be a Bolivian, a Brazilian, a Uruguayan, a Latin American? And also, what does it mean not to be *only* Latin American, Italian, Danish?

I admit that I feel great respect, sometimes tenderness and almost always a certain degree of fear when I see a theatre group pursuing 'the traditions of their land', chasing the Incas, the Mayas, the Aztecs, the Indian cultures, the Basque traditions, the Greenlanders, the Welsh.

Atahualpa and the tradition-in-life

In the autumn of 1974, a Uruguayan director came to the Odin Teatret to study for a few months. His behaviour made a big impression on me. I could tell I had met a great master. This was the first time I heard of Atahualpa del Cioppo. Later, I found his traces in Latin America. Before meeting him, I used to associate him with Bertolt Brecht, partly because they shared a biographical coincidence: exile.

I saw him ten years later in Mexico. He is already more than eighty years old. He has worked extensively in many countries. He still travels a great deal. Despite all he has seen and all of those who have turned their backs on him, he still trusts men. Despite the firmness with which he supports his ideas, he remains curious and open to other people's choices.

Many masters from India or Japan maintain that tradition does not exist: 'I am the tradition. It starts and finishes with me.'

Atahualpa del Cioppo is a master because he is a tradition-in-life. He is living proof of how one can give sense and *Heimat* to one's theatre.

In 1987, UNESCO organized a conference on 'Dramaturgy in Latin America and the Caribbean' in Lima. One night, the Peruvians took the participants to see a performance on the outskirts of the city, in Villa El Salvador, a slum neighbourhood. What the locals managed to create won international recognition and even a recommendation for the Nobel Peace Prize. Villa El Salvador emerges from sand dunes alongside the seashore. After the outdoor performance, the director of the group, César Escuza, invited us for a drink. With emotion in his voice, he told Enrique Buenaventura: 'Our production is dedicated to you, because your writings and your example have guided us.'

Masters are only useful in helping others find their own road and helping them realize the multiplicity of the tradition-in-life.

A house with two doors

The search for an identity in Latin American theatres is realized in the relative absence of a theatre that maintains a continuity with its past.

There are different niches in European theatre. One of these is the so-called 'traditional theatre'. This type of theatre transmits and perpetuates European theatre from the past centuries. The artists and intellectuals who work in this niche refer to Molière, commedia dell'arte, Racine, Shakespeare, Chekhov or Beckett as part of an uninterrupted theatrical continuity.

This continuity does not exist in group theatre. Nevertheless, European theatre groups can be differentiated from 'traditional theatre'. Latin Americans, on the other hand, have nothing to differentiate themselves from. This is why the traditional and group theatres in Latin America share similarities and differences. They are similar because the working conditions are the same for both. They are different because their horizons are different. In Europe the walls of 'The Theatre' form the backdrop (and those who defect from the open space beyond the walls or who are tired from the effort it requires to remain outside them can always attempt to move inside). This is not the case in Latin America.

European groups may be defined by indicating the kind of theatre they do not do or do not want to do. Latin American groups, instead, can only be defined by what they do and their aspirations. This is not an obstacle in the search for an identity among those who make theatre in Latin America, however. A more serious impediment to the search is the alienation from one's ancestral home, from the reflections and testimonies of one's predecessors.

This does not mean that Latin America is short on reflections about the theatre. On the contrary, consider Enrique Buenaventura's and Augusto Boal's impact on one sector of theatre, even in Europe. Nevertheless, a series of circumstances have led to a lack of books. The writings of Dullin, Delsarte, Tairov, Eisenstein, not to mention Stanislavsky,

Meyerhold, Appia, Craig, Copeau, Vakhtangov, and Zeami have either not been published or have limited circulation.

Practical and creative work must be accompanied by knowledge of the past. Being aware of this need, a young director from Mexico City interrupted his budding artistic career to become a publisher. Edgar Ceballos arm wrestles with the ignorance that deprives the present from the breath of the past. He founded the publishing house Escenología, which publishes books on theatre history and practice. He also publishes the journal *La Máscara*, in memory of Gordon Craig's *The Mask*, in which the British director confronted the ignorance of European and eastern performance in the 1920s. Those were the years when the theatre identified itself almost exclusively with dramatic texts.

A sound knowledge of our history ('ours' as theatre workers, regardless of whether we come from Latin America or Europe) is even more necessary, given the fact that our creations and our working techniques last only as memory and must connect to a 'professional memory'.

When approximately twenty years ago, Comuna Baires began working in the margins of mainstream theatre in the Argentine capital, they also published a journal, *Teatro '70*. This journal published neither theatre reviews nor covered current theatre events; it was devoted to the diffusion of the theory and practice of theatre. In recent years, I have met many Latin American colleagues living in their own countries or who have migrated to Europe who maintain that it was this magazine which helped them discover the possible worlds of theatre.

On one hand, our identity is individual, it derives from our biography, from the space and time in which we live. On the other, it is a professional identity, which is free of the limitations of space and time that links people in our profession. It is a matter of two different poles. One cannot exist without the other.

We can imagine the poles as the two doors of the same house, doors to go in and also to go out of when the walls of the house begin shrinking. A poem by Brecht contains a line that belongs to the wisdom of exile: 'Make sure that your house always has two doors.' It refers to sudden escapes, to the fact that one must protect his obligation to resist no matter what. This poem has another significance for those who search for meaning through theatre and who do not accept the world (not even the theatre world) the way it is.

The long night

In 1986, in the Festival of Montevideo, I saw *Lo que está en el aire* (What is in the Air) by the Chilean group ICTUS. 'Ictus' means 'fish' in Greek. It is the Messiah's sign that those who were persecuted exchanged secretly among themselves to recognize each other. The fish is also the symbol of life that moves in the depths. *Lo que está en el aire* was a paradoxical and realistic spectacle. It was a metaphorical story that represented a suffocating reality but, despite this, it defended the possibility of dignity beyond tragedy.

I once asked the Chilean actor and director Héctor Noguera, 'How is it possible that they allow you to make this kind of theatre?' and 'What is the purpose?' He explained that his theatre is no threat to the regime, that its harmless face does not threaten the meaning they give to their work. 'We,' he said, 'Do not produce work against *this* Chile. We work for the parallel Chile.' I was surprised he referred to space rather than time when talking about the future, mentioning a reality parallel to the one he and others like him remain alienated from.

Maybe this is why the actor Roberto Parada refused to cancel the performance the night he was informed during intermission that paid assassins from the Acción Pacificadora (Pacifying Action) had killed his son.

A few months ago, Amnesty International informed the world that the members of the group ICTUS, along with other theatre professionals, had received death threats unless they left the country. They stayed during the long night.

La noche larga was the title of the production by the Peruvian group Cuatrotablas that we saw in Caracas in 1976, when Latin American theatre entered the Odin Teatret's life.

We spent time with Cuatrotablas in 1978, when they organized the meeting of Latin American group theatre in Ayacucho. At that time there was turmoil in the Andean towns due to price increases imposed by the military government. A curfew was ordered. Despite the precarious circumstances, the members of Cuatrotablas did not bend. The curfew did not affect the meeting, nor the presentation of performances during the day.

Times are changing but not necessarily improving. Too many fashions have taken over the bi-dimensional theatre. Some roads of research have opened themselves to me and to the Odin Teatret. We have founded ISTA (the International School of Theatre Anthropology). This has led to the misconception that the Third Theatre phase is finished for us. On the contrary, its meaning remains intact.

When one speaks of influences

I can imagine some readers thinking of a new European influence on Latin American theatre, this time in the guise of 'Odinism'. This is how the automatisms of bi-dimensional thinking operate in the theatre, with its cult of so-called 'originality'.

I was in Latin America in 1973, not for theatre-related reasons. I simply travelled by bus from Cochabamba through the Andes up to the jungle, Iquitos, Leticia from Barranquilla through the Caribbean up to Panama, and then again by bus through Central America to Mexico.

Many of my experiences on that trip, the moments of fear and indignation, reappeared in our production *Come! And the Day Will be Ours* that we presented for the first time in Caracas in 1976. The piece was about the meeting between European immigrants and the natives of North America.

Throughout this trip away from the theatre, I kept thinking about two Spaniards, Gonzalo Guerrero and Jerónimo de Aguilar, who were captured by the Mayas when their ship sank in 1511 on the Yucatan shores. Following their capture, they embraced Mayan culture and became prestigious military men as well as important citizens. When Cortés arrived, Jerónimo de Aguilar rejoined his Spanish compatriots and provided them with valuable information about the language and the customs of the locals. Gonzalo Guerrero behaved differently. He chose his second fatherland and remained with his Mayan wife and children who were the beginning of a new race. He died, shot by a Spanish gun, in 1536, fighting against the soldiers whose cultural origins and roots he shared. Gonzalo Guerrero and Jerónimo de Aguilar represent the two alternatives which come to mind when we think about the meeting among peoples who come from far-off lands: conquest or assimilation.

Who could imagine the Odin Teatret as a group assimilated into Latin American theatre? Nevertheless, the people we have met in Latin America, the theatre groups with whom we have established relationships – through their histories, their performances, and their different cultural contexts – have marked us and our work profoundly. Both *The Million* and *Come! And the Day Will be Ours* were interwoven with Latin American memories and experiences. *Brecht's Ashes*, which was primarily reflections on recent European history and the exile of an intellectual, was nourished by the same anxieties permeating much of Latin America. *Oxyrhincus Evangeliet* (Oxyrhincus is the name of an Egyptian city where important Gnostic texts were discovered) had its roots in our reinvention of the popular riots in Canudos, images of the Brazilian *sertão* and its outlaws, Guimaraes Rosa's visions, Euclides da Cunha's meticulous prose, and *La Guerra del Fin del Mundo* (The War of the End of the World) by Vargas Llosa. Other Latin American presences in our theatre lie in the actors' technique and their practical work. These latter influences are more difficult to explain in words. I will only mention the samba, the way we saw it, remodelled by an actor from Bahía's Teatro Libre, which inspired our training.

If it made any sense at all to discuss 'influences', I should say that in the encounter with Latin American theatre, the Odin Teatret was the one most influenced. However, I believe this is the wrong way of characterizing things.

Gonzalo Guerrero and Jerónimo de Aguilar are not the only possible alternatives. Through the second door in the house, that of profession, a common identity enters. It is hard to tell whose is what. It is especially difficult to distinguish the contributions of one's own culture from influences outside it. Everything we do in the theatre belongs to our professional *Heimat*, the place where we theatre workers are at home.

The members of Cuatrotablas had not seen *Come! And the Day Will be Ours* when they invited us to Caracas to see their production. They had worked in Lima. We had worked in Holstebro. Their actors were Peruvian, ours were all Scandinavian, except for one Italian. Yet we found many elements in *La noche larga* that were very similar to those in our piece, while two or three of our most original solutions were also evident in Cuatratablas's presentation. If time and distance had not made it impossible, someone might have thought one of the two had taken inspiration from the other's work.

When two theatres share characteristics, critics and experts begin rumours very quickly. You can hear words like '*déjà vu*', 'copy', 'bad copy', 'influence', 'imitation', 'acculturation'. Sometimes the rumours become screams, judgements and damning criticism. This is how life in certain theatres is seriously threatened.

A pure Latin American, Brazilian, European, Danish, Florentine or Madrilenean theatre cannot exist. It is not purity that guarantees identity and cultural originality. On the other hand, professional identity has an unavoidable character that cannot be mistaken: its 'transculturality'.

In discussing influences, I would like to clarify something: do not worry if you rely on another briefly. Your paths will eventually separate. Do not concern yourself with similarities. This is the way it is in the flux of life. Everything that is alive ends up finding its own way. Do not obstruct the life of the theatre with ghosts that do not take into consideration the dimension of *ethos*. Only the dead are, in the end, alike.

This article was translated from Spanish by Susana Epstein.

14

The Third Theatre: a legacy of independence

Ian Watson

The Third Theatre, a concept first suggested by Eugenio Barba in 1976, is an idea that was born in Europe but one that has been subsequently shaped by Latin America. Barba's notion of Third Theatre was initially an attempt to context and theorize the independent group theatre movement that exploded in Europe and Latin America during the late 1960s and on into the 1970s. The Third Theatre Manifesto, presented by Barba at the first international gathering of independent group theatres he organized in Belgrade, Yugoslavia in 1976, defined the Third Theatre by differentiating it from what he terms the first and second theatres. Barba characterized the first theatre as an institutionalized activity that is '… protected and subsidized because of the cultural values that it seems to transmit, appearing as a living image of a creative confrontation with the texts of the past and the present' (1986: 193). This is the world of a state-supported and/or a commercial theatre that society embraces as 'Art'. In the Euro-American orbit it is the Royal Shakespeare Company, the Berliner Ensemble, the British repertory system, the regional theatre network in the United States, the State Theatres of Germany, as well as much of the West End and Broadway. His second theatre is the avant-garde. It is a theatre predicated upon 'experimenting, researching, arduous or iconoclastic, a theatre of changes, in search of a new originality' (1986: 193). This is the theatre of Richard Foreman, of Robert Wilson's early years, of Tanztheatre, Tadashi Suzuki and Steven Berkoff. The Third Theatre is, on the other hand, one that:

> lives on the fringe, often outside or on the outskirts of the centers and capitals of culture. It is a theatre created by people who define themselves as actors, directors, theatre workers, although they have seldom undergone a traditional theatrical education and therefore are not recognized as professionals.
>
> But they are not amateurs. Their entire day is filled with theatrical experience, sometimes by what they call training, or by the preparation of performances for which they must fight to find an audience. (Barba, 1986: 193)

This is a theatre in which vocation has usurped profession. Without appearing to romanticize, making theatre for those in the Third Theatre is a way of life, it is not merely a means of expression or earning a living. It is the theatre of Barba's own company, Odin Teatret; it is also the theatre of what in 1976 was Spain's Teatro Independiente (a movement consisting of over ninety groups at the time), a similar phenomenon in Italy made up of more than one hundred groups, and the ubiquitous independent theatre groups of Latin America.

The Third Theatre is a concept arrived at by negation. A type of theatre exists, it is neither the first nor the second theatres, therefore it must be a third type of theatre. For some, this characterization of 'thirdness' implies an inferior status. It flirts with connotations of a Third World reality in which Third Theatre signifies living a hand to mouth existence, lacking a sense of artistic identity, and subsistence survival in the shadows of the far more successful first and second theatres which it secretly wishes to be part of.

To be fair to Barba, this criticism stems more from linguistic happenstance than it does from his understanding of Third Theatre. Classification frequently implies status. To be number three can (though it need not) be read as lesser than one and two. To be third rings of the comparative; first and second are clearly superior in this tune. But Barba is not measuring the attributes of one theatre against another. He merely describes and contrasts three types of theatre in his definition of Third Theatre and nowhere in this discussion does he argue that one theatre is superior to another. He classifies without recourse to a hierarchy.

Despite his attempts to avoid ranked classification, Barba has acknowledged that there is a Third World connotation in his concept of Third Theatre. But he argues that this connotation owes its origins to the discrimination found in both, rather than in equating Third Theatre with a Third World sense of inferiority or its citizens' desire to become part of the First World (1977: 2–3). In the late 1970s Barba even went so far as to identify the sense of discrimination frequently associated with the Third World as a defining characteristic of Third Theatre: 'The groups that I call Third Theatre do not belong to a lineage, to a theatrical tendency. But they do live in a situation of discrimination: personal or cultural, professional, economical or political' (1977: 160–1).

Much of Barba's early thinking on the Third Theatre was done in the context of a diaspora of sorts. Independent groups were springing up in many parts of the world with little contact among them. In his attempt to explain this phenomena he coined the famous metaphor of floating islands in which the groups were 'Like islands without contact between themselves' (19977: 146). The diaspora has changed little in the near quarter of a century since Barba first presented his Third Theatre Manifesto, but much has changed with regard to the contact between the groups and in the nature of those who constitute the Third Theatre.

A major factor in the contact among the groups has been the international group theatre meetings, which are discussed in greater depth below. The meetings have brought many of the leading independent groups together for periods of a few weeks to study, network, and discuss their ideas on theatre. In doing so they have done much to address the isolation of the groups and to affect the relationships among them. In addition to promoting contact, the meetings have encouraged groups to become better trained, to broaden their scope of interests, and to pay greater consideration to aesthetics.

These developments have led to Barba reassessing his notion of Third Theatre. He acknowledges that the Third Theatre is no longer concerned with a particular style of theatre, a single ideology, or alliance of groups bonded together by discrimination. For Barba, the modern Third Theatre is one in which its members are concerned with meaning: 'Today it is clear to me that the essential character of the Third Theatre is the autonomous construction of meaning which does not recognize the boundaries assigned to our craft by the surrounding culture' (1999: 222). The defining characteristic of the Third Theatre is no longer simply its difference from the institutionalized mainstream and the avant-garde. It may, dependent upon circumstances, remain outside these realms or not.[1] Regardless of its relationships, those in the Third Theatre are concerned with exploring and cultivating a language of performance that gives 'an

---

1 There are a number of groups in Latin America which negotiate the borders between the first and Third Theatres or the second and Third Theatres. These negotiations are the product of two interdependent factors in much of the continent. There is little state support for theatre in Latin America and because of this theatre is dominated by independent groups. Galpón in Uruguay, for instance, which produced an array of plays both contemporary and classical during more than twenty years of existence, was for many years thought of as an important voice in Uruguayan culture while at the same time being part of the Third Theatre. Cuatrotablas in Peru is much the same today, as is Teatro Escambray in Cuba and La Candelaria in Colombia.

autonomous meaning for the action of doing theatre' (Barba, 1999: 219) rather than succumbing to commercial considerations or current trends in the avant-garde.

Third Theatre and the international group theatre meetings

The international group theatre meetings have been central to Barba's conceptual understanding of the Third Theatre. As already mentioned, it was during the first of these gatherings that Barba formulated his ideas on the Third Theatre. The meetings have become a response to his metaphorical characterization of Third Theatre as disparate islands. The gatherings bring the islands together in an affirmation of their shared identity. And it has been the shift in locus of these meetings from Europe to Latin America that has had much to do with his re-evaluation of Third Theatre.

As with his notion of Third Theatre, Barba's impetus for and realization of the international group theatre meetings was rooted in his European experience. The first gathering from 21–29 September, 1976, The International Workshop of Theatrical Research, was mounted within the framework of the Theatre of Nations Festival in Belgrade, Yugoslavia under the auspices of UNESCO and the International Theatre Institute (ITI). The two events were juxtaposed, as if in affirmation of Barba's definition of Third Theatre. The main festival included productions by established directors such as Yuri Lyubimov from Moscow's famous Taganke Theatre (*Hamlet, Here the Dawns Are Quiet*, and *Ten Days That Shook the World*), the Paris-based Peter Brook (*The Ik*), Germany's Peter Zadek (*Othello*), Jean-Louis Barrault from France (*La Vie Offerte*) and Poland's Andrezej Wajda (*The Danton Case*) as well as avant-garde pieces by Robert Wilson (*Einstein On The Beach*), Mabou Mines (*The Saint and The Football Players*), and Barba's own Odin Teatret (*Come! And The Day Will Be Ours*). In contrast, excluding the Odin, which already had an international reputation at the time, the meeting of group theatres consisted of small, relatively unknown companies, none of whom performed individually for the public during the Theatre of Nations Festival (though they did, as described in 'The house with two doors', perform collectively on one occasion). These groups included, among others, the Cardiff Laboratory Theatre (Wales), Akademia Ruchu (Poland), Cuatrotablas (Peru), Teatro Núcleo and Libre Teatro Libre (Argentina), El Théâtre Elementaire de Bruselas (Belgium), as well as Teatro di Ventura, Teatro Tascabile di Bergamo and El Centro per la Sperimentazione e la Ricerca Teatrale di Pontedera (all from Italy).

Barba not only organized the Belgrade meeting, he designed the programme which was made up of workshops with master performers (such as the Odin actors, Woiciech Krukowski from Akademia Ruchu, and the Balinese performer Tapa Sudana), lecture/demonstrations in which various groups presented their work methods and techniques, seminars headed by Barba, Jerzy Grotowski and the director of Cuatrotablas, Mario Delgado, the screening of films on theatre, and performances by the groups. The programme also provided ample opportunity for informal encounters among those from the Third Theatre who up to that point had rarely had the opportunity to meet each other. This networking was, arguably, one of the most valuable aspect of the meeting because the encounters over coffee or a few drinks personalized the shared experiences. Difficulties were aired, successes talked about and professional contacts were made that led in many cases to tours or the ongoing exchange of ideas via mail or at following meetings. As Barba might have put it, the islands were in touch with each other.

The success of the Belgrade gathering and the enthusiasm it generated among participants ensured that it was not going to be the last. The second of what has proved to be many meetings, was held from 28 August to 6 September 1977 in Bergamo, Italy under the title of The International Workshop of Group Theatre. The meeting's programme, which mirrored the format of its predecessor, was designed once again by Barba. But despite the similarities in programming, there were two major departures from the inaugural gathering. The first was that Barba was no longer the sole organizer of the event. A group from Bergamo, which had been in Belgrade, Teatro Tascabile, took over the local arrangements under Barba's guidance. The second departure from Belgrade was that the gathering did not have the support of a prestigious arts festival. UNESCO and ITI sponsored the event, as they had the previous year, but the first meeting's success meant that the groups did not need the legitimacy of the first and second theatres to mount an event with international aspirations. Apart from Italy, groups or individual participants came from Spain, Britain, Denmark, Poland, the United States, Peru and Cuba. Once again, Grotowski, whose aesthetics and theatre ethics were an inspiration to so many of the groups, led a seminar; and the role of Asia was enhanced from the Bergamo meeting with the inclusion of masters from Noh theatre (Hideo Kanze), Topeng (I Made Bandem), and Kathakali (Krishnan Nambudiri).

This second meeting of Third Theatre groups, though early in the movement's history, was already establishing patterns, if not traditions, of organization that were to shape later gatherings and the very understanding of Third Theatre itself. The marginalization that is so central to the very idea of Third Theatre, was doubly emphasized in Bergamo. Those who attended had not only turned their backs on the first and second theatres, many of them, as ITI's Jean-Jacques Daetwyler pointed out in his report on the meeting, were from social minorities in their own cultures. These minorities included Eskimos from Greenland, Basques from Spain, urban indigenous Peruvians, Uruguayan émigrés living in Europe, and even one representative of the physically impaired, a deaf actor from the Paris-based theatre of the deaf, The International Visual Theatre (Daetwyler, 1977: 19). In keeping with a marginalized theatre whose members are frequently isolated from each other or from teachers, the Bergamo meeting once again emphasized the sharing of techniques and work methods. Various individuals, including all of the Asian masters, as well as members of the Roy Hart Theatre and The International Visual Theatre, taught or led lecture/demonstration sessions in Bergamo. These teaching sessions were once again augmented with a variety of less structured informal contacts. This networking often played as crucial a role in the long-term relationships among the groups as the more formal activities in the programme.

As important as the celebration of marginalization, teaching and networking have been to the international group theatre meetings and the Third Theatre, arguably the most significant development for the future of both was the emergence of potential leaders within the movement. Prior to the Bergamo gathering, Barba and his Odin Teatret were the embodiment of Third Theatre. The Odin epitomized the Third Theatre, Barba gave it a context and theorized it. But a number of groups who had been in Belgrade returned for the Bergamo meeting. Some from these groups, which included, among others, Akademia Ruchu, the Cardiff Theatre Laboratory, the Roy Hart Theatre and the local organizers of the event, Teatro Tascabile di Bergamo, have in subsequent years become leading figures in the Third Theatre movement. But one stands out above all others, Mario Delgado, the director of the Peruvian group Cuatrotablas. He, more than anyone other than Barba, was going to help shape the notion of Third Theatre (especially in Peru and other parts of Latin America), the future of the independent group theatre meetings, and even Barba's role in them.

Third Theatre and Latin America

As described in 'The house with two doors', Delgado met Barba in 1976 during the Odin's first performances in Latin America at an international theatre festival in Caracas, Venezuela. Barba recognized a kindred spirit in Delgado and invited him and his group to take part in the first Third Theatre gathering he was planning for later that year. Delgado was intrigued by what he witnessed in Belgrade and returned with Cuatrotablas for the Bergamo meeting the following year.

Delgado is, among other things, a man of vision. His experience of a Latin American reality dominated in the mid-1970s by military dictatorships, economic hardship, and a Third World mentality in which theatre was mostly regarded as the irrelevant activity of a tiny, unimportant minority, was tempered by a love of his craft and the dream of what theatre could be. Against a backdrop of penury, indifference and political instability Delgado organized the third meeting of independent theatre groups in Ayacucho, Peru in 1978. This meeting, in an Andean city of some 100,000 citizens 400 miles south-east of Lima, though directed at Peruvian and other Latin American groups, was based on the European models that preceded it. Barba assisted Delgado with organization and played a major role in designing a programme which Delgado insisted should emphasize teaching above all else because he felt that it was important for the Latin Americans to be exposed to the techniques and work methods of their more experienced European colleagues. Given Delgado's implicit acknowledgment of professional superiority on the part of the Europeans, it is ironic that the locus of these meetings, and the Third Theatre that underlies them, has shifted to Latin America. Since the Ayacucho gathering in 1978, there have been six international group theatre meetings, all but one of them has been mounted in Latin America.[2]

The focal shift of Third Theatre from Europe to Latin America was prompted by several factors. First and foremost was the proliferation of theatre groups and the important role some of them played in the cultural life of their local communities as well as further afield. There was little to no government support of theatre anywhere in Latin America in the 1970s and it was only in major cities like Buenos Aires, Mexico City and Rio de Janiero that a commercial theatre of any consequence survived. This lack of support led to the emergence of independent groups that gradually came to dominate the theatre scene in many parts of the continent. It is from these groups that some of the most original and important Latin American theatre artists have emerged; artists such as Atahualpa del Chioppo (from Galpón in Uruguay), Santiago García

---

2   The sole European meeting, The 4th International Third Theatre Encounter, took place from 9 October to 4 November 1979 and was divided between Madrid and the Basque city of Lekeito. The Madrid section of the gathering consisted of workshop demonstrations, seminars, the screening of films on theatre and performances open to the public. The Lekeito programme, which, following the Bergamo model, was organized by Barba and a local group from Lekeitio, Txiruliruli. It was framed as an encounter between groups from Scandinavia and the Basque region. In keeping with its encounter rubric, this part of the gathering placed a much greater emphasis on training, workshops and the sharing of theatre techniques and methods than did the earlier three days in Madrid.

(founding director of La Candelaria in Colombia), Enrique Buenaventura (director of Teatro Experimental de Cali, Colombia), Antunes Filho (from Macunaíma, Brazil), Augusto Boal (of Brazil's Teatro de Arena), Miguel Rubio (Yuyachkani, Peru), and Delgado, all of whose productions and ideas on theatre have extended far beyond the confines of their homelands. These men are but the tip of an iceberg, however. In 1979, Buenaventura estimated that there were more than 2000 groups in Colombia alone (1979: 34). Many of the better-known groups are still in existence. Most have faced political and social discrimination, and all are confronted with an economic reality that would force the closure of their theatres in the United States or Europe. Few actors, directors and designers in Latin America can support themselves through their theatrical endeavours. The majority work as therapists, doctors, lawyers, teachers, even manual workers in order to put food on their tables. But their true vocation is theatre, to which they devote most of their energies. Making theatre is a necessity for these people in a way that it rarely is in the First World. This necessity is, as I suggested earlier in 'Barba's other culture', at the heart of Barba's notion of Third Theatre.

While independent groups came to dominate Latin American theatre, similar groups in Europe lost much of their early impetus. The late 1960s on into the early 1980s witnessed a rise in the number of theatre groups throughout much of Europe. The explosion of idealism and apparently boundless creative drive inherent in the coming of age of the 1960s generation had fostered a plethora of theatre groups in Europe and the United States. These groups were inspired by the revolutionary spirit in the air and by models like those of the Living Theatre, The Polish Laboratory Theatre, the Open Theatre and the Odin.

The fate of the models is telling. Lack of money, internal squabbles, a need to move on creatively and shifts in socio-cultural dynamics in the intervening years has witnessed the end of the Polish Lab Theatre and the Open Theatre while The Living Theatre has splintered and struggles on as a mere shadow of its former self. Barba's group remains intact, but it has shifted much of its attention from Europe to Latin America and become a research centre as much as a company mounting productions.

The one in four survival rate of the models is mirrored in the fates of lesser-known theatre groups. Many of these lesser-known groups have fallen by the wayside and new generations of artists seem to be more drawn to the mainstreams of conservatory training, the security of the first theatre, or the artistic demands of the second theatre than to the challenges of the Third Theatre. Much of the vitality that marked the latter during the 1970s and 1980s in Europe and the United States has been drained.

The shift in focus of the Third Theatre from Europe to Latin America was further consolidated in a change in leadership dynamics. While directors like Delgado and others in Latin America were taking up the challenge of organizing gatherings, fostering networks of independent groups and encouraging the teaching of skills and techniques, Barba's interests had moved elsewhere. In 1979 he founded the International School of Theatre Anthropology (ISTA) to research the connections between traditional Asian performance and contemporary Western theatre. The first ISTA conference was held the following year in Bonn, Germany and even though its organizational structure was in part modelled on Third Theatre meetings, its intercultural research agenda was a far cry from the primary concerns of the Third Theatre. There have been twelve ISTA conferences since the first in 1980. Barba, along with local facilitators and financial backers, has organized all of them. In the same period, there have been six Third Theatre encounters, five of which, as mentioned earlier, were held in Latin America. Most of these meetings were organized by local groups with incrementally less input from Barba. In one case, the Third Theatre gathering in Zacatecas, Mexico in 1981, Barba did not even attend. In the same time period Barba has written only one article on the Third Theatre (1999) while he has published two important books devoted to Theatre Anthropology (Barba, 1995; Barba and Savarese, 1991).

Third Theatre and Peru

The Third Theatre movement in Latin America has been centred in Peru. This is entirely due to the leadership role and organizational skills of Delgado. Following the first meeting in 1978, he initiated and helped organize three subsequent gatherings in Peru and was an organizational adviser to the Zacatecas meeting. The only gathering he did not take part in was the 1987 encounter in Bahía Blanca, Argentina which was mounted by a local group, Alianza, with assistance from Barba and several other of his European colleagues.

The Bahía Blanca gathering, *Encuentro Internacional de Teatro Antropológico* (The International Encounter of Anthropological Theatre) was held from 6–12 April, 1987. This meeting echoed the Lekeitio portion of the Madrid/Lekeitio gathering mounted almost ten years earlier which centred on an exchange between groups from Scandinavia and the Basque region of Spain (for more details on this meeting see note 2). Rather than inviting any of Latin America's leading theatre groups, the organizers planned an encounter between relatively new, inexperienced groups from the predominantly rural south of Latin America (Argentina and Chile) and experienced members of the Third Theatre from Europe. The Europeans were led by members of Barba's own Nordisk Teaterlaboratorium, including actors from Odin, Farfa and The Canada Project, who were accompanied by two Italian groups, Potlach and Tascabile di Bergamo. It was the Europeans' job to teach skills, to show their work and training, and to exchange ideas and techniques, as well as to encourage the Latin Americans to share their knowledge and experience. The reciprocity between colleagues from two separate continents was facilitated by the Encuentro's flexible programme of training, demonstrations, performances and formal as well as informal discussion sessions.

The Zacatecas meeting (10–21 October, 1981), *V Coloquio Internacional de Teatro de Grupo* (The 5th International Colloquium of Group Theatre) grew out of the first Ayacucho gathering. The main organizers of the event, the Mexican group La Rueca, had attended the Peruvian meeting and saw its virtue for Mexico. With organizational help from La Universidad Autónoma de Zacatecas and La Universidad Autónoma de Chapingo as well as financial support from UNESCO, La Rueca's Aline Menassé and Susana Frank designed a programme modelled on the earlier Peruvian gathering with a great deal of help and guidance from Delgado. As in Ayacucho, the primary thrust of the meeting was pedagogical, with many of Mexico's small, experienced groups having the opportunity to attend workshops and seminars led by their more experienced colleagues from Latin America (Cuatrotablas, Peru; Teatro Taller de Colombia, Colombia), Europe (El Temps Fort, France; Farfa, Italy; The Roy Hart Theatre, Britain), and the United States (The Talking Band).

Despite the importance of the meetings in Zacatecas and Bahía Blanca, the gatherings that are central to an understanding of the shifts in Third Theatre, and particularly Barba's place within those shifts, are those Delgado organized in Peru under the name of Ayacucho. There have been three such meetings, the first, as already mentioned, in 1978, and two subsequent meetings at ten-year intervals (i.e., one in 1988 and another in 1998). The only other gathering organized in Peru was the *VII Encuentro Internacional de Teatro de Grupo* (The 7th International Encounter of Group Theatre) held in Cuzco from 24 October – 1 November, 1987. This was a small-scale gathering of primarily Latin American groups called by Delgado as a precursor to the more ambitious and significant *Reencuentro Ayacucho '88*, which he was organizing for the following year to mark the tenth anniversary of the first Third Theatre meeting on Latin American soil.

Given that Lima is the national and cultural capital of Peru as well as where Delgado and his company, Cuatrotablas, are based, it would have seemed an obvious location for the first Third Theatre meeting in Latin

America. Lima is, however, also home to the first and second theatres in Peru. In keeping with the marginalization of Third Theatre, Delgado chose a location outside of the capital but, as one might expect, the choice was not a casual one.

Ayacucho has a deep significance for Peruvians. It is an Andean city, a city of the mountain range that is deeply embedded in what it means to be a Peruvian. But, the city's links to the Peruvian soul are not limited to an accident of cartography. Ayacucho and the region surrounding it (which shares the city's name) are also interwoven historically with Peru's national identity through their importance to the country's independence struggle. It was from the Ayacucho region that Peru's first noteworthy revolt against the Spanish Conquistadors was launched, by the legendary Inca leader Túpac Amaru, in the late sixteenth century. In keeping with Túpac Amaru's courageous stand against colonial hegemony, one of the celebrated figures of the later struggle for independence from Spain was from Ayacucho. María Parado de Bellido, a citizen of the city who was deeply involved with the independence fight, was captured by local colonial authorities and sentenced to death if she did not reveal the whereabouts of the rebel army. She staunchly refused, choosing to sacrifice her own life rather than betray her colleagues. Bellido has become a figure of near mythical proportions deeply interwoven with the Peruvian sense of nationhood. So much so, that even today her trial and execution at the hands of the colonial authorities is periodically re-enacted in Ayacucho's main square.

Ayacucho is also the site of what is often regarded as the most important battle in Latin America's struggle for independence against Spain. Simón Bolívar, who, along with San Martín, is regarded as one of the fathers of Latin American independence, occupied the Ayacucho region in the early part of the ninteenth century. On 9 December 1824, Bolívar's troops, under the command of General Sucre, confronted the Spanish army led by General La Serna on the *Pampa de Quinua* (the Quinua Plain). Sucre defeated the Spanish in what has become known as the Battle of Ayacucho. This battle is frequently cited as the most significant in the war of independence because, following their defeat, the Spanish withdrew from Peru and eventually the whole of Latin America.

The city of Ayacucho is inextricably linked to Peru's independence because, not only did the battle that finally defeated the Spanish take place in the Ayacucho region, but it also led to the region's main city taking the same battle's name. Prior to the Battle of Ayacucho, the region's largest town was called Huamanga. But, following the victory, Bolívar officially changed the name to Ayacucho in honour of the city's and region's roles in the independence of Latin America. The name Huamanga lingers, especially in some of the older institutions, such as the city's university, La Universidad Nacional de San Cristóbal de Huamanga, which was founded in 1677, but the name bestowed by Bolívar is the one most deeply associated with Peru's identity as a nation.

The significance of location for Delgado became even more obvious when he organized *Reencuentro Ayacucho '88*. The meeting, which was held from 19–20 November 1988, could not be held in Ayacucho because the city was in the grip of the notorious *Sendero Luminoso* (Shining Path) guerrillas. It was unsafe to travel to the city so Delgado was forced to find an alternative location. He chose the relatively safe Huampaní vacation and conference centre near the small town of Chaclacayo, about twenty-five miles from Lima. Despite this move, Delgado insisted on retaining the name of Ayacucho in the meeting's title: *Reencuentro Ayacucho '88: the Eighth International Meeting of Group Theatre*. This insistence was not only in deference to the meeting ten years earlier but also to the importance of Ayacucho for Peruvians.

Encuentro Ayacucho '98 was planned as the twentieth anniversary of the original meeting and to commemorate the success of the Huampaní gathering. It was also a celebration of much wider meaning for the country as a whole, because not only was it possible to return to the site of the original meeting, but the site had gained even greater significance for Peruvians in the intervening years. Following the 1980s, the Ayacucho region was no longer only a part of Peru's independence history, it had become a symbol of Peru's struggle with terrorism because of its direct associatiation with the most notorious and successful of Peru's terrorist organizations, *Sendero Luminoso*. Sendero's leader, Abimail Guzmán, began his campaign of terror in Ayacucho. He was a philosophy professor and dean of students at the city's university. He used this base to recruit students, to develop the terrorist infrastructure that eventually became *Sendero*, and eventually as the point from which armed revolutionaries fanned out across the Andes to pursue their scorched earth policy. Ayacucho became a no-go region with the city being a virtual fortress under the control of the army while the countryside was surrendered to the guerrillas.

Guzmán's arrest in 1992 coupled with ex-President Alberto Fujimori's uncompromising pursuit of Peru's terrorists led to the collapse of the infrastructures that supported the various guerrilla movements in the country. Delgado's 1998 meeting was as much a celebration of this collapse as it was part of a history that began in 1978.

The meetings

The 1978 meeting (15–30 May), *3° Encuentro de Tercer Teatro* (The 3rd Encounter of Third Theatre) was modelled on Delgado's experiences at the European gatherings in Belgrade and Bergamo. But there was, as already mentioned, a greater emphasis on teaching in Ayacucho than there had been in Europe. Many of the Latin American groups were axiomatic versions of the Third Theatre. They were marginalized, isolated and inexperienced. This meeting was a rare opportunity for them not only to meet other Latin American groups that shared their preoccupations, but to also be exposed to techniques and ways of working very removed from their own.

The mornings were devoted to workshops led by various teachers, most of whom came from outside of Latin America. They included Richard Armstrong from the Roy Hart Theatre (Britain), F. Didier from the Temps Fort Theatre (France) and Isso Muroa (Japan). But despite the input of these teachers, the gathering was dominated by Barba and his Odin Teatret. Barba's reputation, his writings and his involvement with the organization of the gathering ensured his role as leader. It was his training methods, his dramaturgy and his conception of group theatre that dictated much of the programme in Ayacucho. His actors conducted workshops, the Odin led the way during the public performances that took up much of the afternoon, and Barba's ideas provided a context for the seminars and discussions in the evenings.

The 1988 meeting (19–27 November) saw a shift in emphasis from process to product. This shift reflected a growing confidence in Latin America's Third Theatre. Unlike the 1978 gathering, performance workshops played only a small part in the programme and even these workshops were no longer dominated by foreigners. In addition to European actors from the Odin, Tascabile di Bergamo and Potlach, workshop leaders included performers from the Peruvian groups Cuatrotablas and Yuyachkani, as well as Brazil's Laboratório UNICAMP de Movimiento y Expresión.

The focus of the meeting was on performance. The early morning hours were devoted to the creation of an original work. Participants were divided into groups on the first day of the meeting. Each of these groups was headed by a director who, together with his actors, developed a short *mise-en-scène* from improvisations based on themes given to them by Barba. These completed pieces were then combined into a single ritual-like performance dedicated to Jerzy Grotowski which was presented in the ruins of a pre-Inca city near Chaclacayo to mark the end of the meeting. In addition to signifying the closure of the gathering, performance took up a large part of the daily schedule. All of the Latin American groups presented their works and these presentations were then critiqued in formal sessions led by four critics from different countries: Thomas Bredsdorff (Denmark), Patricia Cardona (Mexico), Beatrice Iacoviello (Argentina) and myself (USA).

Despite the importance of performance, the group of international critics and the expanded role of Latin Americans, the gathering was still dominated by Barba. He led a daily workshop/demonstration session attended by all participants that lasted several hours. This workshop/demonstration focused on his methods of creating performance texts from improvisation. He also chaired several debates and lectures featuring local as well as foreign scholars and journalists.

Barba's prominence was hardly surprising, but it was countered by an unexpected turn of events: some strongly worded criticism of his leadership role. This criticism hinted at a turning point in Barba's 'ownership' of the Third Theatre. He was, and arguably remains, the most conceptually coherent advocate for the Third Theatre; but he is no longer the sole spokesman for the movement. Today he is a master among a select group of equals. The beginnings of this shift in status emerged during *Ayacucho '88* when the full legacy of the previous Ayacucho meeting first became clear and when Barba was attacked as a formalist as well as for what was perceived by some to be a neo-colonial positioning vis-à-vis Latin America. Barba's response to his critics, in turn, suggested an even further change.

Barba's domination of the 1978 meeting encouraged Peru's young and inexperienced groups to adopt his aesthetics and methodology. Many of those attending Latin America's first Third Theatre gathering were either the country's leading theatre groups, or were destined to become them. A number of these groups, and others formed since then who have been nurtured by the likes of Cuatrotablas, Yuyachkani or others of the initial Ayacucho generation, have embraced Barba's approach to theatre as their own. The unfortunate consequence of this, which the emphasis on performance at *Reencuentro '88* made crystal clear, was that many of these groups had become little more than imitations of the Odin. They slavishly copied Barba's fragmented approach to dramaturgy in which the conventional linear narrative is discarded for a visual and oral narrativity.[3] Barba's dramaturgy has evolved over many years with actors he has

---

3   Unlike plot-oriented dramaturgy, which gradually reveals its theme through an unfolding tale that builds to a climax and resolution, Barba's fragmented dramaturgy uses imagery, vocal techniques, sound effects and music to privilege the development of visual themes and paralinguistic musicality over a dramatized story. For a more detailed description of Barba's dramaturgy, see Watson, 1995: 73–103.

worked with since the early 1960s. It calls for a highly skilled use of improvisation, years of training and a clear understanding of the connections between form and content. The more experienced groups at Ayacucho in 1978 took from Barba what they wanted and adapted it to their own approaches to theatre. Unfortunately, their less experienced colleagues attempted to copy Barba and in so doing highlighted their inexperience and failed to find their own voices. As several critics noted during the gathering, it was not so much that these groups discarded what mattered to them, on the contrary, most of them took up themes like political repression and economic hardship which were the Peruvian reality at the time. It was rather that they attempted to adopt a theatrical language that they failed to master and which lacked the conviction of being their own. This led to confused productions that were difficult to understand and in which formalistic traits, such as excessive physicality and vocal tensions, swamped thematics. They were little more than inferior copies of the Odin they wished to emulate.

As noted in an earlier essay ('Barba's other culture'), Barba has often been accused in Latin America of being a formalist, of being far more concerned with dramaturgy, performer training, and acting techniques than with political or social issues. Despite Barba's denials, this accusation was confirmed for his critics in *Ayacucho '88*. Those groups that he most obviously influenced failed because of their focus on form rather than on content. Yet, in most of Latin America, the social value of theatre far outweighs its economic and aesthetic importance. As already noted, it is impossible to make a living in theatre except in a handful of major cities where commercial theatre exists. Equally, a concern with art for its own sake in societies with fragile democracies, human rights abuses, and precarious economies is, understandably, viewed by many as self-indulgent. For these people, theatre has to be a vehicle of social commentary and a catalyst for civil action. Following *Ayacucho '88*, the consequences of Barba's teachings were perceived, rightly or wrongly, by many Latin Americans to subvert the very nature of theatrical activity in their continent.

Another accusation against Barba at the 1988 meeting, and one that had been raised earlier at the Bahía Blanca encounter, was that of a colonial positioning. His leadership role was viewed by a number of participants in colonial terms: he was the 'knowledgeable' European teaching the 'ignorant' locals how to do theatre. Barba was seen by these critics as the new priest rather than a revisited Conquistador. He was not interested in stealing gold from the indigenous population, he was focused on 'converting' them to the 'right' way of making theatre.

I discuss the full parameters of this accusation in 'Barba's other culture', but Barba's response during the group theatre gatherings, initially in

Bahía Blanca and again in Ayacucho, reveals much about the internationalization of the Third Theatre. In a document entitled 'Reflections', distributed to participants at the Ayacucho meeting, Barba took up themes he first addressed in a manifesto, 'Anthropological Theatre', written during the earlier Bahía Blanca meeting.[4] In both of these documents, Barba maintained that those who accused him of colonialism were failing to make a distinction between cultural and professional identity. Barba argued that cultural identity, the question of who we are in relation to our birthplace, to our history, and to our society, is one that can only be answered fully by those inside the culture. But, professional identity, one's training, work ethic, and form of expression can draw on many sources, including ones from outside the culture. Viewing technique as culturally specific is to be blind to what masters from other countries and traditions have to offer. Performers can use the Stanislavsky system, Decroux's corporal mime, and Asian forms such as Noh, Odissi dance and Topeng to build a technique that is their own. Professional identity, for Barba, has its roots in interculturalism.

Consistent with his concern for group theatre, Barba further pointed out that interculturalism need not be limited to individuals, but that it can also be a source for groups to establish their individuality. The South American groups, for example, could draw on the experience and knowledge of the Odin, or other groups such as Tascabile di Bergamo and Potlach, not to copy them, but to take from them what they feel is valuable and adapt it to their own needs. In making these arguments, Barba was shifting the focus of Third Theatre from the local arena to the international stage. He was suggesting that the Third Theatre may be marginalized theatrically but the techniques and the networking that sustain it can be global.

The 1998 meeting in Ayacucho (23–31 May), *Encuentro Ayacucho: 9° Encuentro Internacional de Teatro de Grupo* (Encounter Ayacucho: The 9th International of Group Theatre) confirmed that the Third Theatre had taken Barba at his word. The range, vitality, and calibre of work produced by the groups served to demonstrate how, drawing upon a wide array of inspirations and sources, the Third Theatre has come of age. It is no longer a movement dominated by Barba alone.

In deference to the current breadth of group theatre, lecture/demonstrations monopolized much of the programme during the 1998 gathering. These lecture/demonstrations, referred to as *Banquetes* in the official programme (a cognate of the English word banquet with the same metaphorical implications of a shared meal, savoring, and satiation),

---

4 See the appendix below for copies of these two documents.

were sessions in which select participants talked about and showed aspects of their work. Barba opened this part of the program with a lecture about his methodology and a demonstration by one of his actors. At the end of this three-hour session, however, Barba became a spectator for the rest of the week as a variety of working styles, aesthetics and dramaturgy, took the stage. One of Peru's leading groups, Yuyachkani, followed Barba. The director, Miguel Rubio, introduced actors from the company, each of whom discussed and demonstrated the current research they are conducting into performer training. This research ranges from work with masks to Peruvian folk dance and local traditional stories. Victoria Santa Cruz, the grand old master teacher and director from Peru who is now based in the United States, talked about and showed aspects of her training methods using internal and external body rhythms. These opening *Banquetes* were followed by sessions led by groups from Latin America (La Candelaria from Colombia, Peru's Cuatrotablas, Tablas y Diablas from Mexico, and Luisa Calcumil and El Séptimo from Argentina), Italy (Potlach and La Linea Transversale), Switzerland (Teatro Sunil and Teatro delle Radici), France (Jean Marie Binoche) and Japan (Escuela Kanze).

In addition to the *Banquetes*, the Ayacucho programme consisted of a small number of seminars, a few short workshops and many performances. Again, Barba led one of the seminars, but others were conducted by various people. One was headed by the renowned Spanish playwright and director José Sanchís Sinisterra who lectured on the connections between conventional dramaturgy and collective creation. Another was chaired jointly by the Italian scholar Mirella Schino and the Mexican based critic and director, Bruno Bert, who together led a discussion on the state of group theatre in Latin America and Europe. One of the seminars, *Expresion de Huancayo*, even deviated entirely from the focus on group theatre and examined the reality of people's lives in the local region, particularly with regard to the latter's terrorist legacy.

The move away from teaching at the 1998 meeting was most obvious in the performance workshops that were offered to participants. All of these workshops were one-off sessions outside the official programme. Since the limitation in offerings was matched only by brevity (none of the workshops exceeded two hours), participants were barely introduced to the techniques of performers like Daniele Finzi Pasca, a gifted comic from the Swiss-Mexican group Teatro Sunil, the Odin's Roberta Carreri, and Beatriz Camargo from the Colombian group Itinerante del Sol who ran them.

The workshops, seminars, and *Banquetes*, which were closed to all but participants, were balanced by performances of various sorts that were open to the general public. These performances came closest to the model of a theatre festival and in so doing provided an opportunity for genuine interaction between participants and the local community.

The quasi-festival nature of the performances presented during the *encuentro* was taken one step further by Delgado in 1998 in a bold step that confirmed Third Theatre's move from the margins to centre stage. He mounted an international theatre festival in Lima following the Ayacucho gathering (1–7 June) which featured the Third Theatre groups from the *encuentro*. Barba's latest production *Mythos* was a major festival attraction, but the week-long event, which was a highlight of Lima's cultural calendar, featured over forty performances by eighteen groups from Latin America and Europe.

A shift to the south

Barba remains, as Delgado described him to me in an interview, a master. He is respected by those in the Third Theatre for his conceptual insight, his leadership, his creative work, and his performance research. But to borrow a metaphor from politics, he is more the founding elder statesman than the president or prime minister today. The dynamic of the Third Theatre has shifted from Barba's European homeland to Latin America. Nothing on the scale of the Ayacucho meetings has taken place in Europe in twenty years while organizers in the north of Argentina are already busy preparing for one of the largest gatherings ever.[5] This energy is no doubt due in part to the solidarity such meetings provide for the large number of theatre groups in Latin America, many of whom work in isolation and often face economic hardship and political repression. It is also the product of the dynamic leadership provided by directors like Delgado, Rubio, García and Buenaventura who are recognized throughout the continent as major theatre artists. It is also a consequence of the quality and range of theatrical styles and genres embraced by the Latin groups. Training no longer dominates Third Theatre gatherings. These meetings have become encounters in the true sense of the word as groups demonstrate and discuss their work methods rather than 'sit at the feet of

---

5 This gathering is being planned by El Séptimo, an alliance of groups in the northwest of Argentina, with the help of Mario Delgado. It is to take place in Humahuaca, Argentina. The meeting is only in the planning stages and, given the logistical and economic difficulties of such an enterprise, it is possible that it will not be realized. Nevertheless, the initiative, desire and stubborn will needed to organize such a meeting are obvious to the most casual of observers. Having attended *Ayacucho '98* and witnessed at first hand the dynamic energy of the Third Theatre movement in Latin America, I am confident that, should the planned meeting by El Séptimo face insurmountable obstacles, another gathering elsewhere will replace it.

the master' who will teach them how to do theatre. The groups have each constructed their identity in Barba's anthropological sense, drawing on whomsoever feeds their artistic sensibilities with little regard for geography.

Even though it is Barba's ideas that are the root source of the Third Theatre meetings and his organization of them in their formative years that remain the model for the gatherings, he is little more than an adviser to the current leadership. The organization of *Ayacucho '98*, for instance, was totally in the hands of Delgado and the Peruvian quasi-governmental agency PromPeru that provided money and public relations expertise. They consulted with Barba and they invited him and his group to take part. But he and the Odin actors were much like other leading participants: they conducted a lecture/demonstration, Barba led a seminar, one of his actresses presented a workshop, and the group performed. Neither Barba nor his actors played a leadership role as they had done in the 1970s and 1980s. They, in fact, spent a great part of their time at the 1998 gathering doing what all of their fellow groups did, observing the work of others.

This shift has to be a source of pride for Barba. His floating islands are firmly secure and no longer need a navigator to guide their journeys to each other. His legacy is a mature Third Theatre that celebrates him but no longer needs him.

Interview With Mario Delgado, 29 May 1998, Ayacucho, Peru

IAN WATSON Why did you organize *Ayacucho '98*?

MARIO DELGADO There were two meetings in Europe prior to the encounter we organized in 1978 in Peru. There were a number of gatherings, like those in Zacatecas, Bahía Blanca and Madrid, between the first Peruvian meeting and the second in Huampaní in 1988, but continuity of the Peruvian gatherings was all important for us. We wanted to organize a meeting every ten years here in Peru. Through this kind of continuity you can see growth, developments, changes.

IW What changes did you see from 1978 to 1988?

MD In 1978 many things were just beginning. By 1988 a uniformity had been generated, there was basically only one aesthetic. But today there is a range of aesthetics in group theatre. Some of the older groups are now part of the mainstream, they have become institutionalized. This is a positive thing because they have a permanency they didn't have in the past. But at the same time there are new proposals. There has also been a decline. Some of the important, older groups have split up. Many of the young people are disillusioned because it is so difficult to hold a group together today. Nevertheless, if the idea of the group is going to survive, it is the young people who have to do it. The older generation are the vanguard, they are the ones doing the pushing, but it is the young who must continue the adventure.

IW   The young most frequently embrace the new. They are, undoubtedly, the ones most responsible for the 'range of aesthetics' that you talked about. But is this new range limited to Peru or are you referring to the whole of Latin America?

MD   All of Latin America and Europe also. Look at the mask work of Binoche, a group like Sunil, or the Italian organization of groups, La Linea Transversale, all from Europe. These are countered by the Argentinean collective, Séptimo, or the participation of an artist like Sanchís Sinisterra in our gathering. Sanchís Sinisterra is a leading Spanish playwright and director. Ten years ago it would have been impossible to imagine that someone like Sanchís Sinisterra would be in a festival of group theatre. He had doubts about coming when I invited him. He thought that the Odin's influence was everywhere. But I told him it was not so. Groups have changed and they have their own identity and the groups need you as a dramaturg. Sanchís Sinisterra is now very happy to be here. His prejudices are gone and he is very open. Binoche and Sanchís Sinisterra came here with many prejudices and now they no longer have them.

IW   How important do you think the group theatre meetings have been in generating these changes and developments?

MD   They are basic, essential, fundamental! To reunite people twenty years after the first meeting in Ayacucho was something very important. Not only to embrace each other in nostalgia but to look at each other and to see how each of us has grown. Every group has something, but it also lacks something; we are seeing this here and now. We can share limitations, changes and experiences here today. For example, listening to Eugenio Barba discuss the work of Teatro Sunil with such enthusiasm, it's incredible that a master like Eugenio can still be amazed by something new in group theatre. The other aspect of this most recent meeting was to give a public face, a profile.

IW   A public face to the groups or to Ayacucho?

MD   If it were not for Ayacucho this meeting would not have taken place. Ayacucho is an isolated city, a city away from everything; it is a cultural city, even if it doesn't have a theatre of its own. But it is not only a place, it is also a public. It is possible for us to create a relation between our work and the people here. You can sense the involvement of the people with the theatre groups and the event in general. This engagement inspires the groups, gives them energy. So when the groups return to their homes, they will keep on fighting within their solitary existence, but with Ayacucho as a constant reference, a place that you know you can return to. Ayacucho, an Andean city with mythical links to Latin America's history, has become a frame of reference for group theatre.

IW   Let me ask you something else. You have taken this notion of the group meeting and made it very much something of Latin America. But its roots are really with Eugenio Barba. What do you see as Barba's legacy in all of this, in what is happening here?

MD   Eugenio's legacy lies in his escape from traditional theatre, in his commitment to the marginal. He makes contact with Latin American theatre because it is marginalized and he identifies with the marginal. This is why he feels more comfortable here. Many Latin Americans embrace Barba's ethics while employing his techniques and methodology. But Latin America continues to grow and today we have the feeling of being equal partners with Barba rather than his pupils. For me this is very important. It recalls Brecht who created a way of making theatre in response to the Europe of his day. But today, Brechtian theatre is more relevant here in Latin America than it is in Europe. If Brecht were alive today, maybe he would have become a kind of Barba.

IW   That may explain Barba's relationship to Latin America. But what of the other side? What does Barba bring to the Latin America of today?

MD   Eugenio gives us a mirror to look at ourselves. He does not prompt us to look to Europe for models, he suggests we look at our own continent as a source of growth. It is clear today that no one attempts to do Barba's theatre.

IW   I agree. One of the major differences I am aware of from the *encuentro* ten years ago is that in 1988 I saw little Odins everywhere, now I do not see any.

MD   It is even more. Eugenio and the Odin have their teaching sessions at this *encuentro*, as do many others. I am the leader of this gathering, however, with all the problems that go with that. Even I get into conflict with the Odin and Eugenio because of the company's requirements etc., but the Odin has to adapt itself to this new order.

IW   Talking of a new order, what is the connection between Ayacucho, the group meeting, and the government-backed organization PromPeru?

MD This is the first time that the groups have received support from the state of Peru for such a meeting. The support has come from PromPeru. But apart from the money, the organization's commitment to Ayacucho is instructive. PromPeru promotes Peru in general, but it has a special project in Ayacucho because the city is so important to our history. Ayacucho is Peru, symbolically speaking. Any future of Peru has to go through Ayacucho. This is where our interests coincide. Both Cuatrotablas and PromPeru want a social benefit for the people of Ayacucho. We want to help the people of this region, we want them recover their happiness, their strength, their pride and to try and let them forget the guerrilla. If we can do this for Ayacucho, we can do it for Peru.

The interview was conducted by the author during *Ayacucho '98* and translated from Spanish by Flavia López de Romaña.

References

Barba, Eugenio (1977), 'An offense against nature', *Rampelyset* (Denmark), interview with Per Moth.

Barba, Eugenio (1986), *Beyond the Floating Islands*. New York: Performing Arts Journal Publications.

Barba, Eugenio (1995), *The Paper Canoe: A Guide to Theatre Anthropology*. London and New York: Routledge.

Barba, Eugenio (1999), 'A legacy from us to ourselves', in *Theatre: Solitude, Craft, Revolt*. Aberystwyth, Wales: Black Mountain Press, pp. 216–25.

Barba, Eugenio and Nicola Savarese (1991), *A Dictionary of Theatre Anthropology: The Secret Art of the Performer*. London and New York: Routledge.

Buenaventura, Enrique (1979), *Le maschere, il teatro*. Milan: Feltrinelli.

Daetwyler, Jean-Jacques (1977), 'Third Theatre in Bergamo', *International Theatre Information* (summer-autumn): 19–20.

Watson, Ian (1995), *Towards a Third Theatre: Eugenio Barba and the Odin Teatret*. London and New York: Routledge.

Appendix

Anthropological theatre. A document presented to participants at the Bahía Blanca Third Theatre gathering by Eugenio Barba

Theatre Anthropology is the study of human being's biological and sociocultural behaviour in performative circumstances.

Anthropological Theatre is a theatre in which the performer confronts his own identity.

The notion of identity stems from the Latin, *Idem*, which means what does not change, what remains the same. Each human being has an axis, a centre, a kernel of values which orients him to life's circumstances, oppositions and obstacles. In the case of the performer, this identity manifests itself through his craft. The concretization of this craft explores an historic and biographic horizon, which determines the artistic results. As with any cultural expression, these results are relative to the performer's experience, heredity and vision of the world. It is this relativity which gives to each individual his uniqueness in front of others. In the same way, a theatre group should manifest its relativity in order to define itself in front of others.

The Anthropological Theatre underlies the uniqueness of the individual, of each actor, of each theatre group, of each historical-cultural horizon. It implies a travel through one's own history and culture, and provides the means of strengthening the individual's axis-identity, giving each of us a separate profile. But at the same time it supplies the tools for meeting in a territory where we are all equal. A territory that consists of the performer's material presence which is the same and unchangeable in any place. This presence is one's professional identity, which permits the performer to go behind his artistic temperament and the artistic results or style of a culture to discover the common principles of scenic presence which can be applied to his own exploration. This professional identity belongs to a transcultural theatrical history built by masters and creators who preceded him. Therefore an actor from Polynesia can develop his professional identity by orienting himself to the values and experiences of masters from other cultures.

Anthropological Theatre only exists if it is based on a polarization. On the one hand, the question: who am I, as an individual in a determined time and space? And on the other, the capacity of professional exchange between individuals who may be far removed from one's own time or geographic location.

It is through exchange, rather than in isolation, that a culture can develop, that is, transform itself organically. The same process applies to individuals and theatre performers. Therefore in professional exchange one's historical-biographic identity is fundamental when confronted with its opposite pole, the meeting with otherness, with what is different. Not to impose one's own horizon or way of seeing, but rather to provoke a displacement which makes it possible to discover a territory beyond his known universe.

The Anthropological Theatre means protecting one's own axis, overcoming insecurities and self-defence in order to expose oneself to confrontation, disorientation, and crisis, so that the theatre can respect life's law of continual flow and change.

(Eugenio Barba, Bahía Blanca, April 1987. Translated from Spanish by Susana Epstein)

Reflections. A document presented to participants at *Reencuentro Ayacucho '88* by Eugenio Barba

1 Third Theatre culture does not depend upon styles or fashion. It relates to an attitude that does not rely on the rules of conventional productions. It is a theatre that runs parallel to the prevailing theatre or to the kind of theatre that is respected the most by cultural institutions and the press. Given the dramatic situation in which certain countries find themselves, these

theatres may be a form of civil resistance against personal humiliation, social and economic injustice, under-development, fanaticism and violence. This was reaffirmed at the 8th International Meeting of Group Theatre – *Reencuentro Ayacucho '88*, which took place in Lima, Peru (*sic*), from 19 to 27 November 1988. A gathering that was an homage to Jerzy Grotowski whose example of intellectual, emotional and professional awareness served as a model for the previous meetings in Belgrade (1976), Bergamo (1977), Ayacucho (1978), Madrid (1979), Zacatecas (1981), Bahía Blanca (1986) and Cuzco (1987), all of which have left traces in the development of group culture that has modified and enriched contemporary theatre.

2 The Third Theatre highlights a reality, which requires the overcoming of theatrical ethnocentrism in order to be understood. It also relates to all the scenic 'anomalies' that constitute our century's tradition of theatrical reforms, from Stanislavsky to Brecht and Grotowski, while fulfilling those personal needs that call for alternative human relationships through working in the theatre.

3 Group theatre may look exceptional or marginal within the theatrical landscape, but it reveals aspects of performance that belong to the very nature of theatre: a collective art, which like all art, involves a search. Third Theatre's search, however, is collective.

4 The Third Theatre's search is for identity. An identity with two faces: one looking to our specific historical, social, and cultural context; the other to the professional that unifies us, despite different languages, traditions and origins. The work in the profession is what allows us to develop our differences. The goal of these meetings is to compare these differences.

5 Theatre Anthropology, in the sense of 'the study of human behaviour in a performance situation', might link diverse theatrical traditions to specific individual and group traditions, but while this link unifies, it differentiates and is the opposite to the process of homogeneity.

6 The different types of groups that constitute the Third Theatre and the variety of works they produce make it a true social laboratory. This Group Theatre can be experienced as a mirror that puts the hesitations, dangers and utopias that define and threaten us into perspective. It allows for the dialectics between cultural and professional identity. It places what is different about the groups into a social context through the multiple relationships it generates between them and their spectators.

7 Contradictions and discrepancies are a necessary condition to grow. Those that were discussed at *Reencuentro Ayacucho '88* generated a framework for self-reflection. Critics and scholars who consider this parallel theatre as a relevant artistic and social manifestation also contributed to this process. They treat it as the most respectable theatre while maintaining a coherent line in their professional ethics. Future meetings must keep and deepen the dialectics between reflection and action.

(Eugenio Barba, Lima, Peru, November 1988. Translated from Spanish by Susana Epstein.)

15

About islands and woods: notes on a journey to the Odin Teatret

Miguel Rubio

Miguel Rubio, the director of Yuyachkani, is one of Latin America's leading theatre directors. He is at the forefront of group theatre in the continent and, as the following article attests, has a long history with Barba. Rubio, along with his former wife, Teresa Ralli, formed Yuyachkani in Peru in 1972, with the express intention of using theatre as a catalyst for change in a society they perceived as corrupt and unjust. Rubio's reputation is built upon a politically committed theatre and an aesthetic that combines elements of Bertolt Brecht's political ethos, Barba's techniques, a cadre of Latin American influences including, among others, Santiago García, Enrique Buenaventura, Atahualpa del Cioppo and Augusto Boal, and a deep understanding of traditional Andean performance evident in the dances, music and costuming of its public, open-air festivals. In this article, Rubio traces his reactions to Barba from his initial meeting with him at the first Third Theatre gathering in Latin America in Ayacucho (1978), where he rejected what he perceived to be a formalist aesthetic, through to his present relationship, one that calls for engagement and dialogue rather than dismissal or blind acceptance. The chapter was originally published in Spanish in the Mexican theatre journal *Máscara* (Año 4, No. 19–20, October 1994–October 1995). (Ian Watson)

As I was travelling to meet Santiago García at the Bogotá airport for our flight together to Holstebro where we were to join the Odin Teatret's 30th anniversary celebrations, I found myself thinking, 'What has knowing the Odin for seventeen years meant to me?'

A few hours earlier in Manizales, Santiago said, 'I am going to eat a plate of Barba's spaghetti and get back.' The single plate was a reference to the fact that we were only going to spend a weekend in Denmark.

We travelled for twenty-four hours and arrived at 6 o'clock sharp in the Black Room, one of the Odin's five workspaces at their Holstebro headquarters. Despite the length of our journey, we arrived on time, so Eugenio did not have to delay his welcoming words for the opening part of the celebrations, entitled 'Traditions and Founders of Tradition', on our account.

Such a long trip gave me time to reflect upon how many times we had met with the Odin, with Eugenio, or with anybody involved with the company. The first time was during *Ayacucho '78*, the now famous *Encuentro de Teatro de Grupos* (Meeting of Group Theatres) organized by Cuatrotablas. On that occasion, my response to their participation was one of rejection and a denunciation of what I saw as a disturbing influence in Peru and in Latin America in general. For us, it was a time of discovery, a time to explore a theatre that we could call 'ours'. We were struggling for a national dramaturgy rooted in our Latin American heritage and leftist politics.

Time passes, as Pablo Milanés would say, and life teaches us many things. Luckily, we have changed. I remember Eugenio saying to me only recently, 'because we, as old Marxists …' (*sic*).

When the Odin travelled to Venezuela in 1976 for its first encounter with Latin America, the continent's theatre was deeply concerned with its own historical times and the agenda was very clear. Those theatre groups that, thanks to Enrique Buenaventura's initiative, had evolved a new means of making theatre, were the cells in which we were rehearsing what we imagined ought to be man's future, democracy with a collective lifestyle at its foundation.

Names, event, ideas, journals all come to mind: Bertolt Brecht, the Cuban Revolution, Augusto Boal, Atahualpa del Cioppo, the independent theatres of Argentina and Uruguay, the Living Theatre, María Escudero, Santiago García, Enrique Buenaventura, Peter Schumann and his giant puppets denouncing the Vietnam War in New York, the Manizales Theatre Festival, the *Conjunto* magazine, collective creation, masks, dances, street theatre. These share much in common with Latin American theatre of the time, the identity of which was best captured by Magaly Muguercia's metaphor of an axe. That is, a theatre battle hardened by the inclination to change society.

Yet, despite its vitality, the Latin American theatre of those days was stuck, much like a top spinning in place. A re-evaluation of the potential for an authentic theatre was called for. It was time to explore our pre-

Hispanic past and the transformations wrought by history from those ancient beginnings to contemporary times.

The Spaniards brought their theatre, but what did we have prior to their arrival? The Odin's presence felt like an invasion by the *new Spaniards*. 'What are they?' I kept wondering. 'Are they the harbingers of a new religion?' Their mystical attitude bothered me. I remember them working all day and smiling very little in Ayacucho in 1978. The clown skit they presented was, in fact, not very funny at all. One morning, as they were going around the marketplace on their huge stilts, a child screamed, 'Mom, big gringos have just arrived!' It was Tage Larsen who was hopping around with Roberta Carreri. That child's reaction was truly the way we all felt. We wanted to know who they were and what they wanted.

Another morning, during breakfast, I approached Tage, who was eating dressed in black with a red tie and hat in what was an obviously performative manner. I asked him, 'And you, whom do you impersonate? With the disinterested expression of a cowboy from a Western movie, he replied, 'Myself.' This truly confused me and I thought that in addition to their Messianic bent, the people from the Odin were crazy. During the intervening years, I have come to understand that Tage was working at the boundaries of his extra-daily presence, at that point where presence subtends impersonation.

We used all our resources to defend ourselves in Ayacucho. It had already been difficult enough for us to attend such a 'petit bourgeois' meeting at a time when there was a forty-eight hour strike in Lima against the military dictatorship and our colleagues wanted us to stay in the city to support the demonstrations in the streets. Our presence in Ayacucho indicated that we had chosen the theatre over solidarity!

A new era began for Yuyachkani in Ayacucho, as I believe it did for many of us who were there. But we had arrived with too burdened a guilty conscience to remain silent, we needed to make our voices heard. I remember my *compañeros* urging me to respond to Eugenio's opening lecture in which he maintained that no one could make revolution with the theatre. 'What a shame!' I thought. But when I went back to Lima this and other such statements gave me a lot of food for thought and discussion.

We did not remain silent in Ayacucho. We did not present any pieces, but we sang revolutionary songs. Who would have guessed that many years later we would sing them again in Holstebro during the welcoming lunch organized by the Odin for Yuyachkani, or that Eugenio would want us to sing them every time we meet.

Despite the objections and rejections, the meeting in Ayacucho generated strong conducting threads of an invisible current. The centre of energy was provided by the restless Odin actors: in the streets, in the peasant communities, at markets and most especially in the barters they mounted as a way of exchanging work. The group would arrive in a given place and present a performance, following which the community would respond with an artistic piece of its own. Little was said in these encounters because the levels of interaction prompted by this kind of activity were beyond words. It was amazing to see the answers that emerged once the group had made contact with the community through exchange without any attempt to preach or to patronize. I must admit that we learned a lesson here that helped me rethink our way of making contact with our audience. I realized then that we had often done the wrong thing by bringing 'correct ideas' to the people.

The Odin's production *The Book of Dances* was one of the productions the company performed often on the outskirts of the city. This was a fascinating piece built from fragments of the actors' training, the group's experiments with stilt-walking, their playing of musical instruments, and the company's work with pageant flags.

The Odin actors were not directly involved in the *Encuentro*. They were its peripheral support, the bell that was constantly signalling an event somewhere in Huamanga. Sometimes we would run just to witness their meetings with the people. Many of us were torn between an ideological rejection of a group of actors that gathered an audience to say 'nothing' to them and a fascination with the links they were able to establish with spectators. We, who believed in 'an urgent theatre', thought that it was a waste to see the circle of spectators these gringos gathered merely to spread their energy! We were in the process of building a theatre based upon the ideological premise that we were all part of a popular culture. The investigations of our traditions had led us to attempt to incorporate them into our theatre. We used to take a long time studying these traditions, while at the same time researching our audience in order to be able to reach it better. The Odin was reversing the paradigm: through the exchange in barter, popular culture was becoming a means for the local community to research the Odin's group culture!

Yet, this understanding of group culture is problematic since it can be used to justify the appropriation of virtually any sign from a traditional culture under the guise of collective incorporation. We felt a natural affinity with those cultures that the Odin had borrowed. We could not appreciate any other value in their work than that of usurper. They seemed to us to be a new type of Conquistador who enjoyed going around the world displaying the trophies acquired in their travels: costumes, masks, objects and the arrogance of believing that they could genuinely assimilate signs of other cultures through training. When I found out that they were foreigners everywhere, even in Holstebro, and that in order to communicate among themselves during rehearsals they had to first agree upon which language they were going to use, I found myself asking, 'Where *are* these people from?'

I think that our obsession with identity, our need to come to terms with our individual national roots as well as the collectivity implied in being Latin American, was making us hypersensitive towards the Odin's hybrid experiments.

Barba's concept of Third Theatre, originally conceived at the first group theatre meeting in Belgrade some two years prior to our gathering in Ayacucho, attempted to place many different theatre proposals in the same bag. Eugenio's 'floating islands' metaphor has a similar agenda; but, the Third Theatre label, which he used to identify a vast movement of marginal, isolated theatres that were neither 'official' nor avant-garde, was an especially troubling characterization for us. It clearly had overtones of 'the marginal'. In addition, the idea of being in a third position sounded wrong to us. Third positions lack prestige and appear historically conciliatory as well as devoid of radical rhetoric. In our eyes, this third position did not openly oppose the power or the establishment. We did not wish to be part of a passive marginal condition. However, I must admit that despite the limitations of Barba's idea of Third Theatre, it has helped many groups around the world to identify their similarities.

The Odin has produced a seism in Latin American theatre and, in my opinion, the foundations of this seism were laid in Ayacucho. The choices of what things we accepted from the Odin and what others we rejected were influenced by our already emerging theatre movement. A movement which, even though it suffered from a rhetoric of extremism, was very clear about what was needed. It was a theatre based on revolutionary ideas with conservative forms and a lack of clear technical guidelines for the actor. This conservatism and especially the lack of clarity for the actor provided an opportunity for the Odin to suggest alternatives. When we met the Odin, we came to learn about a theatre system rooted in the most important traditions of the West and East. This system was not fully understood by those who delighted at what they saw. They all too often digested it poorly and imitated its forms without regard to the principles underlying them. Unfortunately, this generated a proliferation of 'little Odins', followers who seemed to be cut by the same pair of scissors that shaped the original and whose performances looked inorganically similar to those of their mentor.

I am still struck by finding myself travelling to Holstebro with Santiago García. Along with other masters such as Atahualpa del Cioppo,

Augusto Boal, Enrique Buenaventura, and Vicente Revuelta, he has brought reflection as well as Bertolt Brecht's plays and ideas to Latin America. Santiago belongs to a different theatre tradition from that of Eugenio; he is one of those whose theoretical premises and theatrical strategies have their origins in Brecht. His merit, in my opinion, does not lie in his staging of Brecht's pieces, but in the way in which he has created a uniquely Colombian and Latin American theatre based upon the German writer's seminal teachings. This is one of the reasons why Santiago is a teacher, a master road builder. He has taught many of us how to use the theatre's universal traditions and contemporary ideas to invent our own theatre; he is a man always ready to learn.

Surprising as it maybe to some, Barba's books were studied in depth at the permanent Workshop that Santiago directs at the *Corporación Colombiana de Teatro* (Colombian Theatre Corporation). These studies were a major influence on the Colombian performer César Badillo, a member of Santiago's La Candelaria group, and the book he wrote *El Actor y sus Otros* (The Actor and his Others). These influences are most readily evident in Badillo's discussions in his book of how an actor is formed by the group theatre ethic, collective creation and Brecht's ideas. In addition, his exploration of the various national and Latin American approaches to dramaturgy, their uses of fiction, dreams, thoughts and his own experiences as a theatre worker are all examined through a dialogue with Barba's ideas in *A Dictionary of Theatre Anthropology* and other texts.

Badillo's book and Santiago's attitude are instructive. All too often the Odin Teatret and Eugenio's work have prompted an extreme reaction: either total approval or total rejection. I have frequently encountered criticism based on common places, from people who neither knew the Odin's work, nor were familiar with Eugenio's writings. Fortunately, time and distance have tempered these excesses, but in the past subjectivity and prejudice all too often reigned.

I remember once in Colombia, someone asked me if I had seen the Odin's *Brecht's Ashes*. 'No,' I replied. 'Neither did I,' he said, 'but I've heard that it is an insult to Brecht's memory and work.' In fact, I never saw the production. I was very curious because I had seen photos from the piece in which Iben Nagel Rasmussen, an Odin actress, wears a hat from Cuzco and carries a pair of scissors typical of those used in a folk dance from the Ayacucho region.

Another time, someone told me that the production favoured the Red Brigade terrorists. 'It must be,' I thought, 'given Barba's obsession with polysemy, paradox, and the polyhedron image.'

I always think of Eugenio Barba's and the Odin Teatret's presence in Latin America as a motivating force, a polemic, something extreme and disconcerting.

Thinking about them during this long journey is like remembering a history shared with companions; a history that is somewhat like a pendulum swinging between things that draw me closer to them and others that separate us. What is clear to me is that the Odin's presence among us as Latin Americans has curiously helped us to know better who we are, and helped us to relate to each other in ways beyond merely learning new performance techniques together.

Some people associate Yuyachkani with the Odin in a mechanical, simplistic manner. Invariably during an international event, in interviews, or in reviews of our productions, there will be some comment about the connections between us. Initially, I was very uncomfortable with these comments. Sometimes I found myself 'defending' the Odin, mainly because what people were discussing only demonstrated their ignorance of the group. Obviously, one can disagree with Barba, one can reject his aesthetic choices, but one would have a hard time disputing that he is a contemporary theatre innovator, a master with a pedagogical vision rooted in a theoretical and practical system founded upon an ethical approach to the theatre. This vision is especially valuable during a time dominated by pragmatism, minimal effort and artifice. Barba and the Odin work with the basic raw materials of theatre, with its fundamental core: the actor and his presence. In doing this, they confirm to us that we can do without everything on stage except the orchestration of energies embodied in representation and the performer's presence.

Time has not gone by in vain, though. In recent years, a lot of ice has been broken and many prejudices have disappeared. We have changed, as have our friends at the Odin. They have learned something in this continent, after all. They have realized that influences are mutual. In the beginning, it was clear that people had to listen to the master. Meanwhile, he appeared much more interested in conducting his research in Bali, Japan, and India than in Latin America. I remember during the International School of Theatre Anthropology (ISTA) meeting in Bologna when Raquel Carrió, a Cuban critic and researcher, wanted Latin Americans, many lacking a sense of rhythm, to learn a rumba so that Eugenio could incorporate it into his *Teatrum Mundi*, a production that he mounts at the end of every ISTA. Unfortunately, Raquel's enthusiasm was not enough for us to learn the rumba steps. Much to her disappointment, she said: 'When this man eventually discovers the beauty of African-American Caribbean culture, his life is going to change and he is not going to need to travel so far to continue his research. Mark my words, man!' Many of us believe, in fact, that this should be Eugenio's next step in his relationship with Latin America. Possibly it is already beginning.

When Nitis Jacon, the director of the Londrina International Festival in Brazil, organized the first ISTA to be held in Latin American in her home city in August 1994, she insisted that Eugenio include a local performer in the meeting. This was how Augusto Omolú, a Brazilian dancer who incorporates the Afro-Brazil universe of the Candomblé into his performances, became the first Latin American member of ISTA's pedagogical team. Barba also mounted a version of *Othello* with Omolú.

The kind of work Omolú and others have also begun to investigate, that is, performance forms shaped by our Latin American traditions, could be strengthened if we had a greater opportunity of comparing our traditions with those of the pedagogical teams at ISTA. One such comparison could be with the latest research we have begun at Yuyachkani. In the past, we have explored highly codified Eastern movement forms like t'ai chi as starting points for our work. In more recent times, we have invited our own masters of popular culture to incorporate traditional dances into our training. In doing this, we have been looking for the principles embedded in the dances that are equivalent to those that Eugenio has identified in his Theatre Anthropology research. This type of comparison enables an intercultural dialogue to generate from the technical norms of one's own culture.

Theatre has existed for thousands of years on this continent, but colonial aggression has repressed many indigenous types of theatre and martial dances. Nevertheless, we can perceive traces of many of these forms that have survived due to cultural resistance. These traces, which are evident syncretically in a variety of artistic manifestations, are not always understood. They are often minimized under the title of folklore, a term created outside the continent to describe the 'strange' uses and habits of the people native to it.

We already have the foundations of a new type of relationship in which we are not cast as mere spectators. We can discover much more together if we are prepared to understand, as Barba says, that the history of theatre is not only concerned with what is ancient but with what is new.

Many years after having conceived his controversial notion of Third Theatre, which to many of us seemed an attempt to establish an international category of homogenized aesthetics, Eugenio has suggested a broadening of criteria that I would like to acknowledge.

In his article 'The Third Theatre: the legacy from us to ourselves' he writes: 'The Third Theatre ... is not a theatrical style; it is not an alliance of groups; still less a movement or international association; nor is it a school, an aesthetic or set of techniques' (Barba, 1999: 216). Later, in the same article, he argues that:

> The difficulty in understanding what the Third Theatre is depends on the search for a unitary definition which fixes in one mould the meaning of a theatre reality which is different. But the Third Theatre may be defined precisely by the lack of a common unitary meaning. It is the sum of all these theatres which are, each in its own way, constructors of meaning. Each of them defines in an autonomous way the personal meaning of their doing theatre: what Jouvet called 'the legacy from us to ourselves'. (1999: 221)

This was the spirit that prevailed during *Reencuentro Ayacucho '88*, organized once again by the stubborn industry of Mario Delgado and Cuatrotablas. The seeds for this meeting were planted a year earlier, in Cuzco, where, surrounded by the beautiful landscape of Urubamba, preparations were made for the meeting that was to take place the following year. In his closing remarks in Cuzco, Eugenio stressed his professional links with his totem grandfather, Stanislavski, and with his other grandfathers, Meyerhold, Vakhtangov, Copeau, Eisenstein, and his most important grandfather of all, Grotowski. He also said:

> During this week, watching the lecture demonstrations and the training sessions of the Peruvian groups, I realized that I am confronted with a unique phenomenon; today, there is no other country on this planet where the process of learning has so much in common with the principles of Theatre Anthropology which lead to a personal codification for the performer. This is extraordinary.

These two thoughts have remained with me since that meeting in Cuzco.

Other points Eugenio made in the same address echo the 1960s. 'It was women,' he said, 'who created group theatre at the beginning of the century in England; women who were fighting for their right to vote. This is perhaps the genetic thread that makes women so strong in every group theatre that I have encountered.'

The quality of our gatherings has changed a lot since that first meeting in Ayacucho in 1978; not only in Peru, but also elsewhere in Latin America. Even though the festivals we have mounted are important and have given us the opportunity to compare our work, they have also become shop windows of sorts, where things are on display, but there is not enough time or space for serious exchange. In the past, we had meetings that allowed us to analyse the state of our theatre; we would diagnose its strengths as well as its faults and prescribe manifestos of solidarity along with other means of unity. Acknowledging who we are has also been very important to us. This process was, however, primarily intellectual. The group theatre gatherings I attended following *Ayacucho '78* focused on practical work which started very early in the morning and continued until late at night. At these gatherings, the word 'exchange' gained meaning for me for the first time because I was able to see how other colleagues worked, how experience can be systematized, and how actors could articulate their work process. When we meet today, it is common for us to discuss training workshops and/or the details of artistic exchanges without them being thought of as 'an alternative pedagogy'; these have become part of our conventional work experience.

As discussed in 'The Third Theatre: a legacy of independence', it was not possible to mount the 1988 group theatre gathering in Ayacucho because the Shining Path guerrillas controlled the region. The meeting was held, instead, in the *Centro Vacacional Huampaní* (Huampaní Holiday Resort), fifty kilometres from Lima. A few days before the meeting, the Odin planned a brief, secret trip to Ayacucho. When I learned about it, I joined them. I wanted to witness this visit. We travelled together on the only available flight that day. When we arrived at Ayacucho, the plane had to circle the airport and was unable to land due to bad weather; we returned to Lima. Eugenio, against his financial manager's advice, decided to rent two small planes which would attempt to land in Ayacucho by avoiding the bad weather. I was invited to join the group. We finally landed at Ayacucho airport in the afternoon, long after anyone had been expecting us. The only people at the airport were two military units, one from the army, the other from the air force. They questioned us about the purpose of our visit. The small planes departed for Lima leaving us in a tense stalemate with the military at the airport. Finally the commander said: 'Well, if you are artists, as you say, why don't you do something for our troops?' 'Of course,' Eugenio replied, 'but there is one small detail, sir, when we give a performance, we ask for an artistic response in exchange, a barter.' The actors prepared in less than fifteen minutes, though it felt like one to me. This time the stilts did not appear in the market; instead, they transformed the tarmac into a huge stage while the soldiers abandoned their harshness and produced small cameras from their backpacks to take pictures of the performance. I could not believe my own eyes. It was even more incredible to hear the soldiers sing school songs with shy voices as their contribution to the exchange.

Once the unexpected barter was over, the Odin marched towards the city. The march was led by Mr Peanut, who, with his impeccable tails and skeleton head, disguised the exhaustion of the actress wearing the costume on the long walk to Ayacucho, an Andean city which is more than three thousand metres above sea level. How was Mr Peanut to know that this march was nothing compared to what was going to happen to him later in Chile, when the Odin visited the *Palacio de la Moneda* (The

Ministry of Finances) in Santiago and General Pinochet, finding it distasteful to host death, resorted to ordering his *carabineros* to beat him up brutally?

When they managed to knock Mr Peanut to the ground, the *carabineros* were surprised to see a woman, the actress Julia Varley, appear from inside the character's clothes. The *carabineros* are still confused about Mr Peanut's identity and whereabouts.

More than thirty groups, the vast majority from Latin America, and about two-hundred and fifty theatre workers from different parts of the world came together during the last days of November 1988 to participate in the 8th International Encounter of Group Theatre (*Reencuentro Ayacucho '88*).

Peru was living through violent times that had even spread to the capital. Up to a few hours before the meeting, we were not sure if it would take place. As well as blackouts, which were common due to strikes, the water was contaminated and the employees at the *Centro Recreacional Huampaní*, where the meeting was to take place, refused to work. In addition, the government was indifferent to the event. The foreign visitors were perplexed; as for us who were used to such difficulties, this was just one more obstacle to overcome.

Despite the organizer's initial goal of only exploring performance and dramaturgy, these circumstances were a catalyst to discussions about what it means to make theatre in a context of crisis. It was useful for us to realize that our techniques are the result of what we need in order to face our daily reality. The meeting was different from the previous encounter in Ayacucho; politics were no longer the source of polarization, they were now incorporated into the work. In my view, the two most important aspects of the gathering were, on the one hand, the examinations of acting technique in the workshops entitled the Taxidermy of Performance, which provided the opportunity for critics to examine the work done by the groups. And, on the other, the various dialogues, such as Eugenio's morning lecture demonstrations, the paper 'History, violence and theatre in Peru', presented by the Peruvian journalist Juan Larco, and the heated discussion, 'Suing the group theatre', between the critic and writer Alfonso La Torre and the Italian scholar Ferdinando Taviani.

We built bridges between our differences. Eugenio argued that 'contradictions and discrepancies are a necessary condition for growth'. This spirit of inclusion and confrontation accompanied us throughout the entire time we were there.

I am sure that by the end of the meeting it was clear to everybody that group theatre has a variety of aesthetic options, has diverse manifestations, and cannot be defined by a single philosophy. Group theatre is an ethic. An ethic which unifies us, yet leaves enough room for each of us to discover an individual and social meaning that is the product of our own reality.

This realization has strengthened us. Despite our differences, we have built solid links and the understanding that, even if our origins and artistic ideals differ, we are unified by our need to meet.

During this journey, our companions from the Odin Teatret were able to create relationships that transformed space, language and culture into relative terms by highlighting what underlies them: the human condition and how we human beings transform this condition and our ideas into action.

Now I can see that in underpinning performance forms from various traditions there are principles that make them similar and allow them to establish a dialogue. This is why I am not surprised that Sanjukta Panigrahi from India could hold long work sessions with Augusto Omolú from Brazil without being able to exchange one word (after all, they never knew each other's language!).

This is also why I am also not surprised about coming from so far to celebrate this thirty years of utopia.

Translated from Spanish by Susana Epstein

References

Barba, Eugenio (1999), 'A legacy from us to ourselves', in *Theatre: Solitude, Craft, Revolt.* Aberystwyth, Wales: Black Mountain Press, pp. 216–25.

IV

A dialogue with Eugenio Barba

16

The conquest of difference: an electronic dialogue

Eugenio Barba and Ian Watson

This dialogue was conducted via email with Ian Watson in New York and Eugenio Barba travelling between his Odin Teatret headquarters in Holstebro, Denmark and a teaching assignment in Cairo, Egypt. The dialogue took place over a three-month period between early December 2000 and the second week of March 2001.

IAN WATSON On more than one occasion, you have described your theatrical heritage as one that incorporates masters of both the East and West. This heritage, in conjunction with your ISTA research, and your talk of the performer's professional rather than cultural/ social/personal identity locates your own professional identity at the crossroads of many cultures. How would you characterize your work at these crossroads? Is it intercultural, multicultural, transcultural, or something else altogether different?

EUGENIO BARBA Nowadays intercultural and multicultural have become categories which seem to have an easily comprehensible meaning for many people. But if I ask myself whether these categories are of any use to me when reflecting on my craft or whether my activity as director falls within them, then I am struck by perplexity and many questions arise. Long before these words became commonplaces, the social and cultural plurality within each European nation was a known fact. The history of our continent is scarred by wars of religion, class struggle and hegemonic languages and cultures repressing others. Theatre history had brought to light the seismic consequences of the European Reformers' 'intracultural' journey at the beginning of the twentieth century and their assimilation of performative elements from their respective popular and religious backgrounds – circus, cabaret, music hall, liturgies or devotional ceremonies.

The mere fact that people of different traditions or origins come together is not relevant in itself. It can signify one of two things: either that their differing cultural identities are combined in a sort of complementarity, in the form of various 'specializations', or else that this contact represents a need to distance oneself from one's own respective origins in order to create or integrate a new *heimat*, an artistic home. In the latter case, insistence on the multicultural aspect as a starting point is not pertinent and conceals the problem instead of illuminating it.

Multiculturalism is a possible perspective for examining a theatre phenomenon. The relevance of this perspective, however, needs first to be demonstrated. When the Berlin Philharmonic Orchestra engages an Italian conductor, is it choosing intercultural dialogue or is it making a choice from within the 'village' of classical music? And what if the conductor is Indian or Korean? When does the difference in origin become the most important factor, and when not?

To be even more specific: is this conversation between Ian Watson and Eugenio Barba a dialogue between two people who are involved in theatre, one as a scholar and the other as director and leader of a group? Or is it an example of the different ways in which a southern European and an Anglo-Saxon view theatre? Is it a confrontation between two particular biographies and forms of cultural message: on the one hand a Scot who, for many years, was professionally active in Australia and now teaches in an American university, and on the other, an Italian who was trained in Poland and has worked for more than three decades in Denmark? Which of these different differences is the most significant when describing our ongoing dialogue?

IW From which perspective would you consider it pertinent to speak in personal terms about the intercultural or the multicultural?

EB Rather than the path of aesthetic, sociological or anthropological abstraction, I would choose a concrete biographical point of departure. Here we can detect the experiences which determine the stand we take, the artistic results of this stand and the words through which we express it.

In my adolescence in the deep south of Italy, I had only to travel a few hundred kilometres to the north to feel like a foreigner. And as a child of a bourgeois family, I ignored the manifestations of the 'people's culture' in the village of Gallipoli where I grew up. Many years later I read with amazement in the anthropologists' books that I had been living in the midst of *tarantismo*, the tarantula syndrome, with trance, music and dances structured in a therapeutic-performative ceremony of whose existence I had not the faintest knowledge.

I studied at a military school for three years, but at the age of eighteen, rejecting the discipline, I fled as far away as possible. In Norway, as an immigrant, I had to cope with the vital problem of how to integrate in a context where habits, mentality, relationships between the sexes or in the working hierarchy constituted for me a real cultural trauma. I had to readjust my bearings radically. For instance, my knowledge of history. I had been taught that in 1936 Italy had occupied Ethiopia in order to civilize its barbaric population, but the Norwegians and their books told me of a war of extermination.

I left my bourgeois milieu and the warm, Catholic southern Italy because I didn't identify myself with my country's history, myths, longings and ideals. I became an emigrant, a redneck worker in a totally opposite universe: cold Protestant Norway. In its proletarian world I discovered class struggle, the efficiency of a strike and solidarity, but also xenophobia and racism. I was a 'dago', a wop. I had to learn to think and speak in Norwegian, always straining to decipher the subtext of words and behaviour around me. My existential condition made me 'different', and this position was never neutral. For some Norwegians it was a pejorative feature, for others a positive and genuine quality.

My yearning to escape from my own Italian background was not replaced by an explicit wish to become Norwegian. Obscurely, I sensed that 'cultural roots' were synonymous with confinement, with a restricted horizon. I wanted to break the ties which limited my mental freedom and to approach the unvoiced dark 'otherness' in myself and around me which a specific culture hindered me from doing. I did not want to be rooted in a nation, a culture or a class. I struggled to let my roots grow in 'the sky', in an ideal country of borderless values and truths which were the fruit of personal strife and conquest.

It still resonates within me, this feeling of enlightenment as if I had inherited the whole earth, all its landscapes and cultures, its manifold past and confusing present. I was eighteen years old and I did not know yet that a legacy always presupposes change, that the heir must bring about this metamorphosis and give birth to new life. Age made me realize that if theatre is discovery, this is based on a resurrection of the past, thanks to the unique individual temperature of each of us. But this past was not encrusted in a culture or a nation. It was the simultaneous and contiguous presence of all pasts.

IW More than curiosity then, it was a yearning to break away from your Italian culture which located you at the crossroads of many cultures.

EB I never attempted consciously to locate myself at such a crossroad. I only longed to be a 'traveller of speed' as I described in my *Theatre: Solitude, Craft, Revolt* [1999: 43–53]. There are people who live in a nation or in a culture. And there are people who live in their own bodies. They are the travellers who cross the Country of Speed, a space and time which have nothing to do with the landscape and the season of the place they happen to be travelling through. One can stay in the same place for months and years and still be a 'traveller of speed' journeying through regions and cultures thousands of years and thousands of kilometres apart, in unison with the thoughts and reactions of men and women far removed from oneself by skin colour or history.

In *The Paper Canoe: A Guide to Theatre Anthropology* [1995], I was aware that my pre-expressive analysis of non-European performative techniques would easily induce a dualistic and mechanical East–West 'intercultural' interpretation, with its recurrent political clichés. In this book I identified myself with the 'culture of transition'. I referred to the European Reformers – those rebels and heretics like Stanislavski, Meyerhold, Craig, Copeau, Artaud and Brecht – as creators of a theatre of transition. Their lives and work had demolished the ways of seeing and doing a performance, had established new relationships with the spectator, stimulated a new awareness of our art as a political, ethical or spiritual agent and had insufflated value and meaning into the entertainment shell of our craft. This attitude has its roots in transition, in the rejection of the spirit of the time and, what is more important, cannot passively be handed down to future generations. We have to choose to be their heirs and 'conquer' their legacy by a lonely effort which personalizes and transforms it.

The reformers – the dead who always remain young – shattered the existing theatre model in Europe, shaping a theatrical ecosystem with various niches and 'small nomadic traditions'. Such 'small nomadic traditions' with fleeting techniques but strong individualistic motivations, are short-lived. However, they move about and evolve if their specific values are embodied by other artists, regardless of place of birth or context. Conquered legacy, which is always embodied, presupposes change. An emblematic example is Seki Sano's destiny, a Japanese who worked with Stanislavski and Meyerhold and became the seminal personality in the development of theatre in Mexico and Colombia.

Of course one can say that Odin Teatret is intercultural or multicultural. It was created in Oslo by Norwegian would-be actors whose Italian-born director had received his professional imprint in Poland. On emigrating to Denmark, Odin Teatret called itself the Inter-Scandinavian Theatre Laboratory and, in addition to its original Norwegian members, took in Danes, Swedes and Finns who did not always understand each other's language. Later on Italians, French, English, Spaniards, Germans, North and South Americans, Canadians, Japanese and Sri Lankans joined too. We travel and sojourn for long periods in many countries and have established a tight network of initiatives and collaboration with performers and scholars from many nations. Our centre in Holstebro is a caravanserai which hosts individuals and groups from all over the world. ISTA, the International School of Theatre Anthropology, is another of our activities that has been going on for more than twenty years.

IW   So you admit that Odin Teatret is intercultural or multicultural.

EB   If you visit the members of the Odin in their homes in Holstebro, you will find plenty of traces both of our individual idiosyncrasies and tastes as well as of mannerisms revealing our cultural and social origins. Furniture, ways of dressing, conduct in our private space, interests, hobbies, political inclinations, religious beliefs, food habits and sexual prejudices clearly denote how little we have in common.

If you examine the set of relationships and norms through which these different individuals have organized themselves, if you delve into their working attitudes and routines, the values to which they are loyal and the dead who are alive in their memory, you will discover an indefinable affinity among all these different personalities, a sort of common 'Odinian ethnicity'. Their behaviour and mentality *in relation to the work*, makes up a micro-culture which is not just the consequence of mixing people from various cultural backgrounds. Only a lazy way of thinking would attempt to explain the complexity, continuity, consistency as well as the many, often contradictory, results of our group by means of the magic formula: 'intercultural'. From an existential, technical, stylistic and aesthetical point of view, Odin Teatret is far removed from other hybrid theatre groups. Similarly it is light years away from purely Danish groups and mainstream as well as experimental companies.

The word 'intercultural', as a cognitive instrument or tool of analysis, does not help to throw any light on, interpret or explain the specific professional identity of the Odin people, the convictions which imbue their work or the inner dynamics which have allowed the same core of people to remain together and active for more than thirty-seven years. Odin Teatret's history and commitment, which make it unique, unrepeatable and at the same time able to withstand new trends and generational changes, have nothing to do with an accidental coming together of a 'foreign legion' of actors, a gathering of artistic temperaments with different passports.

The essential factors are our first years as autodidactic amateurs, the need to justify our choice of the theatre craft and the search for sources of learning in a milieu which was indifferent towards us. More than ideas or theories, constraints lead towards unsuspected solutions. One such constraint – fundamental in the shaping of the Odin's technical and emotional identity – was the emigration from Norway to Denmark. Odin's Norwegian actors had difficulty in making themselves understood by Danish spectators at our new base in Holstebro. For us it was a question of life and death to create performances where the dramaturgy was not based mainly on the interpretation of a text and the understanding of its words, but on proximity and intimacy, on sensual, sensorial, vocal and dynamic ensnaring, perceptible 'actions' or 'attractions' as Eisenstein would have said.

Artistically speaking, the intercultural factors are not determining. More important are the formalized rigour of the chosen performative genre, the aesthetic vision and specific personality of the director, and the 'superstitions' or emotional forces which drive each single artist. In a theatre company the biographical-historical background of the performers – usually called cultural identity – can be very different, even poles apart. The agglutinating factor is the reciprocal agreement to submit to a set of technical principles and to the aesthetic, political or other values which impregnate these principles. The Japanese can be brilliant ballet dancers and North American become appraised Noh or Kyogen performers. None would call the Danish Royal Ballet intercultural, in spite of its French Bournonville technique and the many foreign dancers who are part of it. Danish or Argentinian actors in Tadashi Suzuki's or Bob

Wilson's productions are highly creative in accordance with the artistic and unique universe of these outstanding directors.

IW   You don't mention Hisao and Hideo Kanze, Sanjukta Panigrahi or the many other Asian artists who have collaborated with you. You neglect your travels and field work in Asia or Latin America, your early and still ongoing interest in Noh, Balinese dance/theatre or Kathakali which in the early sixties you were the first Western director to study in Kerala and write about. You don't take into consideration the Asian seminars which Odin Teatret organized since the early 1970s and ISTA, which has contributed to confrontation, debate, practice and reflection since its foundation in 1979.

EB   Your question evokes indisputable facts, which appear as a succession of causes and effects. This is only partially true. Behind the Asian theatres, which entered my life at a late stage, lie other longings, more intimate motivations.

In my withdrawal from my Italian culture the horizon widened, and for many years I immersed myself in books about Hinduism and Buddhism. I even became a merchant seaman in order to visit, as a pilgrim, Ramakrishna's home and temple outside Calcutta. 'My' Asia consisted of a few geographical names inhabited by hermits, philosophers and wandering ascetics: the populous Bengali outskirts of Dakshineswar, the highlands of northern India where Nagarjuna lived, the Tibetan plateau where Marpa and Milarepa dispelled their magic powers, the route through China which Bodhidharma followed, the steppe of the Mongolian shamans. This Asia became a region of the Country of Speed, one of the 'roots in the sky' of my 'flying' home.

When somebody looks at our past, or when we ourselves let our memories flow, we seem to forget the innumerable zigzags, the long deviations and senseless detours. They were not conscious 'searches' for anything in particular, merely symptoms of uneasiness, restlessness, desire for adventure and an irresistible feeling that luck was waiting for us elsewhere. Many sudden and foolish decisions were the result of a fortuitous meeting with a woman, of sympathy or antipathy towards a man. Today I know that it was not just a wish to learn, to risk, to face unexpected situations and powerful personalities. A burning red thread has guided me in my condition of emigrant, of foreigner with 'roots in the sky', in this labyrinth of wanderings, encounters, confrontations, aspirations: the need to protect my dignity and my difference. Looking back now, I clearly discern the ultimate goal: theatre as an island of difference and freedom which has to be conquered.

But let us return to the Asian theatres.

The term intercultural was unheard of in the late 1950s when my interest in theatre was aroused. The striking productions of Bertolt Brecht's Berliner Ensemble, Marcel Marceau's pantomimes which amazed huge audiences with their textless 'physical' exploits and avant-garde texts by such writers as Ionesco, Beckett, Adamov and Mrozek were the cause of considerable ferment in Europe. There was no first-hand knowledge of performances from other continents. Books recorded the interest of Meyerhold, Eisenstein, Dullin, Artaud or Brecht for classical Asian forms. But with the exception of Claudel who had lived in China and Japan, the above mentioned artists had not seen Asian performers on their home ground, only on tour within the framework of European stages and audiences.

As an autodidact I was obsessed with the acquisition of professional efficacy. In spite of my lack of experience, I had to teach my would-be actors. I began with the core of exercises, which I had seen Grotowski's actors doing during my stay in Opole. Some of my young actors had followed courses in pantomime or ballet, so they became 'teachers' in these fields. I relied on books, which could give concrete examples and advice. Stanislavski, Dullin and Vakhtangov were extremely useful. We studied the photos from the European Reformers' pedagogical work and productions and tried to reconstruct the actors' postures as exercises.

I did the same with pictures from Kabuki and the Beijing Opera. From the static image, the actors and I built up a dynamic structure, an 'exercise' which we included in our training. It goes without saying that this reconstruction had very little to do with real Japanese and Chinese acting technique, but this operation had a profoundly stimulating and creative impact on all of us. This applied also to records by different singers, from Italian opera to Armstrong, from Gregorian chants to Yma Sumac, from Indian raga improvisations to the hunting songs of the Pygmies, from Bunraku joruri recitation to Sicilian storytellers. We repeated these intonations, vocal asperities and modulations, in an effort to uncover and revitalize the multiple qualities, possibilities and nuances of the human voice, which we possess at birth and then lose when growing up in a specific language and culture.

During those first years, the various Asian theatres were present in our imagination. In my eyes, these theatres were a sort of theatrical Arcadia with powerful heroines and graceful warriors, fantastic roaring animals, trembling boats on still, clear blue seas, silent mountain peaks … all embodied by the art of the same actor. Excellence of craftsmanship was the model which the Odin Teatret's amateurs wanted to emulate. We did not want to search for 'authenticity' in a mythical Orient with its philosophies, codified techniques and suggestive costumes. Theatre for us was commitment towards the *polis*, the possibility to take a stand and follow the way of refusal. Classical Asian theatres were not the most evident models of engagement.

In 1973, almost ten years after Odin Teatret's beginning, we experienced Japanese theatre, not only its different styles and performances but also the demonstrations of such artists as Sawamura Sojuro, Hisao and Hideo Kanze. The invaluable help of Frank Hof allowed us to organize a seminar in Holstebro which seemed impossible at that time, bringing together under the same roof Kabuki, Noh and Shuji Terayama's contemporary actors.

A couple of years later Odin Teatret organized a seminar on Javanese and Balinese theatre and dance. Here I met I Made Pasek Tempo, the Balinese master who in 1980 was among the founders of ISTA and collaborated with me until his death in 1991. Finally, in 1977, during another Odin seminar on Indian dance and theatre, I met a young Odissi dancer, Sanjukta Panigrahi and her husband Raghunath. It was a reunion with a sister: clever, beautiful, strong and sensitive, courageous and generous. I admired and loved her deeply. I recall the many questions we asked each other, the long conversations at night when everybody else was asleep, her detailed yet suggestive demonstrations and very personal explanations, sometimes with only me present. Sanjukta was not only one of the founders of ISTA, she was its undeniable queen. For me, the immense effort and the painstaking perseverance and struggle to collect funds for an ISTA session were compensated by the expectation of meeting Tempo, Katsuko Azuma, Kanichi Hanayagi, and Raghunath again. But most of all Sanjukta. I have never been able to accept the injustice of her early death.

ıw You speak of Sanjukta and the other Asian performers who have influenced you as if they have been more than guides to your theatrical search. They seem to have affected you deeply and inspired you not just as an artist but as a human being.

EB Yes, more than an inspiration, I feel as though they were my kin who supported me in finding my difference, nourishing my 'roots in the sky'. My first fantasies about Asian theatres, the impact of Kathakali, the many years of mutually concerted efforts with a handful of Asian artists, all this is present in my creative metabolism in a secret, unconscious form. I am very moved by the artists I have mentioned. I feel a deep respect, admiration, even love because of their know-

ledge, rigour, and loyalty towards an artistic discipline, which is at
same time a profession of faith. They mingle together with ot
members from my professional family – European, North and South
American. My meeting with them kept alive a reflecting attitude
which expresses itself as a Socratic, maieutic-like questioning. Let me
explain.

From the very first days of my activity as pedagogue and director
two questions arose. Firstly, why did Stanislavski and Meyerhold
invent the exercises to prepare an actor? My experience showed that
an actor could be excellent in the exercises without reaching the same
quality during the rehearsals and the performance. There was no
automatic connection between the results in the training and the
creative results. Why then do the exercises?

The second question came about after I saw Kathakali in India in
1963. I knew nothing of this theatre form since there were no books
or information about it. I did not understand the language, nor was
I familiar with its code of acting. I knew little of the stories which the
actors were presenting and was confused by the popular and noisy
atmosphere in which the performances took place. However, in certain sequences of the performance, one particular actor was capable
of captivating my attention, bewitching my senses, binding me to
each of his actions. How did he achieve this? What forces or factors
were active in our interaction, based only on sensorial stimulation
and receptivity? Was it a matter of talent, of individual grace and
temperature? Or had technical skill something to do with it? And,
which qualities were essential to this technical skill?

These two questions, or enigmas, became an obsession which still
haunts me. They have determined my fascination on the one hand
for the handing on and the learning process in our craft, and on the
other for the elementary technical factors in scenic communication
between living organisms, i.e., the actor–spectator relationship. My
professional biography is characterized by these two enigmatic
questions: the learning process (the work on oneself), and Theatre
Anthropology (the pre-expressive foundations of an actor/dancer's
craft).

IW You raise an interesting question about your biography when you
mention Theatre Anthropology. Etymologically it suggests a discipline concerned with the study of culture, but some would argue that
it is something different. It is very specifically concerned with performance separate from culture. Whatever its precise meaning, I
think it would be fair to say that you 'discovered' Theatre Anthropology. You developed its concepts, its language, rhetoric, application

and theoretical premises. You are also at the center of every ISTA gathering, which is predicated upon it. Theatre Anthropology could be characterized by some as lacking in a broad enough base to move beyond the concerns of one man. Do you imagine Theatre Anthropology as a discipline that outlives you?

EB You are right about Theatre Anthropology being my passionate concern. It has to do with my origin as an autodidact and with the two enigmatic questions I just touched on: what is the connection between training and artistic results? Do certain essential yet objective principles exist in all genres of acting technique? The attempt to find an answer and research it in depth has led to the twelve sessions of ISTA, to the continuous barter of information between many masters and me, to the University of Eurasian Theatre. These situations allow me to observe at length the work of performers from many genres. Since they come from many countries, or cultures as one now says, people think that I am fascinated by non-European theatres, especially Asian ones. But classical ballet and corporal mime also awake my curiosity and are two of my fields of investigation. Yes, Theatre Anthropology *is* my personal obsession.

I don't know if it will outlive me. For the moment let us stick to the facts.

Any form of communication presupposes misunderstandings. The question is whether these misunderstandings are fertile. I am sometimes bewildered by the various, even bizarre interpretations applied to Theatre Anthropology. Today it is taught in a few universities and in many schools and workshops in different places. If you put the university scholars and the workshop teachers together around a table, they would disagree on the most basic terms. What is a *sats*? Are the principles of scenic presence universal or pragmatic? And the biggest mouthful of all: what is pre-expressivity?[1]

However, their discussion would reveal not only disagreement or confusion but also interest in the concreteness of the field which Theatre Anthropology explores. It is a field which is studied according to the different levels of organization of the two hemispheres in which an actor moves: that of the process and that of the results. This study is not guided by ideas, theories or aesthetics, but by material factors such as weight, stance, gait, sight and the quality of tensions and energy. These tangible factors make the actor's 'flow of life', or scenic presence, perceptible to the spectator.

---

1   For a thorough discussion of Barba's technical terms see Barba, 1995 and Watson, 1995.

Concreteness must here be understood in its etymological sense: *cum crescere*, to grow concomitantly. An artistic process is more similar to the growth of a jungle than to the evolution of a specific project. Hence the importance of the levels of organization, the grasping of the complementary aspects of repetition and innovation, i.e., the score and subscore, and the awareness of the many psycho-somatic factors which an actor brings into action to induce an 'effect of organicity', of 'life' in the spectators.

Acknowledgement of these principles in the various performing techniques as well as other questions investigated by Theatre Anthropology have spread to many niches of the theatre's ecosystem and even to some academic circles. This elementary knowledge is now so prevalent that it has become anonymous, as though it belonged to the baggage of competence which has been in existence for a long time. In other words, it is no longer associated with Eugenio Barba, ISTA or Odin Teatret.

I W Do you think that the ISTA pedagogues, the master performers from the East and West, should take away anything from ISTA, or are you only concerned with your own research?

E B A meeting between performers who present their professional experience reciprocally is never a one-way process. If it is extremely enlightening for me to watch what and how a Japanese or Balinese actor/dancer teaches his pupils, the same must be said for them when they see me work with my actors who have twenty-five, thirty and even more years of experience. It is very strange that anyone could consider such masters merely as inert receivers of my professional concerns. On several occasions they have expressed the different phases of their reactions during our collaboration within ISTA. In *La scuola degli attori* edited by Franco Ruffini [Milan and Florence: Casa Usher, 1981], in *The Tradition of ISTA* edited by Rina Skeel [Brazil: FILO, the International Festival of Londrina and the Universidade Estadual de Londrina, 1994] and in *The Performers' Village* edited by Kirsten Hastrup [Denmark: Drama, 1996] they explain in their own words what it is that they get from ISTA, the motives which bring them back again and again, the kind of challenges they meet, and also their changing awareness towards the master–pupil relationship and their own performing tradition.

Of course, if I disappear, there will be no more ISTA. So I suppose you can say that it is a very personal project, that its continuity is my concern, that I am the centre from which this adventure of mutual inspiration and friendship emanates. I have already talked about the two enigmatic questions which motivate my efforts to keep it alive.

But there are also other reasons. One is the pleasure of creating a utopian fiesta, a potlach-like banquet, which hosts masters of ancient traditions and anonymous youngsters from Third Theatre groups, curious scholars and friends whom I love. I like ISTA because it is a paradoxical space. It costs almost half a million US dollars to implement this 'performers' village' during fourteen days, half of it in isolation. This extravagantly exorbitant amount is collected by organizers who are usually theatre groups or individuals belonging to the Third Theatre with no easy access to financial funding. Only a strong motivation, a belief in the impact of ISTA in their professional milieu, and superhuman efforts can make an ISTA session possible.

My concern combines my interest in the actor's embodied knowledge with my attachment to the master-friends and scholar-friends. It makes me live rare moments of an experience which I can only call 'freedom'. It overtakes me mostly at the night, when the daily activities are over and I visit one of the artists on the ISTA staff. I ask him or her the most naive or intricate questions and they try to give an answer, demonstrating it sometimes with a stance, a posture, a tension, a step, a dance. They make an effort to grasp my sentences, to understand which part of their experience I am referring to through terms which do not exist in their terminology: organic, dramaturgy, pre-expressivity. They translate and describe to me words and metaphors from their working language which are connected to the appraisal of an actor's skill. There is patience and also a desire to protect me, to aid this friend whom they have seen ageing, yet persisting with the same inquisitive, childish questions.

This is my research at ISTA, a solitary and individual one. I attend again and again the same classes and watch the same working demonstrations which reveal to me new perspectives when observed from the point of view of the particular theme adopted by that ISTA session. Only in my final speech do I let my observations, perplexities, unexpected associations and connections be structured into a consistent flow.

It is generally thought that if people work individually on their own, and later meet, this moment of encounter is one of evaluation and contributes to reaching a unitary vision. At ISTA the exact opposite is the case. The moment of encounter is one of disorder in the research, of turbulence, confusion, without a common programme. It is a time for questioning. Everyone draws her own conclusions, according to her specific working environment, whether theatre or university, practice or theory. The conclusions are very diverse, often not comparable. They may not even refer to the same field.

Another fundamental question has to be asked: what is the influence of the profession which we practise on our way of thinking? As I touched on earlier, we do not derive solely from a country, a language, a culture, but also from a craft. The emphasis placed mainly on the country of origin is justified when we consider the processes of immigration and uprooting, or multiculturalism as a social problem involving various ethnic groups. But such exclusive attention becomes a limitation or a blind obsession when applied to relationships between single individuals and artists. It imposes a social perspective as this was the only determining one. There is a great difference between establishing a relationship with Indians in general, and collaborating with Sanjukta and Raghunath who, amongst other things, are also Indian.

IW   Nevertheless, wouldn't you say that there is an element of colonialism at work in ISTA, at least in so far as the model of observation and study is frequently one in which the 'wise' Westerners observe the 'others?'

EB   The study of the 'other' is not despicable, and of course you start from what you know, applying the criteria of your own professional or historical-biographical background. It is what you do with the results of this observation that can raise moral doubts. One can study an ethnic minority in Denmark to assert the superiority of the Danish culture. And one can study an ethnic minority in Denmark to make politicians aware of certain particularities which should be taken into consideration in a pluralistic democracy.

I am a Westerner, a European who grew up in southern Italy, an economically underdeveloped region, neglected by the central government and discriminated against by the northern Italians. After the Second World War the southern Italians, together with the Portuguese and the Spaniards, emigrated to the northern European countries in search of work where they were treated as pariahs. As I told you before, this was also my lot as an emigrant when I earned my living as a welder, sailor and longshoreman for many years. But in the evening I took possession of and appropriated any knowledge which I felt could help me towards intellectual autonomy. I did not think in terms of countries – Russia, Paraguay or Australia – nor of cultural specificities – Eastern or Western. Francis of Assisi and Teresa de Ávila were alongside Mirabai and Hakuin, General Giap with Clausewitz and Che Guevara.

As a foreign worker, I often felt excluded. When I began as director, I was an amateur, together with a few teenagers who had been turned down by the theatre school. I belonged to the theatre lumpenproletariat, which is to be found across all borders. I called it Third Theatre, bearing in mind the discrimination which is inflicted by the theatre's first world.

The history of Odin Teatret, and mine too, has its origins in indifference and rejection by the theatre milieu. My daily, almost insuperable obstacle was to teach these trusting teenagers *how* to be actors and *why* they should continue with a rigorous training which was incomprehensible at that time: exercises, silence, no discussion, absolute precision and discipline. I tried to find the reasons for this *why* in the biographies – and not only the ideas – of the theatre reformers which I read and interpreted based on my own situation. This is the beginning of the discovery of the 'subterranean' history of theatre without national frontiers and going beyond the divisions in continents and epochs such as we find in history books. The essence of this subterranean dimension is *ethos*, a matrix which is the embodiment of certain norms, ways of thinking and practices of the craft. It was this *ethos* that I found in Sanjukta, Katsuko, Tempo and Fabrizio Cruciani with whom I founded the ISTA, all now dead.

One can call colonialism my attitude during the ISTAs when I observe masters from West and East, North and South presenting their 'first day of work' and the first technical rudiments they have learned from their masters. It can also be called fetishism, superstition or faith that in these simple postures and stances is encapsulated a knowledge which I have to decipher. Facts about our life and work speak, but always according to the words and views of those who tell them.

Could one not assert that there is an element of colonialism in this desire to enforce a multicultural perspective? Does this tendency not contain the imposition of just one particular problem amongst many? Undoubtedly it is a burning problem, but because of its incandescence in certain areas, it tends to dictate its own demands in every situation, smothering all other questions and possibilities. Does there exist a discussion, dispute, relationship and confrontation in which it is not possible to uncover a trace of colonialism, of an inequitable exchange?

The problems of colonialism cannot be avoided when referring to relations between European, American, Asian and African countries. But we must also accept that the legacy of colonialism cannot invade our entire mentality, preventing us from giving full weight to relationships between individuals who are specialists in adjacent fields.

At ISTA, what is more relevant: the meeting of people from different cultures, or the meeting of different colleagues from the same craft? A true multicultural encounter also takes place when a Noh actor performs with a Nihon Buyo dancer for the first time, as happened at the Bielefeld ISTA. Why is it so difficult to accept the view that people who meet are not just artists from different cultures, but colleagues of a common profession, gathering together to inspire one another and broaden their knowledge? There is a risk of falsifying the experience of ISTA through exaggeration, looking on it as a multicultural and aesthetic project and not for what it is: a wandering village of men and women sharing the same craft.

IW Do you think it is fair to say that there has been a shift in ISTA over the years from a genuine research endeavour to one in which already confirmed findings are presented to participants who have little space to engage you or other ISTA staff in a dialogue about those findings?

EB The most drastic shift over the years has been the duration. The first two sessions lasted two months each. Since then, the duration has been of about two weeks, of which half has been a 'closed session' and the rest has been open to the public with a symposium, demonstrations and performances.

ISTA began as a gathering of actors and directors of theatre groups who, after some years of activity, felt the need for new stimuli. I thought that stimulation could be provided by meeting inspiring theatre historians, Asian masters I admired, as well as Odin actors, Dario Fo, Orazio Costa, Ingemar Lindh, Keith Johnstone, Clive Barker, Jerzy Grotowski and Tom Leabhart. I have invited many Western actors and directors to give demonstration of their work and experience. They have declined politely because it was not clear what was expected from them since ISTA was not proposing a workshop.

The first two ISTAs offered me the possibility of concentrating on my two disturbing questions: the relationship between training and artistic results, and the material factors of an actor's presence which contribute to captivating the spectator's attention. But if you read carefully through the schedules of all the twelve sessions, you will discover that all of them are organized more or less in the same way. In the morning the artistic staff teach some basic positions and gaits from their respective traditions. Then there is a part with different names: bazaar, gipsy-time, barter, 'chaosmos'. Here the participants join freely in groups according to specific interests, exchanging and exploiting their heterogeneity and experience as well as that of the artistic staff. You will see spontaneous gatherings about masks, commedia dell'arte, improvisation, martial arts, voice training, singing, the conditions of

Colombian or Cuban theatre. In the evening there are performances, only for the participants, in an intimate setting. They may be followed by comments, both from the performers, or from me.

The only ISTAs which did not follow this pattern were the ones in Holstebro and Copenhagen. They were structured as masterclasses with practical explanations by the invited artists. Until 1994, demonstrations of the principles of Theatre Anthropology were part of the daily programme. This is no longer so, but during the 'bazaar time', Lluis Masgrau, an assistant and colleague of mine, proposes films and videos of past performances as well as learning methods from the perspective of Theatre Anthropology.

When I started ISTA I had only one clear idea – and this determined the repetitive choice of the same artists and the same core to the programme. I can best sum up the idea in this way: in order to find any 'recurrent principle' within the techniques of the various genres, I had to use performers with codified styles. They would be able to repeat – always in the same way – a score, a form which contained the information I was looking for. Therefore ISTA began with Asian classical masters, Ingemar Lindh, trained by Etienne Decroux, and Toni Cots, an actor from Odin Teatret. Each of them taught the participants for a week what they themselves had learnt during the first days of their career. In this way I could be sure that the participants would not learn Odissi or Buyo dance, Balinese Baris or mime scenes. Even more important, these lessons allowed me to sit and watch the masters repeat the same dynamic patterns, which aroused many questions in me. At night I visited them and bombarded them with questions.

The secret of ISTA is not group research, but solitary observation of the same elements or factors. Those who come again to ISTA are faced with the frustration of experiencing only variations of what they have seen previously. They seem to forget that the theme of each ISTA makes it possible to study these elements from another point of view.

What changes is the theme, the perspective which an ISTA session adopts. When, in Brazil, the subject was 'Tradition and Founders of Traditions', I discovered how inert the term 'tradition' was for me since it did not help me in a practical way to uncover new aspects of the history of my craft. And how fertile was the expression 'founders of small nomadic traditions' in understanding the mutation of European theatre in the twentieth century. One of the results of the ISTA in Wales was the coining of the term 'subscore', thus enlarging and deepening that territory of an actor's working process which is not included in Stanislavski's subtext. The ISTA in Umeå threw light on the many reasons which Stanislavski and Meyerhold followed in inventing the practice of exercises.

I feel I have achieved a victory over the mutism of my two enig-matic questions when new terms and ways of seeing help forge an operative terminology as well as dissipate the fogs of abstract expla-nations. In certain cases I have gathered my reflections in books such as *The Paper Canoe* or *The Secret Art of the Performer* written in col-laboration with Nicola Savarese. Some of the latest observations have been published as articles, mostly in *The Drama Review* and *New Theatre Quarterly*. But the majority of my 'discoveries' lie dormant in a dozen or so notebooks crammed with odd sentences, words in many languages, floating terms which I have not yet had the time or else am still unable to translate into efficacious thought.

IW Your 'discoveries' dormant in notebooks suggest another of your concerns, 'the subterranean history of theatre', which I understand you, together with Nicola Savarese and the Italian scientific staff of ISTA, are writing a book about. Has this 'subterranean history', or the yet to be formulated 'discoveries' influenced or been present in your work over the years?

EB In the work with actors, a director reacts to that which 'functions', is 'alive', 'organic' and contains an ambivalent or 'hermaphroditic' vibration, expanding the possibility of the meanings that the direc-tor wishes to convey in a particular sequence of the performance. This efficiency is not based on theories but on an ability to suggest, on inventiveness, pragmatism, intuition which reacts to material stimuli: the actions of the actors, even their faults, misunderstand-ings or fortuitous events. These are some of the factors which guide the relationships and the working process involving actor and direc-tor. However, when we *a posteriori* transform our experience into awareness and try to communicate it through words, we have a tendency to justify and bend the results according to our own tastes, theories, ideologies and aesthetics. For me this process of transform-ing experience into awareness and reflection took place within the historical framework of the European theatre reformers I talked of earlier and of course my three years of collaboration with Grotowski.

I feel that my professional origin, as well as Odin Teatret's, is con-nected to amateur theatre and its role in the anthropological muta-tion which our craft underwent in Europe in the twentieth century. This mutation was not the result of an evolution, but of the defla-gration of the unitary theatre universe, and the simultaneous growth of many theatres whose diverging techniques, visions, aims and even spectators constituted a galaxy. Theatre no longer existed, only *theatres*, in the plural. A kaleidoscopic fragmentation which is even more evident today.

Many protagonists of this mutation did not belong to the professional milieu, but were outsiders – amateurs like Antoine, Stanislavski, Appia, Jacques Dalcroze or poets and writers such as Mallarmé, Paul Fort or Strindberg. They had not been conditioned by the norms and the well-proven know-how, nor by the lifestyle, mental habits and routines of the professional milieu. The constraints of their contexts and their personal beliefs forced them to shape their own 'small nomadic tradition', i.e., new ways of thinking and proceeding, with unprecedented techniques and objectives.

This handful of reformers shattered the theatre model prevalent in Europe. They were the catalysts for a 'big bang', for the explosion of 'Tradition' and the creation of 'small nomadic traditions' with specific ideals, pedagogical approaches, acting principles, social and aesthetic aims and even a particular audience. Theatre was no longer a continent, but an archipelago, each island attempting to build or break down a tradition, to create faiths, to implement its own technical and aesthetic dialect. Even more inflammatory was their questioning of the ultimate goal of the craft, which until now was only a commercial enterprise. Must theatre demand a conscious attitude from its members, make them take a stand, assume a responsibility towards their work, their spectators and the events of their time? Their efforts verged on metaphysics, an aim beyond the physical yet transient parenthesis of the performance: an artistic, didactic, political, ethical, revolutionary, nihilistic or spiritual dimension.

European twentieth century theatre sprang from an Oedipean bubo, not only because it killed the authority and the model of tradition which had generated it, but also because, like the adolescent Oedipus, it set out on a wandering solitary yet personal search for meaning, origins and identity.

IW   So, you see this 'explosion of Tradition' or 'big bang' as the demise of a unitary model of theatre and the origin of multifarious performance cultures that are clearly evident?

EB   We witness such a condition daily. In New York, a Broadway actor and a performance artist from Soho are autonomous and incommunicable planets in the galaxy I spoke about before. The same applies to Noh and Kabuki, classical ballet and modern dance, as well as groups like Gardzienice or Yuyachkani when confronted, for example, with a municipal theatre in Germany. All have different techniques, ways of thinking, objectives, spectators and so on.

Performative multiculturalism is not dangerous, it does not end in bloody confrontations, the mediocrity of its results do not kill and intolerance is usually kept to a verbal level or expressed through indifference. The whole picture becomes more complicated if we speak of a multicultural society and the role of the theatre in it.

When we call a society multicultural, we have the impression that we are not expressing a judgement but merely underlining the plurality of its components. We are in fact indicating an ambivalence.

The multicultural condition is never experienced as neutral, but rather as a threat or a value. It is a threat when imposed by economic and social conditions that escape the control of the individual. On the other hand, it is considered a value when it is the result of a choice. A multicultural or multi-ethnic group, festival, orchestra, theatre or association appears in a positive light purely through its composition, even before we are aware of what it produces or how it produces it.

This very positive value attributed to multiculturality is the other face of its threatening aspect. Since society seems to us to be divided and fraught with internal struggles, oases of peaceful cohabitation between groups and individuals from different cultures appear as fortunate and exemplary islands.

Today, the term multicultural does not so much define a society made up of different groups, but rather a reality in which the differences are problematic. Differences become *problematic* when they gravitate towards two specular ways of destruction: homogenization or reciprocal rejection.

Homogenization and rejection are not opposite alternatives, but two different levels of culture. The superficial homogenization (the same styles of dress, the same food, the same film or sports stars, the same standards of information, the same performances) is connected with a profound need to delve into the foundations of one's own specificity and ethnic origins in order not to be overwhelmed by the surrounding multicultural confusion.

In a society with problematic differences, theatre becomes a paradoxical space.

In a strict sense, a *paradox* is not a bizarre opinion but a coherent thought which originates from principles different to those on which common opinion and prevalent theories are based. The paradox, though not refutable, does not prevail: it does not conquer, yet it is not conquered. I am thinking about all of this when I speak of the paradoxical space of theatre.

The 'common places' of the theatre, in European culture, have for centuries been in the centres of cities. Theatres were the place, the symbol and the monument of a unity of national, urban or class culture. In the nineteenth century their façades resembled those of other temples of bourgeois civilization such as museums and the stock exchange. Outside these renowned and respected 'common places', other theatre spaces appeared, divergent or in opposition: arts and avant-garde theatres, studios, *théâtres de poche*, ateliers, talleres, workshops, laboratories, off and off-off theatres. Their polemic dialogue with the 'common places' of theatre has been a fertile force in the performative traditions of the twentieth century.

Outside these two complementary spaces a 'Third Theatre' grew up.

Together with my group, Odin Teatret, I travel around the world for half of the year. Only the smallest fraction of this time is spent as guests of subsidized and respected theatres. Most of the time we are travelling in the spaces of the Third Theatre. Everywhere I go I find milieux composed of motivated minorities, people who thirst after action and transcendence through theatre.

IW Has transcendence anything to do with ideology, with the vision of a better society or new beliefs? Or is it related to the tendency to reach back into history and find the roots, the original sources and the collective rituals which the present age has cancelled but which theatre may help to recreate?

EB The word transcendence sounds philosophical or religious. For me it indicates the contrary: something without a doctrine, that has to do with the values guiding the modest and precise conduct of the artisan. It makes me think of the apparent solitude of the anarchic craftsmen who fought for the freedom of Catalonia and whom Hans Magnus Enzensberger met in exile, as well as their capacity to retain their dignity and sense of revolt through anonymous crafts.

There is a lot of 'transcendent' theatre today in our multicultural society. Compared to the periods in which the renowned theatre seemed to be the only point of reference, today there is a multitude of performance forms many of which exist in those regions where the social wounds are deep: in prisons, hospitals, amongst immigrant communities and those who are marginalized. In other words, always outside the territories of that particular culture frequented by theatregoers.

I feel attracted by this paradoxical space of theatre which is a turbulent one, far from the lights and the attention of the experts and opinion makers. This contradiction nourishes my reflection: the neglected, marginal theatres are for the most part trying to find new meanings and values for a practice which seems destined to remain as a glorious relic of a society which is fast disappearing.

I have experienced theatre as emigration. It has allowed me to move around within the many classes and cultures of various societies and to defend my own identity without being transformed into an identifiable individual. The value of the theatre is in the quality of the relations it creates between individuals and between the different voices within a single individual.

I do not believe in reciprocal understanding. I believe in selfish exchanges, in an unmotivated solidarity between different human beings who do not pretend to understand each other. I believe in the immutable separateness of those who act together. The fruit of their action may, however, be common and unitary.

I believe in theatre as an empty ritual, not because it is futile and senseless, but because it is not usurped by a doctrine. Here, everyone can ride his or her own 'difference', can uncover it, reinforce it, without suffocating that of the others.

Until the beginning of the twentieth century, the natural space of theatre people has been the fluid and derisory dimension of travel in which cultural identity was not defined by geographical or historical limits, but by the efficiency of a craft. For centuries, while the theatre was subjected to the tyranny of pleasing and success, censorship and social scorn, actors lived a life of exile, cut off from the most precious and respected norms of the society around them.

Today many people choose one of the theatre's 'small nomadic traditions' as a means of safeguarding that part of themselves which lives in exile. This exile is not an amputation or a humiliation. It is a conquest. Or, in other words, it is a *political* action. It involves taking a stand, not always declared or even conscious, but concrete and active, against a society that is afraid of its many souls.

IW One could say that barter takes place in this paradoxical space as a sort of empty ritual, one without a doctrine to support it. Barter may also be a negotiation at crossroads or merely an exercise in two cultures viewing each other momentarily as they meet for a brief moment where their roads intersect. Do you regard barter as something beyond what some might call a shallow cultural exchange in which strangers do little more than metaphorically shake hands?

EB Before being realized, a barter requires many days of preparation, in certain cases even weeks. It is not the consequence of a spontaneous meeting, a clash of sympathies, but of a well-considered policy of relationships, interactions and finalities. The contacts which Odin Teatret establishes with individuals and associations are the hidden motor of the event, its subscore or rather its occulted goal. These contacts always build on measurable interest and the local partners must clearly perceive the concrete advantages they may draw from a barter, how it may benefit their purposes.

When Odin Teatret decides to do a barter, it is extremely selective in choosing its 'scouts' – the local organizers – well aware of what they represent in *their specific context*. In communist countries they could be dissidents, in Latin America communist students or Catholics inspired by the Theology of Liberation. One has to keep in mind that a major objective of any barter is the duration of its effect. In addition to building up the event, the local organizers must exploit its possible positive consequences for their own aims once Odin Teatret has left. A successful barter gives prestige and trust to the local organizers. Therefore, Odin Teatret must have a sound knowledge of whom it is supporting and why.

Imagine a theatre group from Belize arriving in New York and wanting to do a barter with your neighbourhood. Would you go there to recite a Scottish ballad while Susana, your Argentinian wife, rejoices at the prospect of dancing a tango to an old record of Gardel? Would you both feel an enthusiasm, shared by all your neighbours, to show the living seeds of embodied memories which make up your neighbourhood, this fragmented community of which you are a part?

I have my doubts that you or your neighbours could be persuaded to participate just by reading a small poster on the door of your pub or by Belizian actors announcing in the street their desire for a cultural exchange. But if your little son insisted on you and your wife taking an active part in a school party, then you would probably join in *without even knowing that you were involved in a barter*.

It could begin with a Belizian actor speaking with a couple of the more active teachers of your son's school. These would appreciate that the Belizians would perform their dances and songs without compensation (one normally never speaks of theatre, it scares people who are not accustomed to it, and theatregoers have an already in-built reaction: watch, applaud and go home. They would not understand why they should also perform afterwards). The teachers could realize the beneficial effect of a gathering where new pupils could mingle with older students, playing and singing a composition of their own, or be involved with their teachers and parents in presenting short sketches. The children, happy to perform, would push their parents to participate in this party where nobody would think of judging the 'performers' according to artistic criteria. You would come as your son's father who happens to be a Scot and recites a poem from his schooldays. Grandparents could sing a lullaby from their childhood, in their native Czech or Chinese. Under the pretext of a school party which is also enlivened by foreign artists, younger and older children, parents who have never met each other, teachers and different generations would mix organically in a sort of festivity which started with no ostensible motive. In the course of the evening, Belizian songs and dances would alternate with the school band or chorus, a ballet scene, the disabled pupils playing a sport, a short sketch produced for the occasion, acrobatics on skateboards, a display of martial arts, a simulacrum of rituals or religious songs, even if the parents aren't believers. And everybody would taste the cakes that the mothers, or fathers, had baked at home from an old family recipe. Such situations revitalize existing relationships, establish new ones, create unprecedented dynamics, uncover potentialities, implement possibilities, help to shape an 'identity' for the school vis-à-vis the foreigners. And let us not forget that these foreigners, through the quality of their entertainment, may be able momentarily to suspend the prejudices of their hosts.

IW   A barter presupposes a dramaturgy which is flexible and adaptable to each specific situation, but does it always have a 'hidden' purpose such as you have described?

EB   The rhythm, the dramaturgy, the *mise-en-scène* and the scenic space vary according to a precise subtext which has been more or less agreed between the theatre group and the local organizers. In popular neighbourhoods, with prevailing confusion and vivacity, barter may be rigorously structured, while in a rather bourgeois school it can flow with relaxed anarchy. The foreigners can present themselves first, followed by the numbers chosen by the organizers. Or else the barter may develop as a flow of scenes mixing the foreigners with local representatives. It can be shaped as a meandering, in which the audience strolls along the 'mansions' watching local performers and foreigners. When a traditional theatre in Coventry was our host, the event took place in the diffuse noise of a central square; with a cultural organisation in the outskirts of Buenos Aires we chose the old traditional theatre venues, where most of the participants came for the first time. In a poverty-stricken quarter of Santiago, we demanded as a prologue to the barter that the children clean a littered ground, which the organizers wished to turn into a playground. Our explanation was that we Danes are obsessed with hygiene.

All this 'Machiavellism' is possible only if one finds politically and culturally motivated individuals, or a group with whom you feel an affinity and who sees a benefit in arranging a barter. They know their neighbourhood, its topography and history, the people who live there, the resources, the limits and the possible provocations. These 'scouts' assume the burden of establishing and convincing contacts, making them meet to rehearse, printing and spreading information, etc. They must find any necessary equipment such as benches with which to build a circle and to seat spectators during open-air performances. Permission may have to be sought from the local authorities and private individuals to attach a projector or a screen to the wall of a house, a supermarket, a monument and so on. Most of all, the barter is a way to make the host group grow, face new challenges, unusual situations and discover a different role within the framework of their activity.

When the barter occurs in a prison, a psychiatric hospital, a refugee camp, an old people's home or in a kindergarten it is striking to follow the dynamics of the preparation, the expectations and fantasies which arise, the demolishing of conventions, habits or rules, the change of attitudes and the awakening of a feeling of self-worth and self-respect. In a refugee camp outside Holstebro, at the end of the barter, when all the effervescence had died down, an elderly man fetched a *sash*, a Balkan string instrument, and started playing and singing to himself. The Danish social worker at my side was astonished. For several months, since his arrival from Bosnia, that man had refused any communication, seeking protection behind a wall of silence. A barter is a seed you plant. You must do it in a careful and competent way. It may bear fruit if the people who organize it can keep alive the fragile social 'u-topia', 'no-place', which barter ephemerally represents.

A barter can provoke many contradictory reactions in a spectator who is an outsider. He may have difficulty in grasping the underlying logic of the event and watches the 'happening' as it were a performance, regarding the expressions of the community as a fortuitous assemblage of quasi-cultural manifestations deprived of a genuine expressivity. It may seem that the theatre group imposes rules, which don't belong to the community, and introduces alien habits which evoke associations of cultural imperialism. Many outsider-spectators are not moved by or in any way involved in what is going on around them. But the secret key is not so much what appears to take place between people as what happens inside each of them.

For me barter is a 'Trojan horse' through which Odin Teatret makes itself welcome in a community. The huge wooden beast sets in motion a series of reactions and the defending walls of the different members of the community crumble for the short duration of the barter. The longevity and probable growth of these reactions reside outside the horse: not in the actors' intentions but in those who let them in. The organizers have in their hands the destiny of a barter, the burden and the task to preserve its effects and cultivate them in the routine of grey, daily relations and activities.

IW It is interesting, given that barter is frequently viewed as being less central to the Odin's *raison d'être* than performance and research, that one of the most famous and widely circulated photographs of the company is a picture of the group engaged in a barter. I am think-ing of the photograph looking down upon an open, expansive field in which the Odin and their hosts are gathered in a near perfect circle as the barter is in progress. It is a stunning photograph. But is this all? Does the photograph and its frequent use by the company hint at something more, how central is barter to you and your work?

EB Barter means exchange, a reciprocal but short-lasting commitment, an effort to reach out towards 'otherness', in oneself and outside of oneself. All Odin's endeavours spring from this tension.

I like that photograph for many reasons. It is an effective graphic ideogram created by a young Dane, Peter Bysted, who is now a well-known designer. It is a picture of a barter in a Peruvian village near Ayacucho. There was no suitable space for the barter in that small community, so we chose a field outside the village. It was as if the meeting-exchange was a truce and the place a no man's land. The shape of the circle does not allow you to distinguish the foreigners from the locals. All are simultaneously actor and non-actor, partici-pant and observer. The image evokes a sense of integration and com-munion, yet also solitude, like a political gathering or a ceremony drowning in the vastness of nature. The lonely figure, near the small hut in the background, reminds me of myself in such situation: I am in the circle and also out of it, detached.

Yet the photo does not move me because of these arguments, but for other and mute reasons, which refuse to be tamed by words. It speaks to the dragon who protects the gold within me.

IW What relationship, if any, do you see between your ideas on barter, how you engage it in your work, and its use by other theatre groups influenced by you? What relationship do you see between your barters and the likes of Mette Bovin who adapted your ideas to serve anthropological research?

EB Barter is not the result of any originality by me or any of my col-leagues. It sprang from constraints. In *Theatre: Solitude, Craft, Revolt*

I have described its fortuitous origin when Odin Teatret did not have a production to show and was thus not able to present itself through an artistic result to the rural population of an Italian village [1999: 114–25]. Others have picked up the barter and applied it according to their needs, purposes and contexts. Theatre and dance groups, scholars as well as the anthropologist Mette Bovin have adopted it. So it is and should be, with ideas and practices which may be stimulating no matter where they come from.

Odin Teatret does not 'own' barter, and even if it is a genuine expression of our history and vision of the world, we don't feel poorer or in any way exploited or misunderstood because a group in India or Bolivia is making use of it. Anyone can claim it. To my eyes, taking possession of it turns barter into a process that you have to conquer, thus forcing you to define your own personality, political beliefs, professional viewpoint and responsibility.

IW   Talking of ownership. There has not been an international Third Theatre gathering in Europe in over twenty years, but there have been a number in Latin America in that time. Would you say that the Third Theatre movement has moved beyond your solitary leadership and become a multi-vocal entity with this shift in its focus from Europe to Latin America?

EB   If you remember my definition of Third Theatre, it will be evident that I never was its solitary leader. I simply labelled a particular theatre culture in different societies which critics and historians usually disregard. Or, if you like, I invented a name for the many niches in the theatrical ecosystem which are not taken into consideration. I wrote explicitly that Third Theatre does not imply a specific style, it is not an alliance of groups, a movement or international association. Nor is it a school, an aesthetic or a set of techniques. It is not a trend. Third Theatre is a definition of theatre people who are far from traditional or avant-garde theatre, and who try to shape their own 'why'.

The three meetings which Odin Teatret organized in the 1970s in Belgrade, Bergamo and Lekeitio/Madrid have a continuation in the sessions of ISTA whose participants belong to the galaxy of the Third Theatre.

In the last twenty-five years, artists or cultural activists belonging to these theatrical niches, aware of their common condition, have kept in contact under different forms. One of the most recent meetings was held in May 2000 at the University of California-Berkeley where thirty-five community arts practitioners identified their historical roots as the Little Theatre Movement in the early twentieth century, the Federal Arts Projects during the Depression, the civil rights movement in the 1950s and 1960s, and the founding of Alternate ROOTS in the 1970s. Many also mentioned Paul Robeson, Augusto Boal, Chicano theatre, Afro-Cuban culture, Brecht, Chaikin, Keith Johnstone, the Bread and Puppet Theatre, the Living Theatre and even Linda Montano's and John Cage's experiments. This meeting is one of the many examples of Third Theatre in the USA. They refer to themselves as 'community' or 'community-based' theatre discussing in depth the difference between these two definitions. Jan Cohen-Cruz describes this motley aspect of North American theatre in her recent article in *New Theatre Quarterly* [2000].

In the Arab world, where censorship is the rule and free expression is limited, there exists on the one hand a government controlled theatre and, on the other, a commercial one. In Egypt, where martial law has been in place since 1981, the few theatre groups want to follow a 'third road', as they call it. In 1990, in spite of the fact that the Ministry of Culture had cancelled the Cairo International Festival because of the Gulf War, these groups labelled themselves 'free' and managed to organize an alternative festival. A similar attempt was made in 2000, but this time they were unsuccessful.

Finally, let me mention the dozens and dozens of companies in Italy which name themselves 'invisible'. Throughout the 1990s they held annual meetings in the form of very original festivals lasting up to forty days. The names these groups use to differentiate themselves from traditional or avant-garde theatre, from government institutions or commercial enterprises are different, but they all belong to the theatrical culture which I call Third Theatre.

IW As the number of Third Theatre gatherings organized in Latin America attest, the Third Theatre has an important resonance throughout the continent. Does this help explain why the Odin spends a great deal of time performing and teaching in Latin America, or why you have lectured, taught and travelled so much there? Why are you so committed to Latin America?

EB I met some Latin Americans who made me fall in love with their continent. In the course of the years they impressed me with their stubbornness, questioning, integrity, results. The constraints which are imposed on them, the conditions under which they work, the need to break their isolation and create their own difference – they call it identity – all this reminds me of Odin Teatret's biography. I am fond of these men and women, of their voices, the colour of their hair and skin, the wrinkles on their faces, the compelling and trusting way of relating to me by youngsters who could be my grandchildren.

My steps were often decided by the bonds of affection, gratitude and loyalty towards a few people I met. Neither aesthetic ideas nor artistic ideals were my best teachers, but the mute condition of the emigrant and the privileged responsibility of a director with a handful of individualistic yet faithful actors and collaborators. My country consists of what I have learned and its inhabitants are those individuals, dead or alive, who give meaning to my life. Theatre is the unique condition in which I affirm my difference. I cross its territory as a 'traveller of speed', driven by an insatiable longing for freedom, which I know I can only quench by confronting the other with all my vulnerability.

References

Barba, Eugenio (1995), *The Paper Canoe: A Guide to Theatre Anthropology*. London and New York: Routledge.

Barba, Eugenio (1999), 'Written silence', in *Theatre: Solitude, Craft, Revolt*. Aberystwyth, Wales: Black Mountain Press, pp. 43–53.

Cohen-Cruz, Jan (2000), 'A hyphenated field: community-based theatre in the USA', *New Theatre Quarterly*, Vol. 6, Part 4, No. 64: 364–78.

Watson, Ian (1995), *Towards a Third Theatre: Eugenio Barba and the Odin Teatret*. London and New York: Routledge.

CONTRIBUTORS

METTE BOVIN is a Danish anthropologist who did much of her early field work in West Africa. After writing and directing the play *The Game About Nigeria* for an ethnographic museum exhibition in the late 1970s, she began to explore the relationships between theatre and anthropology. This led to her work with the Odin Teatret and ISTA.

I NYOMAN CATRA is, as touched on in the introduction to Chapter 4, one of Bali's leading performers as well as teachers and is on the faculty of the National Institute of the Arts (STSI) in Denpasar, Bali. In addition to his work at ISTA, he has studied in the United States as a recipient of fellowships from the Fulbright Foundation and the Asian Cultural Council.

FRANC CHAMBERLAIN is Senior Lecturer in Performance Studies at University College, Northampton in England. He is a theatre artist and scholar interested in training and theatre practice across cultures. He is a former editor of the theatre journal *Contemporary Theatre Review* and General Editor of the Harwood Theatre Series. He is currently preparing a series on theatre training for Routledge.

TONY D'URSO is a Milan-based photographer who has worked extensively with the Odin Teatret. His photographs have been used to illustrate numerous books on the Odin and Barba's work. He is co-author of two book-length photographic studies of the Odin, *Lo Straniero Che Danza* (with Ferdinando Taviani, Cooperative Editoriale Studio Forma, 1977) and *Viaggi Con/ Voyages With: Odin Teatret* (with Eugenio Barba, Editrice Alfeo, 1990).

RON JENKINS is, as mentioned in the introduction to Chapter 4, the Artistic Director and Chair of Theatre at Wesleyan University in the United States. He is author of *Subversive Laughter* (The Free Press, 1994) and *Acrobats of the Soul* (Theatre Communications Group, 1988). He has conducted research into Balinese performance for over twenty years and has attended ISTA on numerous occasions where he has worked extensively with the Balinese troupes involved.

IBEN NAGEL RASMUSSEN has been an actress with Eugenio Barba's Odin Teatret since 1966. In addition to being a performer, she is a leading figure in the European group theatre movement, a teacher and director.

MIGUEL RUBIO, as explained in the introduction to Chapter 15, is the director of the Peruvian theatre group Yuyachkani. He is one of Latin America's leading theatre directors and is at the forefront of the group theatre movement in the continent. He is especially interested in politically committed theatre that combines extensive training, collective creation, and an aesthetic rooted in a deep understanding of traditional Andean performance.

NICOLA SAVARESE teaches theatre history and performance at the University of Rome Tre in Rome. He has also taught at Bologna University and was a research scholar at the Getty Institute for Research in Los Angeles for nine months (1999). He is both an actor and a scholar who has written extensively on Asian theatre. As mentioned in the introduction to Chapter 2, he is one of the founders of ISTA, and continues to be a senior adviser to Barba on all matters concerning the organization. He also collaborated with Barba in compiling the *Dictionary of Theatre Anthropology: The Secret Art of the Performer*, published in English by Routledge (1991).

MARIA SHEVTSOVA is Professor of Drama and Theatre Arts at Goldsmiths College, University of London. Her research areas include the work of contemporary European companies and directors (notably, Brook, Mnouchkine, Dodin), and socio-cultural and interdisciplinary issues in relation to performance and the theatre. Her recent publications include *Theatre and Interdisciplinary*, which she edited for Theatre Research International (2001).

NIGEL STEWART is Lecturer in Theatre Studies at Lancaster University in England. He is a dance artist and scholar with a special interest in the relation of movement analysis and notation to hermeneutic, phenomenological and environmental aesthetics. He is presently co-editing *Performing Nature: Explorations in Ecology and the Arts*, to be published by Peter Lang.

FERDINANDO TAVIANI, as touched on in the introduction to Chapter 2, is a professor of theatre at L'Aquila University in Rome. He is one of the founders of ISTA, and is the Odin's unofficial historian, having written a book (*Il Libro dell'Odin: Il Teatro-Laboratorio di Eugenio Barba*, Feltrinelli, 1975, 1978) and numerous articles on the company's development over the years. He also acts as a literary advisor on many of Barba's Odin productions.

IAN WATSON is Deputy Chair of the Department of Visual and Performing Arts as well as the Coordinator of the Theatre and Television Program at Rutgers University-Newark in the United States. He is the author of *Towards a Third Theatre: Eugenio Barba and the Odin Teatret* (Routledge, 1993, 1995), and the editor of *Performer Training: Developments Across Cultures* (Harwood, 2001). He is also on the board of *New Theatre Quarterly*.

INDEX

Literary works can be found under the author entry. Theatrical productions can be found under the director or producer entry. The various journals referred to in the text are grouped under the general heading of 'journals'. The numerous theatre groups mentioned in the text are grouped under the general heading of 'theatre groups'.

Acción Pacificadora 194
accultured 47, 56
Adamov, Arthur 241
Aeschylus 65
Aguilar, Jerónimo 195–6
Aguire, Dardo 189
Aguirre, Coral 189
Ajima, Natsuko 78–9
Amaru, Túpac 207
Améry, Jean 190
    The Intellectual in Auschwitz 190
animation culturelle 123
Anthropological Theatre 218–19
Antoine, André 252
Appia, Adolphe 193, 252
Arba, Boureima 150
Armstrong, Richard 209, 241

Artaud, Antonin 1, 8, 22, 53, 57, 65,
    186, 237, 241
Asian Cultural Council 59
Ayacucho xv, 11, 172, 189, 194, 203,
    207, 209, 213–14, 216–17, 220,
    206, 208, 210, 212, 218, 223,
    225–6, 229–31, 259
Azuma, Katsuko 29, 30, 32, 72, 76–8,
    242, 248

Badillo, César 226
    El Actor y sus Otros 226
Bakhtin, Mikhail 116
Bali/Balinese
    actor/dancer 9, 15, 59, 64–5, 245
    dance/drama 76
    dance/theatre 240

performance/performer 60, 63, 65, 80

technique 63–4

Bandem, I Made 59–60, 65, 201

Barba, Eugenio
'Anthropological Theatre' 212
Dictionary of Theatre Anthropology: The Secret Art of the Performer xii, 14, 30, 36, 226, 251
The Paper Canoe: A Guide to Theatre Anthropology 14, 33, 237, 251
'Reflections' 212
Shakuntala 9
Solitude, Craft, Revolt 237, 259
'The Third Theatre: the legacy from us to ourselves' 228

Baris 250

Barker, Keith 249

Barong 1

Barrault, Jean—Louis 43, 200
La Vie Offerte 200

barter (s)/bartering 9, 11–13, 94–126 *passim*, 128, 141, 143–4, 148–9, 153, 155–7, 159, 162, 166, 170, 174, 185–6, 188, 224, 230, 255–60
barter community 98–9, 100, 103–4, 108
deep cultural exchange 106
event narrative 99–100
invested community 97
shallow cultural exchange 106
socio-cultural narrative 100

Barucha, Rustom 23, 28–9, 33
Theatre and the World: Performance and the Politics of Culture 28

Baudrillard, Jean 122

Beckett, Samuel 192, 241

Beijing Opera 241

Béjart, Maurice 82–3

Berkoff, Steven 197

Berlin Philharmonic Orchestra 235

Berliner Ensemble 197, 241

Bert, Bruno 213

Bhabha, Homi 3, 14, 24, 105, 108–9, 179–80

Binoche, Jean-Marie 213, 216

biomechanics 23, 25, 31

bios 46, 49–50, 119

BITEF (Theatre of Nations Festival of Belgrade) 187

Black Theatre Cooperative xii

Blues 81

Boal, Augusto xvi, 124, 192, 204, 221–2, 226, 261

Bodelsen, Anders 151

body-in-life 56–7

Bogart, Anne
The Medium 5
Viewpoints 5

Bogdanov, Gennadi 22, 23, 25, 31

Bohannan, Laura 143

Bolívar, Simón 207

Borges, Jorge Luis, *The Dead Man* 177

Bourdieu, Pierre 125–6

Bovin, Mette 96, 151, 259–60
Dances in the Sand – A Meeting between Europe and Africa (16mm film) 146–7, 151–2

Brecht, Bertolt 1, 43, 124, 170, 186, 191, 193, 217, 220–2, 226, 237, 241, 261

Bredsdorff, Thomas 210

Brook, Peter 1, 4, 14, 95, 108, 178, 200
The Ik 200
Mahabharata 13
Orghast 4

Buddhism 240

Buenaventura, Enrique 192, 204, 214, 221–2, 226

Bunraku 241

Butoh 78–9, 85, 86

Bysted, Peter 259

Cage, John 261

Cairo International Festival 261

Calcumil, Luisa 213

Calvino, Italo, *Invisible Cities* 164

Camargo, Beatriz 213

Candombe 10, 96, 100, 104–5, 115

Candomblé xvi, 31, 82, 84, 171, 177, 228
Caracas Festival 10, 170
Cardona, Patricia 210
Carlson, Carolyn 25
Carlson, Marvin 101, 104
Carrió, Raquel 227
Catra, I Nyoman xiv
Ceballos, Edgar 193
Centre for Performance Research xii
Chaikin, Joseph 98, 261
Chaplin, Charlie 148, 152, 156–7
Chauduri, Una 108
Chekhov, Anton 192
Chen, Xiao-mei 30
Chow, Rey 32, 180
Christoffersen, Erik Exe 117, 120, 124–5
Claudel Paul 241
Clifford, James 3
Cohen-Cruz, Jan 261
collective creation 175
commedia dell'arte 192, 249
Copeau, Jacques 15, 186, 229, 237
Corporación Colombiana de Teatro 226
corporal mime 31
Cortés, Hernán 195
Costa, Orazio 249
Country of Speed 237, 240
Coventry Arts Alive Festival xii
Craig, Gordon 186, 193, 237
   The Mask 193
Crisafulli, Fabrizio 163, 166
cross-cultural/cross-culturalism 3, 4, 6, 8, 9–10, 12, 62, 64
Cruciani, Fabrizio 36, 248
Csikszentmihalyi, Mihaly 86
cultural pluralism/plurality, 2, 6, 7–9, 11, 15, 25, 30, 110, 170, 234

da Cunha, Euclides 177, 195
Daetwyler, Jean-Jacques 202
Dalcroze, Jacques 252
Daniela (Regnoli) 160, 165
Danish Royal Ballet 239
Dasgupta, Gautam 108

de Bellido, María Parado 207
De Marinis, Marco xiv, xv, 14, 33
De Toro, Ferdinando 24
Debray, Régis 123
Decroux, Etienne 1, 15, 23, 71, 186, 212, 250
   belle courbe 48
   déséquilibre 48
del Cioppo, Atahualpa 191, 203, 221–2, 225
Deleuze, Gilles 122
Delgardo, Mario 11, 180, 185, 201–5, 207–8, 214–15, 229
Delsarte, François 192
Derrida, Jacques 46, 53–4, 122
   différance 55–7
Devi, Rukmini 1
Didier, F. 209
Dionysus 65
dramaturgy/dramaturgical 11, 47, 191, 176–7, 209–11, 231, 239, 246, 257
Dullin, Charles 192, 241
D'Urso, Tony 128, 130–1, 138–41

Ecole Jacques Leqoc xii
Egger, Geert 152
Eisenstein, Sergei 1, 192, 229, 239, 241
Ekblad, Stina 25
El Centro per la Sperimentazione e la Ricerca Teatrale di Pontedera 200
Emerson College 59
Encuentro Internacional de Teatro Antropológico Bahía Blanca/International Group Theatre Gathering (Bahía Blanca, 1987) 95, 97, 205
enculturated 42, 47, 78
Ennosuke II 43
Escenología (publishers) 193
Escudero, María 185, 222
Escuza, César 192
Eurasian performer 56–7
Eurasian theatre xvi, 47, 49

Euripides 63, 65
  The Bacchae 60, 62
European Mime and Physical Theatre
  Workshop Symposium xii
extra-daily 47–9, 56, 144, 151, 223

Faust 60
Federal Arts Project 261
Festival of Caracas 184, 188
Festival of Montevideo 193
Festuge 9
Filho, Antunes 204
Flores, Palonino 146
Fo, Dario 115–17, 124, 157, 178, 186,
  249
Foreman, Richard 197
Fort, Paul 252
Foucault, Michel 119, 122–3
Frank, Susana 206
Freilich, Erving 145, 156
Freud, Sigmund 53–4
Fujimori, Alberto 208
Fusco, Coco xiii

García, Santiago 184, 203, 214, 221–2,
  225–6
Geertz, Clifford 3, 15–16, 113
Genet, Jean, *The Maids* 160
Giacchè, Piergiorgio 24
Giménez, Carlos 184–5
giullari 112, 116
Glass, Phillip 81
Globe theatre 63
Goffman, Erving 97
Gómez-Peña, Guillermo 13
Gómez-Peña, Guillermo and Coco
  Fusco, *Two Undiscovered
  Amerindians Visit* xiii
Gramsci, Antonio 115–16
griot 150, 152–3
Grotowski, Jerzy 2, 14–15, 22, 33, 82,
  170, 174, 178, 187, 201, 209,
  220, 229, 241, 249, 252
Guattari, Félix 122
Guerra, Ruy 177
Guerrero, Gonzalo 195–6

Guevara, Che 8, 11, 123, 247
guru 68
Guzmán, Abigail 208

Hamidou, Moussa 147–8
Hanayagi, Kanichi xiv, 22, 53, 60–1,
  71, 242
Harrer, Heinrich 106
Hastrup, Kirsten xvi–vii, 8, 21, 26–7
  *The Performers' Village: Times,
  Techniques and Theories at
  ISTA* 76, 245
Hinduism 240
Holmberg, Allan 155
Holstebro 2, 20, 42, 67–8, 80–1, 95,
  101, 144, 146, 160–1, 171, 177,
  183–4, 186, 221–3, 225, 234,
  238–9, 242, 250, 258

Iacoviella, Beatrice 210
improvise (d)/improvisation 41, 78,
  82–6, 98–100, 113, 129, 134–5,
  140, 160, 162, 175, 209–11,
  241, 249
inculturation 42
Innes, Christopher 8
intercultural/interculturalism 1, 3,
  5–7, 11–13, 21, 39, 43, 63, 79,
  82–3, 106, 108, 112, 119–20,
  124–5, 144, 179, 212, 228, 144,
  234–5, 237–9
International Center for Theater
  Research/Center International
  de Recherche Théatrale
  (CIRT) 4, 95
International Group Theatre
  Gathering/*Encuentro
  Internacional de Teatro
  Antropológico Bahía Blanca*
  (Bahía Blanca, 1987) 95, 97,
  205
International Workshop of Group
  Theatre (Bergamo, 1977) 201
International Workshop of Theatrical
  Research (Belgrade, 1976) 200
intracultural 235

Ionesco, Eugene 241
ISTA (International School of Theatre
    Anthropology) xii–xviii
    passim, 1, 2, 6–7, 9, 12, 14,
    20–74 *passim*, 76, 80, 99, 110,
    114, 116, 120, 144, 170, 171,
    181, 194, 205, 227, 234, 238,
    240, 242, 244, 245–50
    Teatrum Mundi 9, 13, 30, 61, 62,
    227
ITI (International Theatre Institute)
    184, 200–2
Izumo, Takeda, Miyoshi Shoraku and
    Namiki Senryu, *Chushingura*
    82

Jacon, Nitis 228
Jarrett, Keith 81
Jazz 81
Jenkins, Ron 24
jo-ha-kyu 76, 77
Johnstone, Keith 249, 261
journals
    Conjunto 186, 222
    The Drama Review xii, 157, 251
    La Escena Latinoamericano 183
    La Máscara 193, 221
    New Theatre Quarterly xi, 58, 181,
    250, 261
    Performance Research xii
    Teatro '70 193
Journey to the West (Chinese novel)
    62–3
Jouvet, Louis 229

Kaba, Jean-Pierre 147–8
Kabuki 4, 9, 14–15, 28, 43, 48, 70,
    76–7, 82–4, 86–7, 241–2,
    252
Kanze, Escuela 213
Kanze, Hideo 201, 240, 242
Kanze, Hisao 43, 240, 242
Kathakali 1, 2, 5, 13–14, 67, 201, 240,
    242, 243
Kershaw, Baz 107
Khan, Kubla 164

Kristeva, Julia 46
    intertextuality 55, 57
Kropotkin, Piotr 117–18, 121
Krukowski, Woiciech 201
Kustov, Nikolai 23
Kyogen 239

L'Aquila University 36
La Torre, Alfonso 231
La Universidad Autónoma de
    Chapingo 206
La Universidad Autónoma de
    Zacatecas 206
La Universidad Nacional de San
    Cristóbal de Huamanga 208
Laksmi, Desak Made Suarti 63–4
Lama, Dalai 106
Langfang, Mei 1, 43
Larco, Juan 173, 231
Leabhart, Thomas 22, 23, 31, 71, 249
Lindh, Ingemar 249–50
Little Theatre Movement 260
Livingstone, Robert 12
Lizot, Jacques 146
logos 40, 46, 50, 55
Londrina International Festival 228
Lyotard, Jean-François 122
Lyubimov, Yuri 200
    Hamlet 200 *see also* Shakespeare,
    William
    Here the Dawns Are Quiet 200
    Ten Days That Shook the World 200

Mahapatra, Kelucharan 22, 67
Mallarmé, Stéphane 252
manis 52
Manzalis Theatre Festival 222
Marceau, Marcel 241
Martín, San 207
Masgrau, Lluis 250
Mauss, Marcel 118, 125
maya 63
McLuhan, Marshall 5
Meldolesi, Claudio 36
Menassé, Aline 206
Meyer, Hans 190

Meyerhold, Vsevelod 1, 15, 23, 186,
    193, 237, 238, 241, 242, 251
Meyerholdian 48
Milanés, Pablo 222
mise-en-scène 8–9, 13, 37, 47, 51, 55,
    57–8, 177, 209, 257
Miura, Hisako 53
Mnouchkine, Ariane 1, 101
    Les Atrides 13
    Shakespeare Cycle 4, 13
Molière, Jean-Baptiste Poquelin 192
Montano, Linda 261
mudra (s) 51–2, 56, 67
Muguercia, Magaly 22
multicultural/multiculturalism 3, 4, 5,
    6, 9–12, 83, 85, 110, 179,
    234–5, 238, 247–9, 253
Muroa, Isso 209

Nambudiri, Krishnan 201
Natyashastra 2, 22
New York Theatre Workshop 5
Nihon Buyo 22, 29, 72, 76, 79,
    249–50
Nobel Peace Prize 192
Noguera, Héctor 194
Noh 1, 4, 6–7, 15, 43, 83, 201, 212,
    239–40, 242, 252
Nordisk Teaterlaboratorium/Inter–
    Scandinavian Theatre
    Laboratory 20, 170, 206, 238
nritti 70
nritya 70

Odin/Odin Teatret xi, xii, xiii, 2, 7–11,
    21, 29, 34, 36, 76–85 *passim*,
    95–124 *passim*, 127–30, 135,
    143–4, 146, 149, 151, 153, 159,
    161–2, 171–2, 180–1, 183–6,
    188–9, 191, 194–6, 198, 201–2,
    204, 206, 209, 210–12, 215–17,
    221–7, 230, 232, 234, 238–42,
    245, 248–51, 254–5, 258–61
    actors
        Carreri, Roberta xvi, 76–87, 96,
        142, 146–53, 155–6, 213, 223

Cots, Toni 250
Ferslev, Jan 82
Larsen, Tage 223
Nielsen, Tina 52, 55
Rasmussen, Iben Nagel 51–5, 84,
    128–41 *passim*, 226
Varley, Julia 51–5, 231
Wethal, Torgeir 53, 84, 135
film
    Theatre Meets Ritual 115
productions
    The Book of Dances 129, 135, 137,
        224
    Brecht's Ashes 195, 226
    Come! And the Day Will be Ours
        176, 195, 196, 200
    Ferai 8
    Judith 85, 86
    The Million 9, 30 195
    Min Fars Hus/My Father's House
        113, 131, 159
    Mythos 214
    Ornitofilene 8, 11, 176
    Oxyrhincus Evangeliet 85, 86, 125,
        177, 195
    Talabot 8, 11, 82, 99, 177, 183
    Traces in the Snow 76, 86
Odissi dance/Odissi 6, 7, 22, 28–9, 48,
    52, 67–8, 72, 74, 76–9, 86, 99,
    212, 250
Ohno, Kazuo 79
Omolú, Augusto xvi, 71, 171, 177, 228,
    232
onnogata 1, 14, 22
Orixà/Orixà dance 71, 177
Ortiz, Fernando 5, 29
Oshala 82
Osterwa, Julius 186
Otello 177
Otelo 171, 177

Pan Cultural Arts: Shobana Jeyasingh
    xii
Panigrahi, Raghunath 9, 67, 242, 247
Panigrahi, Sanjukta xii, xiv, 9, 22,
    29–30, 32, 51–3, 55, 65–78

passim, 98, 232, 240, 242, 247–8
Panthéâtre xii
Parada, Roberto 194
Pardo, Enrique xii
Pasca, Daniele Finzi 213
Pavis, Patrice 4, 29, 33, 51
Paxton, Steve 25
PCI (Italian Communist Party) 120
Peirano, Luis 170
Pelto, Pertti 155
Piers, Stephen 25
Pinochet, General Augusto 231
Polo, Marco 164
potlach 159, 162, 163
Pradier, Jean-Marie xvi, 173
pre-expressive/pre-expressivity 6–7, 14–15, 22–3, 30–1, 33–4, 49, 50, 52, 54, 56–7, 119, 237, 243–4, 246
Primer encuentro de teatro antropológico (First encounter of anthropological theatre) 189
PromPeru 215, 217–18
Pronko, Leonard 15

Racine, Jean 192
Ralli, Teresa 221
Rama, Franca 124
Rangda 62, 65
Rasmussen, Knud 8
recurrent principles (of acting) 47–9
   dynamic opposition 52, 56
   reduction 52
Reencuentro Ayacucho '88 206, 208, 210–11, 219–20, 229, 231
Reencuentro Ayacucho '98 (Encuentro Ayacucho: 9º Encuentro Internacional de Teatro de Grupo – Ayacucho 98) 208, 212, 215
Revuelta, Vicente 226
Roach, Joseph 104
Robeson, Paul 261
Rockerfeller Brothers Fund 59

Ronconi 178
ROOTS 261
Rosa, Guimaraes 195
Rouch, Jean 147
Royal Shakespeare Company 197
Rubio, Miguel 11, 180, 204, 213–14, 221
Ruffini, Franco 36
   La scuola degli attori 245
Russian Ballet 43
   Karsavina 43
   Massine 43
Ruzza, Luca 163

Said, Edward 32, 109, 110, 181
Sano, Seki 238
Santa Cruz, Victoria 213
Satie 81
sats 244
Savarese, Nicola 251
Schechner, Richard xv, 1, 98, 104, 108
   Between Theatre and Anthropology xvii
Schechner, Richard (with Willa Appel), *By Means of Performance* 5
Schino, Mirella 213
Schumann, Peter 222
score/physical score/performer's score 42, 47, 50, 52–5, 54, 85–6, 98–9, 245, 250
Sendero Luminoso (Shining Path) 208, 230
VII Encuentro Internacional de Teatro de Grupo (Cuzco, 1987) 206
Shakespeare, William 63, 149, 177, 192
   Hamlet 143 *see also* Lyubimov, Yuri
   Othello 228 *see also* Zadek, Peter
   The Tempest 60, 63, 65
Sinisterra, José Sanchís 213, 216
Skeel, Rina, *The Tradition of ISTA* 44, 245
Sojuro, Sawamura 242
St Denis, Michel 15

Stanislavasky, Constantin/
    Stanislavskian 1, 14–15, 22, 33,
    77, 186, 192, 220, 229, 237–8,
    241–2, 251–2
  Stanislavsky system 212
Strindberg, August 252
STSI (National Institute of Arts –
    Bali) 59–60, 65
subscore 245, 250, 256
subtext 50, 86, 251, 257
Sudana, Tapa 201
Sulerzhitsky, Leopold 186
Sumac, Yma 241
Suteja, Ketut I 52, 55
Suzuki, Tadashi 1, 197, 239

t'ai chi 81, 228
Taganke Theatre 200
Tairov, Alexander 192
Tamasha xii
Tanztheatre 197
Tara Arts xii
Tarenzi, Danielo 163
Taviani, Ferdinanado 36, 108, 120–1,
    128, 160, 173, 231
Taymor, Julie 12
Tempo, I Made Pasek 242, 248
Terayama, Shuji 242
Theatre Anthropology xvi, 1, 6, 7, 12,
    14–15, 22–4, 28, 30–4, 38–9,
    42, 46–9, 51, 53–4, 205, 218,
    228–9, 243–5, 250
theatre groups
  Akademia Ruchu 200–2
  Bread and Puppet 186, 261
  The Canada Project 206
  Cardiff Laboratory Theatre 200,
    202
  Comuna Baires 172, 174, 193
  Contradanza 185
  Cuatrotablas 11, 109, 172,
    174–5, 180, 185, 196, 200–2,
    206, 209–10, 213, 218, 222,
    229
    La noche larga 185, 194, 196
  El Séptimo 213, 216

El Teatro Elementaire de Bruselas
    200
El Temps Fort 206, 209
Farfa 206
Galpón 203
Gardzienice 95, 252
ICTUS 194
The International Visual Theatre
    202
Itinerante del Sol 213
La Candelaria 175, 204, 213, 226
    Guadalupe años sin cuentra 184
La Linea Transversale 213, 216
La Rueca 174–5, 206
Laboratório UNICAMP de
    Movimiento y Expresión 209
Libre Teatro Libre 172, 174, 185,
    200
    El Rostro 185
The Living Theatre 178, 186–7, 204,
    222, 261
Mabou Mines 200
    The Saint and the Football Players
    200
Macunaíma 204
Open Theatre (the) 186, 204
Roy Hart Theatre 202, 206, 209
Tablas y Diablas 213
The Talking Band 206
Teatr-Laboratorium/Polish
    Laboratory Theatre 186, 204
Teatro Alianza 189
Teatro Campasino 124
Teatro Campesino 186
Teatro de Arena 204
Teatro delle Radici 213
Teatro di Ventura 200
Teatro Escambray 175
Teatro Experimental de Cali 175,
    204
Teatro Independiente 198
Teatro Libre de Bahía 185, 196
Teatro Núcleo 172, 200
Teatro Potlach 109, 206, 209,
    212–13
Teatro Sunil 213, 216

Teatro Taller de Colombia 206
Teatro Tascabile di Bergamo 99,
        109, 200–2, 206, 209, 212
Tercer Mundo 174
Théâtre de l'Unité 121–2
Théâtre du Soleil 101
Yuyachkani 11, 99–100, 109, 174–5,
        180, 204, 209–10, 213, 221,
        223, 227, 228, 252
Theatre of Nations Festival 200
Third Theatre 107, 112, 117–18,
        120–1, 123–4, 171–4, 179, 181,
        186–8, 194, 197–215 *passim*,
        219, 221, 225, 228–9, 246, 248,
        254, 260–1
Third Theatre Manifesto 197, 199
3º Encuentrao de Tercer Teatro
        (Ayacucho, 1978) 209, 222,
        229
Tokyo Ballet 82
Topeng 201, 211
training 68, 71, 79, 80–5, 94, 113, 128,
        144, 153, 160–1, 163, 170,
        173–6, 198, 209, 211, 213–14,
        241, 243–4, 248–9
transcultural/transculturality 3–4,
        6–7, 30, 33–4, 37–9, 43–4, 47,
        151, 160, 196, 219, 234
traveller of speed 237
Triangle xii
tribangi 48, 74, 83, 87
Turin Symphony Orchestra 189
Turner, Fred 29–30
Turner, Victor xviii, 97

underscore 50–3, 55
UNESCO 118, 187, 191, 200–1, 206
University of Eurasian Theatre 244

*V Coloquio Internacional de Teatro de
        Grupo* (Zacatecas, 1981) 206
Vakhtangov, Yevgeny 186, 193, 229,
        241
Vargas Llosa, Mario *The War of the
        End of the World* 8, 177, 195
Via Negativa 15
Volli, Ugo 36

Waits, Tom 80, 81
Wajda, Andrezej 200
        The Danton Case 200
Watson, Ian xv, xvi
        Towards a Third Theatre xi
Wesleyan University 59
Wilson, Richard 197, 200
Wilson, Robert 200, 240
        Einstein on the Beach 200
Winther, Frans xviii, 9
Wirth, Andrzej 4

Yanomami (Indians) 95, 144,
        185–6
Ybema, Walter 146

Zadek, Peter 200
        Othello 200 *see also* Shakespeare,
        William
Zarrilli, Phillip 23, 24, 81
Zeami 1, 22, 193